A Modern, American
Orthodox Pastor

A Modern, American Orthodox Pastor

The Homilies of Father William Olnhausen

Father William Olnhausen

James Scarpaci MSW and Michael Huber ThM, MA,
editors

ISBN: Softcover   978-1-4500-7887-0

To order additional copies of this book, contact:
Xlibris Corporation
1-888-795-4274
www.Xlibris.com
Orders@Xlibris.com
60481

Table of Contents

Within

Introduction

The precipitating incentive for this project came from coeditor, James Scarpaci, a colleague and friend of mine. Credit goes to him for the idea for this volume which, otherwise, likely would not have come to fruition.

Jim and I practiced together as psychotherapists in the same clinic a number of years ago and we kept in touch after I left. Recently I had the profound honor of introducing Jim to the Holy Orthodox Church and by the grace of the Holy Spirit he and his entire family were chrismated into St. Nicholas Antiochian Orthodox Church in Cedarburg, Wisconsin. Being impressed with the quality of the messages by the priest of St. Nicholas, Father William Olnhausen, Jim suggested we preserve some of the best and representative messages of Fr. Bill's in a keep sake that would roughly coincide with the 20th anniversaries of both St. Nicholas as a church and the Orthodox ministry of Fr. Bill.

For the past several years I have been honored to have served as the Vice-chairman of the church council of St. Nicholas. This presented me with an opportunity to represent the church along with Fr. Bill at the Antiochian Archdiocese convention in Palm Springs of July 2009. I will recount only one impactful event that occurred at this convention that relates directly to the work at hand.

On two separate occasions, while milling through a sea of black robes in the crowded hallways of the hotel's convention center, several priests, spontaneously and without provocation, seeing me with Fr. Bill, unabashedly pronounced Fr. Bill to be the best priest in the Archdiocese.

Believe me, having spent 18 years of direct observation of Fr. Bill and his ministry, neither I nor anyone else at St. Nicholas would mount any kind of argument against that. But I didn't have any other significant experience with any other Antiochian Orthodox priests. I had converted directly from the Evangelical Protestant church and St. Nicholas was all I knew except a coinciding brief period when I attended a different Orthodox church. For this reason these proclamations by other priests who certainly knew much better than I did astounded me.

This experience altered greatly my perception of this current project. Given the fact that it is obviously next to impossible to conduct a verifiable and reliable research study proving the claim of these priests, none the less, it set into motion an idea of presenting the homilies of Fr. Bill from recent years at St. Nicholas that could also illustrate the character and qualities of a modern, American Orthodox priest that are indicative of such a claim.

It is my intent to not overstep my bounds with this project. This is not an attempt to set forth a manual of how an Orthodox priest ought to be. It is simply both a celebration of a priest and his messages and an attempt to extend and deepen the ministry of his words for the spiritual and Orthodox advancement of its readers.

This is not, therefore, a simple compilation of some of Fr. Bill's best messages, though that would be worthy in and of itself. It is a humble attempt to set forth the qualities of this priest that seem both exemplary and ordinary as illustrated by his homilies.

I have thus categorized several of these qualities and used a block of messages, not in any particular order, to try to accomplish this. I introduce these chapters with observations and insights of my own given my own personal experience of Fr. Bill for nearly the entire length of his Orthodox ministry. I would sincerely ask the forgiveness of the reader and any member of St. Nicholas if I have made any observation or statement in error. I recognize that the comments are from my own narrow experience and likely differ from others.

With regard to Fr. Bill's homilies something ought to be said about an additional method of communicating spiritual truth that Fr. Bill only initiated relatively late in his Orthodox ministry—the children's sermon. When Jim and I asked Fr. Bill to submit copies of his homilies there were no representations of his children's sermons.*

---

*   Since the writing of this Introduction Father Bill published one of his children's sermons which is found in the appendix.

Quite frankly I have never been a fan of the children's sermon. I have seen way too many pastors attempt children's sermons and fail to integrate substantive spiritual depth at the child's level—depth that could simultaneously speak to the hearts of adults.

Fr. Bill's children's sermons are the clear exception in my opinion. I believe some of the credit for this belongs to C.S. Lewis whose writings had an obvious impact on Fr. Bill's life. Fr. Bill was a long time member of the C.S. Lewis Society and the method and spirit of *Narnia* permeates Fr. Bill's children's sermons. I will mention only one but notable example.

Father was very fond of presenting the same children's sermon every year for Pentecost. As the children stood round about him in front of the festal icon Father would have a child loosely hold a piece of paper up in front of her. Father would then blow and have the paper waft back and forth without any perceptible force acting on it to illustrate the behind-the-scenes activity and power of the Holy Spirit in our lives and in the world.

I chuckle to myself when I hear *The Chronicles of Narnia* referred to as children's literature. Yeah, right! It is far more adult literature disguised as children's literature. This is the way of Father's "children's" sermons. I suspect that Father believes many at St. Nicholas were just as much edified by his children's sermons as his adult ones.

This quality of being at a child's level (reminiscent of our Lord's invitation to the children, Luke 18:15-17) is reflected, humanly and humorously, by Fr. Bill in other ways. Besides the depth and seriousness of the liturgical rites Father thought it childlike fun to smoke out parishioners with the censor and laughed in quasi-sadistic joy as he splashed congregants with holy water for Epiphany. Professionally, I find this notable since the personality style of Fr. Bill is one that is not typically associated with child motifs.

I should also comment briefly on the title of this work which I personally insisted on. This is written in a time of Orthodox history in the United States where the pervasive issue of the day is Orthodox organizational or administrative unity. I have already mentioned that Fr. Bill is an Antiochian priest in the Antiochian Orthodox Church (see Acts 11:26 where the disciples were first called Christians in Antioch). And, make no mistake about it, Father and our whole congregation have frequently rejoiced and celebrated in the precious gifts handed to us by the Church of Antioch. But Father Bill is representative of the overwhelming majority in the Antiochian Church supporting American Orthodox unity. (Where is the "American Orthodox Church" in the middle of Romania?)

In addition, Fr. Bill is, as are the editors, a convert to Orthodox Christianity. This has brought a distinct perspective and message to his homilies that I comment on later in this work. However, Father has repeatedly and unequivocally stated his deepest appreciation for "cradle Orthodox." He always saw this as a great advantage for the church, the best of both worlds that harmoniously contributes to the whole, especially in these United States at this time in history. I believe nothing filled the heart of Father with more pride than the harmonious and loving relationships among the many varied backgrounds of the members of St. Nicholas. He would take every opportunity to boast that our Bishop Mark experienced visiting St. Nicholas as a haven of rest and peace.

Finally, mostly for the benefit of those who may read this but have never personally heard Father speak, I can never remember a time at St. Nicholas when it wasn't difficult hearing what Fr. Bill had to say. It seems as long as I can remember we have been trying to correct bad acoustics in the church nave by various methods and electrical gadgets. This, admittedly, is complicated by my own hearing problem and Fr. Bill's publicly self-confessed "mumbling" at times in his speaking delivery. Fr. Bill will never be mistaken for a TV evangelist and that's how we love it.

My wife, Cindi, told me this morning that what distinguishes Father's style of speaking from other pastors' is that he speaks to his parishioners as a loving father to his beloved children, not as a preacher talking down to the people. Naturally this experiential element will be somewhat missing from a simple reading of Father's homilies. We've included a chapter on the pastoral quality of loving and hope that the select homilies will communicate this adequately.

It has been a wonderful and spiritually invigorating experience reading and rereading Father's homilies for this work—some of which I originally missed hearing first hand. It is my prayer that the reader will experience the same.

Michael Huber
September 26, 2009
The Translation of St. John the Theologian

Chapter One

Obedient

What is obedience? The story of Eden perhaps gives us the best example of what it is not. And perhaps this is a sufficient answer. Some might be surprised that this question might even be asked. But consider the multitude of individuals raised in certain ethnic, cultural, religious and/or familial backgrounds where "obedience" was a life or death proposition filled with fear of punishment. There was no choice. One either obeyed or got whipped for it. Such embedded psychic images then get projected onto God as the ultimate authority figure. "Obedience" then becomes something other than what it was intended to be.

We submit, therefore, as the opening selection of Father Bill's homilies the story of both his conversion to Orthodoxy and the beginning of St. Nicholas Church. Why? Because it is a story of authentic, Christian obedience—the story of a man who encountered something greater than himself and out of sheer wonder and conviction, awe and love, willingly allowed himself to be guided and led by this "Higher Power." This is the true nature of submission, or obedience.

Appropriately then, "The Miracles of St. Nicholas" is a fitting follow up. It is the same living St. Nicholas, who "spoke" to Fr. Bill, who guides and shepherds St. Nicholas Church. He is the pastor behind the pastor.

Some of Fr. Bill's most enjoyable and penetrating homilies included his reports from his overseas trips (usually to Greece) on sabbatical. One of Fr. Bill's great contributions in his homilies is this deeply recognized experience of something larger at work. He would repeatedly say this of the Orthodox Church—where the Spirit of God guides and guards His people. This is in contrast to the current state of affairs in most of the Western Church where it is believed our own "wisdom" and "creativity" is better. This sounds a lot like Eden doesn't it?

His "2006 Trip Report" (the first selection in Chapter Two) is just one fine example of his appreciation and obedience to the Larger/Greater which left him often expressing experiences of humility. It is impossible to isolate one trait of Fr. Bill's in each, identified homily. The pastoral attitude and method are clearly conveyed with Biblical/cultural accuracy and even some humor which was always not far away.

What Orthodoxy calls "obedience" could perhaps in some sense be analogous to the recently popularized phrase "paradigm shift." The following homilies titled "Ten Years Later," "Twenty Years Later" and "What I've Learned" eloquently speak to Fr. Bill's life of openness and willingness. Is not the paradigm shift from anthropocentric to theocentric, in fact, Orthodox obedience?

HOW ST. NICHOLAS CHURCH, CEDARBURG, CAME TO BE
December 6, 2006

I am convinced that in the year 1985 earth time, the Lord Jesus must have said to Saint Nicholas, "We need an Orthodox church on the north side of Milwaukee. Go work on that Olnhausen fellow."

Sometimes we remember things wrong, so yesterday I went back to the original source, my travel journal. I remembered it right. Here is the entry for Saturday, August 3, 1985, written at the Orthodox Academy on Crete where I was attending a conference. I was not Orthodox then and had no intention of becoming Orthodox. That evening we had visited the local Bishop Irenaeus and had supper with him and some of his people in the courtyard outside his chapel. It says we arrived during a Baptism, though I don't remember that. I do remember him and his priests sweetly singing *Phos Hilaron* at sunset on that lovely summer evening. Here is what I wrote that night: "Wonderful! Such joy! Bishop Irenaeus is a holy man. This is the way the Church should be . . . don't forget the Bishop's face: serene, holy, happy." I did not forget his face. Two weeks later in Athens I saw his face again in an icon store near the cathedral. On Saturday, August 17th, I wrote that the "St. Nicholas icon has the happy holy look of the Cretan bishop." Only later did I come to see that it was Irenaeus who looked like Nicholas. (Many Orthodox bishops eventually come to look more or less like Saint Nicholas, for he is the prototype Orthodox pastor.) I had to have that icon, that face of Bishop Irenaeus, so I spent considerably more than I intended and bought the Saint Nicholas icon. Though I didn't yet know it, Saint Nicholas already had me on my way to Orthodoxy. The last words in my journal written just before we landed in Milwaukee were, "The Greek church has a remarkable integration with everyday life—icons in buses, stores, cabs, houses. The Church is concerned with social needs of people. It seems to go far deeper than the Christian veneer of Western Europe. Why?" I felt I had to know. I had to find out why, and you can see what it led to.

Actually I think Saint Nicholas had been working on me before that. My first experience of "forever" came when I was a little boy, and I asked my mother, "How long has Santa Claus been alive?" She answered, "Always, I guess" and suddenly for the first time my mind opened up to eternity. I always was attached to Saint Nicholas. At my old Episcopal Church in Mequon we celebrated Saint Nicholas Day. We had someone dressed as Bishop Nicholas come and collect toys for needy children, as we did here last Sunday. So it felt natural when I came home from Greece to hang my new icon of Saint Nicholas on the wall of my church and light a candle before him. Now I was about to learn how icons work. One day a woman said to me, "Have you noticed how his expression changes?" I said "Nooo . . ." and I started watching. Sure enough, not that the paint moved. It didn't. I can't explain it, but sometimes he was happy, sometimes sad, sometimes stern, sometimes pleased. Someone said, "It's just reflecting your feelings at the moment." So I began to check that. Sometimes this was so, sometimes not. Sometimes I would be in a good mood and he would be looking very displeased, or it could be the reverse.

The truth was that I was not often in a good mood. I was discovering that I needed to be Orthodox; that Orthodoxy was what I had always believed; that I had been trying to be Orthodox outside the Orthodox Church. I knew I needed to go home. And while this was a wonderful discovery, I couldn't imagine how to do it, for we had a family, one child in college, one nearing college age. How could we afford to make the change? And as a pastor, I felt I couldn't just abandon my people. Was there a way to make my Episcopal church into an Orthodox church? Again, I couldn't imagine. One evening I was in a particularly glum mood, depressed, frustrated. I walked over and looked at Saint Nicholas. You can see how he had already drawn me into relationship with him. And for the first and only time (I've never been able to see this again in the icon), he looked smug, like the proverbial cat who had swallowed the canary. I lost my cool. I said to him, "How can you hang there on that wall looking so pleased with yourself, when I'm so miserable?" And then, and I don't mean I heard words, it wasn't like that, again I can't explain it, he told me that he had Saint Nicholas Church well under way, and if I didn't get in his way it was all going to be just fine.

After that, things began to move. Not that I was relaxed about it. Often, I was a nervous wreck. But Saint Nicholas kept at it. I was invited to visit a weeping icon at Saint Nicholas Albanian Orthodox Church in Chicago, where I was given the courage to go back to my church and start talking about Orthodoxy. About this time, a couple of quite amazing things happened to move me towards Orthodoxy and into the Antiochian Archdiocese, but that also is another story. Finally, my Episcopalian bishop fired me for promoting Orthodoxy. I said I wasn't leaving without that icon. That was no problem! So, with Father Peter Gillquist's guidance and the blessing of His Eminence Metropolitan PHILIP, His Grace Bishop ANTOUN came and he founded our Orthodox mission. Father Tom Hopko from Saint Vladimir's Seminary, who knew nothing of our Saint Nicholas connection, sent us a relic of Saint Nicholas which is now embedded in our altar. We submitted three names for our new church to Metropolitan PHILIP, who named us Saint Nicholas Church. When we bought this building, we had our first services on the next major feast day which was Saint Nicholas Day of course, just twelve years ago today. The money we need has always just arrived often in very unexpected ways (that's also another story) for which one of our early treasurers, Lou Chambers, coined the term "the Saint Nicholas factor." It still kicks in regularly. When there have been problems, I have gone to Saint Nicholas, and sometimes results have come within hours. When I mentioned to him in passing that we needed more children, more young families around here, it took a couple of weeks for the surge to begin, and now look! That wonderful icon I bought in 1985 now presides at the entrance to our church to make the point that this truly is Saint Nicholas' Church. This is not really our church. It's his. This is his work.

One last thing, maybe ten years ago, after all this had happened, Khouria Dianna and I were at Milwaukee Irish Fest, where they had a genealogy table, and a sign which said, "Trace your family roots." My mother was a Collins, her father was Irish, and I'd always felt especially close to that side of my family. So I looked at the chart, and my mouth dropped. It said, "*Col*lins: derivative of Ni*chol*as." Did Saint Nicholas have all this in mind even before I was born?

Holy Father Bishop Nicholas, continue to intercede with Christ our God to save our souls.

THE MIRACLES OF SAINT NICHOLAS
2004, revised in 2007

First let's look at miracles. Usually they are defined as extraordinary unexplainable events, performed intentionally by God. Actually in the Orthodox and Scriptural understanding everything (not just miracles) fits that definition. We believe that everything exists and all things happen by the immediate action of God. We and the whole cosmos exist because God right now says "let it be"; otherwise we would cease to be. The "laws" of nature operate because God moment by moment causes them to do so. Gravity works because the Holy Spirit of God right now pulls things down. He could just as easily choose not to do so. Even sin and evil exist only by his permission and power. Now, God does some things regularly for our good (again, gravity, since sticking to the surface of the planet is to our benefit), and some things God does rarely or maybe once, which is what people usually mean by miracle. But God does it all, both that which happens according to the "laws" of nature, and that which we call miraculous. In this paper I am speaking of miracles in the popular sense: extraordinary events. Such miracles are a sign to us that God is not limited by what we understand or expect; there is always hope. Miracles are signs of what the Kingdom of God is like: filled with wonders, especially the healing of what ails us.

Christ worked many miracles. About a quarter of the Gospel accounts describe extraordinary happenings, the major ones, of course, being his Virgin Birth and his Resurrection. He has given some of his followers the power to work miracles too, beginning with the apostles in the New Testament accounts. God has a longstanding habit of working through people. If he wants the poor to be fed, he could work a miracle and produce a loaf of bread, but usually he arranges for a charitable person to take some food to them. Likewise he allows certain people to help him work miracles. This didn't stop with the apostles. The history of Christianity is filled with miracle stories. The Orthodox Church has a whole category of saints called Wonderworkers (thaumaturges in Greek). We are still accumulating them. For example, Nektarios the Wonderworker, a Greek saint who died in 1920, has worked countless miracles since then and has become the most popular of modern saints.

One of the great Wonderworkers of the early Church was named Nicholas. Saint Nicholas was born late in the 3rd century in Asia Minor, probably in the town of Patara near the Mediterranean coast. He must have endured the Great Persecution at the beginning of the 4th century, when the empire tried to eliminate Christianity. He became Bishop of

Myra, a nearby seaport. (We have here at our church two stones from behind the altar of his cathedral in Myra, now a ruin. Perhaps Saint Nicholas walked on these stones or the stone floor they came from.) Bishop Nicholas loved his people and his people loved him. Over the years he has become the Church's prototype of the good pastor. There have been many stories passed down about him. Now, it is important to say that we cannot document these stories. He had no biographer as some early saints had, let alone four of them as Christ did. Nicholas left no writings; he did not get recorded on videotape. All we have are stories about him as people passed them down. So far as we can tell they were first written down a couple of centuries after his death, so don't take them for more than they are. Stories can get amplified and refined over the years. But also don't take them for less than they are. The stories tell us the kind of person Bishop Nicholas was and the sort of things he did and which he still does, as you will hear. There are many similar stories from modern times, wonders still performed by Nicholas and other saints, both ancient and modern, living both on earth and in heaven. The wonders done by saints of our day are every bit as startling as these ancient stories of Saint Nicholas, which makes the old miracle stories far more believable.

Here are some of the stories passed down about miracles done by Bishop Nicholas while he was on earth. It was told that while he was still a priest, not yet a bishop, he was sailing to the Holy Land on pilgrimage; a great storm arose, and Father Nicholas by his prayers calmed the sea. Another story tells of three boys who had been murdered by an innkeeper, their bodies stuffed in a pickle barrel—horrible crimes are not a modern invention—and how Nicholas found them and raised them to life again. There is a story of how there was a famine in the region, and the captain of a merchant ship carrying wheat on the Mediterranean was startled to see a man suddenly standing beside him, who begged him to sail his ship to Myra, and then he was gone. So the captain did so, and there was the same man waiting for him at the dock, who was, of course, Bishop Nicholas. A story tells of three military men from Myra who out of jealousy, had been falsely accused of treason and were being held in prison awaiting execution. All attempts to free them had failed until one night the emperor Constantine awoke terrified to see a man standing beside his bed that identified himself as Bishop Nicholas of Myra and threatened the emperor with disaster if he didn't free the men. Constantine checked it out, found the men were innocent and had them released. These were only some of the miracle stories passed down. Maybe even before his death he was called Nicholas the Wonderworker. (There have been quite a number of saints, by the way, who have had the ability to know events from afar, and a few who have been able to remain in one place but also appear elsewhere. One 20th century Greek elder occasionally appeared to people to give them counsel, while those around him knew he had never left his cell. He always denied it, saying it was just someone pretending to be him, but his companions knew better.)

Bishop Nicholas died in the mid 4th century. We don't know the year, but we do know the day, December 6, because holy men and women were (and are) commemorated at services held in their memory on the day of their death and Saint Nicholas Day has always been December 6. Bishop Nicholas died and from his body there began to pour forth a clear sweet-smelling liquid which the Church calls myrrh, for lack of knowing what else to call it, with healing qualities. (This also has happened with a number of saints—Saint Demetrios of Thessaloniki, for example—including a few in recent years.) There began to be many healing miracles. The story of the myrrh might be hard to believe except for one thing, the body of Saint Nicholas is still exuding the same fragrant myrrh. I'm getting ahead of the story, but in the 11th century merchants from Bari in southern Italy came and more or less stole Saint Nicholas' body and took it home, where it is still lying in Saint Nicholas Roman Catholic Basilica in Bari. It is in a quiet place with a holy happy feeling about it, beneath the main church, with a small Orthodox chapel to the left, an encouraging sign of ecumenical cooperation, where the Divine Liturgy is celebrated in Italian. Saint Nicholas' body is still mostly incorrupt (shriveled but still there, not just bones) lying in a pool of clear liquid which upon analysis in the early 20th century was found to have no bacterial content. How do we know this? Because every year on the feasts of Saint Nicholas, his tomb is opened, and a priest removes some of the myrrh. Over the centuries a whole cottage industry has grown up of making fancy bottles to hold and distribute the myrrh. We have some here which I brought back from Bari, for anointing on the feasts of Saint Nicholas. There are still many healings. Small relics of Bishop Nicholas' body have been distributed all over the world, most of which I suppose have flowed out with the myrrh. We have one imbedded in our own altar. These are our physical connections with the real live flesh and blood and bone, myrrh-streaming Saint Nicholas of Myra.

Returning to the early centuries, pilgrims flocked to Myra in great numbers. They took devotion to Saint Nicholas home with them and his fame and his miracles spread through the world, beginning along the Mediterranean and then north into Slavic lands where in Russia to this day more churches are named after Saint Nicholas than any other saint, and west to the far reaches of Spain and Britain where Nicholas was one of the most popular of saints. He came to the New World. After the Protestant Reformation when devotion to saints was mostly abolished,

Nicholas took on a disguise in Protestant regions, for some centuries known as Sinter Klaas in Holland, who became Santa Claus in America. Today he's reemerging as himself again, but that's another story. So this obscure 4th century bishop became and has remained the most popular saint in the world, except for Mary the Mother of God herself. How did this happen? Because of his miracles. People asked for Nicholas' help and often they got it. He is one of those saints who have done their greatest work on earth after their bodily death.

From all over the world come stories of Saint Nicholas' miracles. I recently went on the internet and checked out Saint Nicholas and found 17,990,000 entries. I didn't have time to check out quite all of them! There have been many "ordinary" healings, but let me tell you a few of the more extraordinary stories. They began early. Not long after his death, a ship was sailing from Alexandria with pilgrims headed for Myra, when a great storm came up and the ship was about to sink. The people began to call out to Saint Nicholas to help them. To their amazement the saint himself appeared and calmed the storm. This event is regularly portrayed in icons. Saint Nicholas has long been the patron saint of seafarers who before they go to sea often go to church and light a candle before his icon.

There is a quaint story from old Constantinople of a poor old man and woman devoted to Saint Nicholas who always lit a big candle in church on his feast. One Saint Nicholas Day they had nothing left but a cow. The old woman said, "We're not going to live long anyway; so sell the cow and use the money to buy the candle." The old man did, and went to church and lit the candle. When he got home he found his wife upset. Said she, "An old priest brought the cow back; he said he was a friend of yours, and then he left. Why didn't you sell the cow?" She described the old priest; and then they both realized it had been Saint Nicholas. When the emperor heard the story he gave them money to support them for the rest of their lives.

A story from Ukraine (I don't know the date.) tells of a young couple who were sailing on pilgrimage to visit a shrine, with their little son. The mother fell asleep, and the little boy got away and fell overboard and was lost. They returned home desolate, and turned to Saint Nicholas for consolation. Next morning when the local church was unlocked, crying was heard, and there before the icon of Saint Nicholas lay a very wet little child. They called in the parents and sure enough it was their boy.

Let's take some more recent stories. In the late 19th century there was a man named John Grazes (The story was recorded by his great great granddaughter.) who lived on the island of Patmos where Saint John the apostle received his Revelation. He was captain of his own boat and ferried merchandise between Patmos and other islands in the eastern

Aegean. Being a seaman he honored Saint Nicholas. Once when they were off Patmos a great storm came up so quickly that John and his crew realized they would never make it to port. They prepared to die and began to call on Saint Nicholas. Then they noticed something radiant floating towards the boat and realized it was of all things, the Grazes family icon of Saint Nicholas. John pulled it into the boat and immediately the waters near the boat were stilled. All about them the storm raged with enormous waves, while around them the sea was completely calm, and they sailed quietly to shore with not so much as a drop of rain touching them. (I know a similar story from some fishermen in the Gulf of Alaska involving Saint Herman of Alaska, which took place only a few years ago.) John took the icon back home, but it refused to stay there. (There are many stories of icons that have minds of their own.) Some years later the family noticed the Saint Nicholas icon was missing from the icon corner of their house. They searched, but it was nowhere to be found. Some while later a family friend was walking on the other side of the island and noticed something beside a tree. Recognizing it as the Grazes' Saint Nicholas icon, the friend returned it to them. A few days later it was missing again. John went to the place where his friend had found it before, and there it was again. He took the icon home and said he had concluded that Saint Nicholas wanted a chapel built on that spot. He honored the saint's wishes. The morning the chapel was to be consecrated, the icon was gone again. They found it in the new Saint Nicholas chapel waiting for them.

In 1890 in Sitka, Alaska, a Russian priest, Father Duhov, was visited by a delegation from the pagan Tlingit Aukwanton tribe of Juneau, a seafaring people, who said their prince Yarkon and all the people wished to be baptized. They promised to donate land and build a church there, but the name of the church had to be Saint Nicholas. They told this story: a young Tlingit man had had a vision of an old white man who advised him to go to Sitka and be baptized. The young man soon became ill and called the elders of the village and told them the same old man had come to him again telling him all the people should be baptized. The young man died, but soon other Tlingits began to have the same vision. Bishop Nikolai of the Russian Orthodox Church sent a priest to Juneau and began the baptisms. The entire tribe became Christian and soon built Saint Nicholas Church for they all believed firmly that the old man who had visited them was Saint Nicholas. They had never heard of him before he had appeared to them. Their descendants are Orthodox Christians to this day. They have been instrumental in ending feuding among the native peoples of the region and are still deeply devoted to Saint Nicholas.

In Siberia in a midwinter after the Communist revolution when Russia was torn by civil war, the White Army was retreating. Entering a village they seized a man suspected of collaborating with the Reds, locked him up and assigned a lieutenant to take him out and execute him the next day. That night the lieutenant was sitting alone writing out the formal accusation. There came a knock at the door. He opened it and in walked an old man wearing a black headdress such as Orthodox monks wear and a black rassa (cassock). "Officer," the old man said, "you have arrested an innocent man. Do not kill him." "Who are you?" asked the lieutenant. "I am Father Nicholas from the local church," he answered, and he left. The lieutenant thought it over and decided to release the prisoner. Early next morning he took the man and told the others he would now kill him. Instead when they got some distance away he gave him some bread and said, "Into the woods with you, and don't cross our path again." He returned to the village and went to the church to find the priest. It was locked. He asked a peasant, "Where does Father Nicholas live?" The peasant answered, "He's dead. The Reds shot him years ago." The lieutenant, thoroughly puzzled, got keys to the church, went in, and saw on his right a very unusual icon of Saint Nicholas, portrayed wearing monastic headdress and a cassock. It was the old man who had come to him the night before.

There are many more stories, but would you like to move closer home? How about Michigan City, Indiana, in 1996? At about 6:30 a.m. on the feast of Saint Nicholas, December 6, 1996, Fr. Elias Warnke and Reader (cantor) Timothy Tadros opened the door of Saint George Orthodox Church, Michigan City, to get things ready for the feast day services. They smelled a sweet fragrance like roses which got stronger as they went into the church. As they checked to see where it was coming from, Fr. Elias looked at the icon of Saint Nicholas which was on a stand on the analogion and saw glistening streams of liquid running off it. It came from the forehead, three streams of myrrh. (Weeping icons of the Theotokos, the Mother of God, are not uncommon in the Orthodox Church. I've seen three of them myself, and I know many other firsthand accounts. So far as I know the myrrh always comes from her eyes. Myrrh-streaming icons of St. Nicholas are rare. I know of only one other, at Saint Nicholas Cathedral in Tarpon Springs, Florida. As with Saint Nicholas himself, the myrrh from his icons has come from his body.) The icon at Michigan City was not an original. It was a reproduction printed on paper, laminated and glued to a board, made by the monks at Saint Isaac's Skete in Boscobel, Wisconsin and because it was an imperfect copy they had put it in the reject bin. Father Elias had picked it up because it was free. The myrrh was coming off or through the plastic laminate. There could be no human cause. Only three persons had keys to the church, and besides, they could see the myrrh flowing off of it. (There was an icon in a home in Milwaukee. For years, when the old lady who owned it prayed, it exuded so much myrrh that her daughter complained that she continually had to wipe it up! At Saint George Antiochian Orthodox Church, Cicero, Illinois, in the 1990s, they filled bowls with the myrrh that flowed from their weeping icon of the Theotokos.) As is the usual practice, the priest exorcised the icon just in case (the devil can work wonders, too); the myrrh kept coming. There were some healings. A woman previously diagnosed with untreatable cancer and desperate (She was raising her little orphaned nephew alone and had been told she had two years to live.) was anointed with the myrrh. When she visited the doctor the cancer was gone. A man took myrrh home and anointed his wife who had been bedridden for two years. He left and came back to find her in the kitchen fixing dinner. A woman was apparently cured of chronic alcoholism. Following the usual pattern, the icon exuded considerable myrrh for a while and then it became intermittent and eventually stopped. Don't ask me to explain. I'm just describing. But as I say, I have seen weeping icons.

We can come even closer home to Cedarburg, Wisconsin. The story of how our Saint Nicholas Church came to be through the intervention of Saint Nicholas is not as striking as the others, but it happened to us. (See the article: How Saint Nicholas Church Came to Be) Generation after generation, the miracles of Saint Nicholas continue.

In September 1989, I became a member and priest of the Holy Orthodox Church. Here are my reactions . . .

TEN YEARS LATER
September 1999

What I hoped to find in the Orthodox Church

I was seeking stability in the faith. I sought the Church that Saint Irenaeus had described, which "carefully preserves" apostolic teachings and "proclaims them and teaches them and hands them down with perfect harmony," throughout the world and from generation to generation. By process of elimination, I had concluded that only the Orthodox Church fit this description. I came to the Orthodox Church demoralized and exhausted, war-weary from the losing battle of trying to maintain traditional doctrinal, liturgical and moral standards in western Christianity. In ten years in the Orthodox Church, I have encountered not one disbelieving bishop, priest, theologian or layperson. Certainly there are Orthodox who don't take the faith seriously or who are lax in their practice, but so far as I can see no one denies it or is trying to change it. Orthodox unity in the faith still astounds me. I found what I was seeking.

What I feared as I came to the Orthodox Church

(1) That I would never fit in. Those who have grown up Orthodox cannot imagine how forbidding Orthodoxy can appear to an outsider. I now find it hard to believe that ten years ago people with Middle Eastern and Greek backgrounds seemed very exotic to me. Orthodoxy felt "foreign" and "ethnic" to this German/Welsh/Irish-American. Partly I was a prisoner of my own ethnic background. But also I was afraid I would break some eastern cultural or religious taboo and cause great offense. Orthodox worship appeared very difficult to master, and I was afraid "cradle" Orthodox would laugh at me as I struggled to learn it. I was wrong. Yes, I have encountered some ethnic differences, which have caused me to grow. I have learned to hug and kiss a lot more, and also to express myself more forcefully. (I have had to abandon Anglican subtlety. There's no point in "beating around the bush" with Orthodox people!) I have eaten things I never ate before. The wonderful ethnic diversity of Orthodoxy has been broadening to me in a number of ways. (Ah, the food at our church suppers!) But my fears were unfounded. Though I still make mistakes (just ask the bishops . . .), Orthodox worship has not been as difficult as I anticipated. Furthermore, once you learn it, it holds still: no national liturgical commission is trying to revise and modernize Orthodox worship—thank God! The "cradle" Orthodox who have come to Saint Nicholas have, with almost no exceptions, been sweet and tolerant as I have learned Orthodoxy. Indeed I have never felt so loved in my life. And as for the Antiochian Archdiocese, surely the Middle-Easterners who welcome us into their Archdiocese must sometimes find us converts and our mistakes and peculiar ways hard to take, but I have found only the warmest of welcomes. There has been not the slightest pressure to become anything ethnically other than what I am. After ten years, I feel far more at home in this "foreign" Orthodox Church than I ever felt "back there."

(2) I was afraid I would starve to death. I feared Khouria Dianna and I would have to live in poverty, being supported only by a struggling little mission in a "poor immigrant Church." I was wrong. I can't speak of all Orthodox jurisdictions and parishes—but I am amazed at the amount of money that flows through the Antiochian Archdiocese and through this congregation. My former supposedly wealthy denomination had nothing to compare to Antiochian Village and Conference Center, or to the style of our Archdiocese Conventions and Conferences, or to the proportion of money that goes to good works outside the Archdiocese. I could never have imagined that in ten years our own small congregation would have a fine temple, mostly paid off, and would have given away well over $100,000. The people of Saint Nicholas have supported me more than generously. Khouria Dianna has found it good to work full time, because her health insurance is so good. But we have got our children through college, for the first time in our life we own a home, my automobile allowance allows me to pay cash for my cars, and we have traveled more and farther than ever before in our lives. This has been a great faith-builder: we have far more trust in the power of God to provide. And I was afraid of going hungry!

What else I have found in the Orthodox Church

(1) The Kingdom of God. I have shared this with many of you before: about the fourth Sunday after I became Orthodox, as I stood at the altar at Divine Liturgy, the presence of God and the saints and angels became Real to me. It was not an intellectual discovery (I believed it before), nor was it a new feeling. The Kingdom was just Present, almost palpable. That was how I began to encounter the common Orthodox experience of worship as "heaven on earth" which has continued at every service since then. At worship in my former denomination, I tried hard to concentrate my mind on God and the saints. Now I don't have to. They concentrate on me; they surround me; they encompass me. Words are inadequate to describe the indescribable. But most Orthodox know from their own experience what I'm trying to say.

(2) That Orthodoxy has the power to change lives, beginning with my own: My despair and weariness have turned to hope and energy. Inside, I feel younger than I did ten years ago. And I have seen so many in my congregation turn to God in a new way. Again, I don't deny that there are many nominal Orthodox, and none of us practice Orthodoxy as we should. But I see that the Orthodox doctrine of theosis (that God makes us like himself, makes us holy) is not theory. It is a description of

what actually happens to people in the Orthodox Church. In my former denomination I always felt that I had to change people by my own words and efforts. Here God and the Church do it, and I'm simply one of those being changed.

(3) Not only great joy but also lots of fun! Starting a new mission was hard work on the part of all of us, and just conducting Orthodox worship is exhausting. (Western services now seem so short, so shallow.) But I have never enjoyed myself or laughed so much in my life. This has been a delight.

(4) That the outside world looks odder and odder. Partly this is because American culture has kept changing since I became Orthodox, while Orthodoxy has held still. Things which seemed unconscionable in our culture even ten years ago, on both the left and the right, are now commonplace. But also the world seems stranger to me because Orthodoxy is even more countercultural than I ever imagined. In the liberal western denominations, radical theology, pop worship, women's ordination and "gay" rights are ever more the order of the day—while in Orthodoxy these things are still not even being debated, nor is there any sign that they will be. The western secular world continues to think that politics and economics and education and force can solve our problems, and that a just society can be created by man without reference to God and his truth—while Orthodoxy is God and his truth. I watch the evening news and read non-Orthodox religious publications and just shake my head: what ever do these people think they're doing? Why did I stay there so long? As an Orthodox I feel far less threatened by what's going on outside the Church, and I find that now it makes me sad instead of angry—but the non-Orthodox world looks ever more peculiar to me.

Has there been any down side? Scarcely any. Becoming Orthodox has been overwhelmingly a positive experience for me. However . . .

(1) For some of the reasons mentioned above, I've discovered that Orthodoxy is more difficult to communicate to our society than I would have guessed. In my first enthusiasm as a convert, I felt that if Americans could only be exposed to Orthodoxy, they would rush into the Church. Certainly Orthodoxy is growing in the world—and our Antiochian Archdiocese has grown by leaps and bounds during the past ten years—but I also now see that many modern Americans find it hard to understand Orthodoxy. They are so accustomed to human-centered, man-made religion that they find it difficult even to grasp the concept of God-centered, revealed religion. Many do not see the purpose of

worship. More than a few have come to our Orthodox services (even in English) and have no idea what's going on. "Making America Orthodox" is not as easy as I thought.

(2) As I moved into Orthodoxy and discovered how good it is, for a while I felt unhappy that I had waited so long to become Orthodox. Why did I waste so much time in western Christianity trying to reinvent the wheel, when the real Church was here waiting for me all the while? I could have spent my whole ministry in the Church; we could have raised our children in the Orthodox faith. I'm still sad about this, but I've come to accept that God has his own timing, that he can use even my slowness and stupidity and stubbornness for good.

Would I do it all over again?

Yes! Yes! Yes! These past ten years in Orthodoxy have been the best and happiest and most fulfilling of my life. Thanks to God and thanks to Saint Nicholas for bringing me home.

WHAT I'VE LEARNED IN 70 YEARS
August 24, 2008

At first I thought this might be a short talk. Sometimes I feel I haven't learned much. Then I got to thinking, and yes I have. Some of what follows is directly theological; the rest has been shaped by 50 years of faith. Someone said that what we need to do is not so much think about Orthodoxy—that is well established—but rather think about the world in the light of Orthodoxy. I have been doing that for a long time now. Here are some things I have come to believe:

1) God is real. How can anyone be an atheist or agnostic? The world exists, has design and keeps going; it must have a Creator, Designer and Sustainer. I cannot imagine otherwise. Equally important, God has been moving in my life all these years. He pokes me, prods me, does good things for me. His presence at worship is almost palpable. However, apart from worship, God often *feels* more unreal to me as I get older. (This is not what I expected.) Why? I can imagine three possibilities: When Khouria Dianna and I were in Oregon we drove up to Mount Hood. She wanted to stop and take a picture. I said "No, wait, we'll see better as we get closer." I was wrong. Lower hills got in the way, till finally we got close, made a turn and suddenly Mount Hood almost jumped out at us in all its glory. I *hope* that's what's going on with me and God. But it

could also be because I'm headed in the wrong direction. Or maybe I'm not paying attention. I've learned that often when I don't sense God's presence, often it's not because he's not here; it's because I'm not here.

2) Jesus Christ is the Son of God. I went to seminary believing in God but not believing in Christ. You can do that if you're a liberal Protestant; nobody cares. I soon discovered that theology is complex, and I got so befuddled that I thought of dropping out, when I hit on a plan. I would start not with what little I could figure out but rather with what most Christians always believed, main-stream Christianity, what I later discovered C.S. Lewis had called "mere" Christianity and still later learned is really Orthodoxy. This was one of the two smartest decisions I ever made—the other was marrying my wife. After that instead of my shaping the faith to suit me, I began to be shaped by the faith. I entered into (what was for me) a new world of sacraments, ceremonies, liturgy, saints, the creed and the God who was made flesh and dwelt among us. Quickly Jesus Christ as Lord and God and his love for me became real to me, and I began a lifelong fascination with Jesus. I find the Man absolutely compelling.

Year after year he has become more alive, more profound, wiser and deeper and richer to me. I can't imagine life without him. Orthodoxy has taught me how great he really is. In western Christianity some consider Jesus only a great teacher; others want to confine him to a particular religious experience or to the institutional Church or to the sacraments. Orthodoxy has shown me that Christ is the eternal God who is in all places and fills all things, that wherever in the world there are love, goodness, truth, beauty, mercy, Jesus Christ is there. This has opened up the world to me in a new way.

3) I have learned to trust the Orthodox Church. I was looking for mainstream Christianity, mere Christianity, and in that quest I got burnt elsewhere. Their heart was not fixed on Jesus. Orthodoxy has as many sinners and eccentrics as anybody else. Father Alexander Schmemann, dean of St. Vladimir's Seminary, once on a bad day was heard muttering, "The Orthodox Church is the right church filled with all the wrong people." The truth is all churches, all the world is filled with the "wrong people"—us. That's the only kind of people there are. Actually I have found more love, more good people, in the Orthodox Church than I've ever known before. But Orthodoxy is no escape from problems. Father Peter Gillquist says: If you're looking for the perfect Church this isn't it. The perfect Church is in heaven. But the Orthodox Church (not by any virtue of ours; it is the work of the Holy Spirit) is solid, truly united in what matters most: the Faith. It still amazes me. Thinking about the world in light of Orthodoxy, here are some of things I've learned:

4) It really is love that makes the world go 'round. "Love God with all your heart, soul, mind and strength. Love your neighbor as yourself. This sums up the Law and the Prophets." [cf. Mark 12:30] Someone called Orthodoxy the Church of love. Above all we emphasize community and relationships—with God, the saints and each other. By love we don't mean good feelings. We mean the interrelationships of people, people personally caring about each other. The world is forever restructuring and redesigning things, trying to get control, hoping thereby to make things better. And of course often structures can be improved. But what holds societies and families and churches together is love, people caring about each other. "The greatest of these is love."

5) You can't love people by killing them. Life is sacred, each person from womb to tomb. I have what I hope is a consistent pro-life ethic. Taking human life whether in abortion clinics or in war or in prison execution chambers or just by letting people die because they have no health care is evil. Please, send me a politician who is consistently pro-life.

6) Generally, smaller is better, because it is in small institutions that people can know and love each other. Small institutions produce more personal involvement and responsibility, more caring. In big institutions people often get lost in the shuffle, become just numbers in the system. I am suspicious of all big institutions: big business, big government, big military, big banks, big finance, big media, big labor, even big churches—which is a good thing because God has put me in small churches. I like small local stores rather than big chain stores, even if it costs more. I dislike socialism which concentrates power in big government. I dislike capitalism which concentrates power in irresponsible big banks and corporations. I like the economics of G.K. Chesterton: distributivism, which came out of the 19th century Catholic workers movement. It seeks a world composed as much as possible of small landowners, small businesses, small institutions. Today we're going the opposite direction. America has been taken over by the big guys. How well do you think it's working?

7) The family is the basic unit of society, because family is the only natural human institution that is based on love—just like the Kingdom of God. We can move our politics to the right or the left, we can put as much money as we want into schools or prisons, and it won't work unless we deal with the central issue. Our biggest problem today is broken marriages, broken families, one parent families, weak families where parents care more about getting stuff or getting ahead than they do about loving their kids. Society will never function right till we solve this problem.

8) People need to be free. Love requires freedom. Just on a practical level trying to control people, whether by force or law or manipulation or by laying guilt on them, doesn't work well, not for long. Control works only so long as force is applied; as soon as it isn't people rebel and it's all over. We all need rules, of course. But a family, church or society that lives mostly by rules has already lost it. Love is what glues things together, and love cannot be compelled. Love must be freely chosen—or not. In 70 years I have seen nothing good accomplished by force or control alone. In order to protect the innocent, evil can be restrained by force, and sometimes it must. But ends do not justify means. (I learned that from my eighth grade history teacher's analysis of World War II.) The means we use determine the ends. If the end we seek is to form people who love, who do good because in their hearts and souls and minds they really are good, then compulsion and force won't get us there. I've never told you this story: when I was on Mount Athos I woke up in the middle of the night and maybe it was sleep deprivation but it was also a mystical experience. I looked out my window. Everything was absolutely still except the *shh shh* of the sea, the landscape bright in moonlight, the sky brilliant with stars—and (this was the mystical part, which I can't begin to express) the stars and the planets and the sea seemed to be freely moving in love, choosing to do God's will, and it was that love freely chosen that was holding the universe together—all things, all people moving in harmony freely choosing the will of God. Again, I can't get this into words, but it was vivid, extremely profound, and it has shaped me ever since. This is why I have an intense visceral negative reaction against people, politicians, governments, any who bull their way through life, controlling, pushing, shoving, manipulating and running over people. People must be free.

9) Don't judge people. Love people. Actions must be judged, of course. When Jesus said do not judge [Mt. 7:1], he didn't mean anything goes. He meant: don't judge the worth of people, don't give up on people. Hate the sin but love the sinner just as Christ loves us despite our behavior. It was my mother who taught me: be tolerant. I have learned that when people hurt me or do things I do not approve of, I must try not to judge them. Sometimes I have to apply the Church's discipline for the sake of the community, of course, but I try to make no personal judgments on them, and I wait for the chance to do something good for them. Then sometimes, maybe years later, I find out what they were struggling with at the time that I didn't know about, or how they read the situation in a way that I did not, and I come to understand, and often I wonder why they weren't twice as

nasty or peculiar. Don't put people down. Don't make people into the enemy. God will judge. I don't have to. We are to love people, by the command of the Lord.

10) You may think I'm crazy, but I have come to believe that competition is generally a bad thing. I know: our whole culture, economics, politics, entertainment are based on competition. It's like everything has become a Packers Game, where "winning isn't everything; winning is the only thing." (Vince Lombardi did not invent that saying, by the way.) It's all winners versus losers; get the other guy before he gets you. I challenge you; I'll pay you $50 *cash* if you can find me one verse in the New Testament that glorifies competition between people. The New Testament, the teaching of Jesus is entirely about cooperation and loving people. In New Testament sports images, all can win the race, all can get the prize. Real life isn't winners versus losers. What if we ran marriage like that? No, in marriage the couple loves each other and so both are winners. Or in the Church: actually I've seen churches where they play winners and losers, and when they do everybody loses, the Church loses. In the Church we support and love each other so all come out ahead. It seems self-evident to me that in war there are only greater and lesser losers, no matter who wins. Nevertheless we run politics and the economy and international affairs like sports: destroy the other guy. If we did it the Gospel way, we would seek ways to cooperate, and everybody would win. When I become president (I'm only 70: some think that's not too old.) the first thing I'm going to do is set up a Department of Peace and Cooperation to find ways to resolve conflicts, both national and international. (I won't be elected; this isn't macho enough . . .) And we will start with the teachings of the New Testament. Here's what I would put on the walls of our courthouses: not the Ten Commandments but "Love your neighbor as yourself. Love your enemies. Do good to those who mistreat you." [Lk. 10:27; Mt. 5:44]

11) Truth matters. Christ said he is the truth. [Jn. 14:6] We pray "O heavenly King, Comforter, Spirit of truth . . ." The Ninth Commandment is do not bear false witness: do not tell lies, do not pass along falsehoods whether over the back fence or on the internet. If you're running for president do not tell lies about your opponent. More than once I have voted against candidates with whom I agreed on issues because they told so many lies, ran such dirty dishonest sleazy campaigns. Today the media, the internet, politics, government, advertising are so filled with lies, propaganda and half-truths that we're numb; nobody even seems to care anymore. But if we can't believe what people say society falls apart. If I ever say or write anything that is untrue or inaccurate, please

tell me. And when you pass along stuff that is not true I will continue to set you straight.

12) Honey draws more flies than vinegar. "God so loved the world . . . , God sent his Son . . . not to condemn the world but to save it . . ." [Jn. 3:16] Nor is it my job to condemn the world. Being negative and nasty and sarcastic may attract a radio or TV audience, but in the end it puts people off—or even worse it attracts negative, nasty, sarcastic people. Speak the truth positively in love. Smile. Have fun. Be gentle. Be kind to people.

13) Sit on it. Words said or written in anger or haste can be apologized for, but they can never be unsaid. "If anyone . . . does not bridle his tongue . . . his religion is useless." [James 1:26]

14) Forgive. Let it go. Brooding on past slights just gives people who hurt us continuing power over us. Don't carry this heavy burden through life. Put it down. Forgive and be free of the past.

15) Question authority. My father taught me that. He said: don't be one of the sheep. Be like Thomas the apostle. Think for yourself. Many authorities in this world will say anything in order to keep their power or get money out of you. Beware particularly of religious authorities, especially the ones on television. Question the priest. Don't believe things just because I say so. Think for yourself. Be one of the sheep only if the sheep are following the Good Shepherd.

16) I have learned to love the modern world, despite it faults, dangers and nonsense. I didn't always. For a long time I was a sort of troglodyte, longing for the glories of the past, but by now I've read enough history to conclude that it wasn't any better then, it isn't any worse now. The world has always been a mess; the world has always been glorious. Modern medicine keeps me healthy; without it I'd likely be blind and ill by now. I like indoor plumbing (I remember the outdoor facilities at my grandparents' farm on zero mornings!) and hot showers every day. I love modern communications. The internet has incredible resources for seeking knowledge and researching sermons and papers. On it instantly I can email and even see my loved ones at a distance. (Instead of writing and mailing 80 letters His Grace Bishop MARK can push a button and instantly communicate with all his clergy.) My cell phone allows me never to be cut off from people I love. I can hear gorgeous music daily that was once heard only rarely by a few people in concert halls. I listen to Vespers live from Greece. I love to watch storms on weather radar. Years ago many old people were isolated, bored to death in their rocking chairs; now if I ever get housebound my computer will keep the world open to me. Once only the wealthy could travel, but now I have seen places and done things I never even imagined. Best of all I love the freedom the modern world gives us to be what God calls us to be. Years ago I never

would have or could have become Orthodox. Orthodox were over there and Anglos over here, and we were all too set in our ethnic ways. Now, thank God, here I am Orthodox. Thank God for the modern world.

17) Keep growing, keep learning, keep thinking, keep expanding your horizons. Don't become narrow and closed minded. God is infinite; Christ is universal; heaven is eternal. God intends us to grow in love and knowledge forever. Don't stop now.

But this talk has got to stop now. Turning 70 seems odd and a little scary, but I am so grateful for long years, good health, family and so many people around me who love me and whom I love, and a Church that is built on the Rock. As years go on, I am especially grateful for my faith in eternal life. I believe—because my Lord Jesus Christ said so—that I am still at the *beginning* of a journey that will never end. If I understand it right, our few years in this world are just the preface, the introduction to the great book of life. It is over there that we will start Chapter 1. See, I have learned a few things in 70 years. I think I like being 70.

TWENTY YEARS LATER
September 2009

From 1977 to 1987 I edited a publication for a national Episcopalian organization, trying to preserve traditional Anglicanism. In 1987 I wrote my last editorial entitled "Ten Years Later," pointing out that we had failed and implying that Orthodoxy was the answer. In 1989 I left (actually was thrown out of) the Episcopal Church and became Orthodox, and in 1999 I wrote another article entitled "Ten Years Later," telling of my positive experiences in the Orthodox Church. Now, so quickly, another ten years have passed.

In the past twenty years many things have changed. I who once was 51 am now 71. Khouria Dianna and I have recovered from the anxieties and difficulties of my mid-life change of jobs. (A warning to any considering it: when the man starts over, it is his wife who carries most of the burden.) Our son and daughter are now established in life, and we have three delightful, brilliant, charming, indeed nearly *perfect* grandchildren. In twenty years American politics has blown this way and that, and the categories as always have kept changing.* For twenty years the Episcopal

---

*   I remember when liberals opposed abortion and never even imagined "gay" marriage, let alone it being a basic human right, when conservatives opened the door to communist China and gave us "socialistic" government-imposed

Church and the rest of "mainline" Protestantism have continued to march to the left and have diminished rapidly in numbers,** so that now the American Protestant "mainline" is right wing fundamentalist. Twenty years later, the Middle East is even worse off, General Motors is bankrupt, industries are going down; our great American health care is a mess, commercial TV has turned from comedies to [un]reality shows, commercial radio and TV which once reported news is dominated by loudmouths. The internet, with its vast resources of information and disinformation, and cell phones keep us connected whether we want to be or not. OK, death and taxes are still with us, and Honda still makes great cars, but so many things have changed . . .

. . . and the Holy Orthodox Church is exactly as it was 20 years ago.

Worship, doctrines, moral teachings and structures remain the same, not a single prayer has changed, the same icons still look out at us with the same expressions on their faces. Neither liberals nor conservatives (Do we even have those in Orthodoxy?) are about to take over. One of the best things to stay the same is that his Eminence our Metropolitan PHILIP at age 78 is still going strong, thank God.

But I exaggerate. Some things have changed. Our Antiochian Archdiocese has about twice as many churches as twenty years ago. We have attained "self-rule" status under the Patriarch of Antioch, so that we now have dioceses and diocesan bishops in North America, and a new Bishop MARK of the Diocese of Toledo and the Midwest who is a jewel, thank God again. In twenty years our Orthodox Mission with 25 members has become Saint Nicholas Church with over 225 members. That is "change I can believe in!" ***

But the controversies that consume western Christianity do not seem to touch the Orthodox Church. If anything I think Orthodoxy has become more rooted in the Fathers and the Tradition. The world outside keeps whirling madly, but Orthodoxy stays the same, a fixed star. As the silly joke goes "How many Orthodox does it take to change a light bulb?" "*C H A N G E*?!" Which is good, because what needs to change is

---

environmental and wage and price controls and a multi-billion dollar federally funded interstate highway system, when some Democrats were virulently racist and some Republicans were peace activists.

** I also remember when the Episcopal Church was called the "Republican Party at prayer!"

*** [Ed. note: an obvious reference to candidate Obama's campaign slogan] not Orthodoxy but me. The Orthodox faith doesn't need a makeover. I do. That is what I want to talk about: how Orthodoxy has changed me in the past 20 years—in some ways I did not anticipate, all of them for the better.

1) I got my self back. Not long before I left my old Episcopal church, someone said to me, "I just wish we could get the old Father Bill back"—which startled me. And then I looked at myself and saw how I had changed. I had begun my work as a young priest positive minded, trusting in God and the Anglican system and Anglican people. My approach to parish life was "Let a thousand flowers grow." Over the years, as I saw how many weeds were growing in my Anglican garden, I had become distrustful, narrow and focused on a few controversial issues, negative and frustrated as we lost battle after battle, and control-oriented as the kind of Anglicanism I had believed in disintegrated. I wasn't having fun any more. I was becoming cranky. I found myself shaking my finger at people during sermons. Looking back, I see now that I became Orthodox for psychological reasons as well as for theological reasons. I wasn't myself any more. I needed to get my self back.

While I was still Anglican, Father Thomas Hopko warned me that Orthodoxy possessed "absolute theological unanimity," and if I became Orthodox I would have to give up being a valiant defender of the faith and learn to be just "one of the guys." It sounded good. I half believed him. I checked Orthodoxy out carefully and saw no signs of disbelief anywhere. No matter, when I first became Orthodox I waited for the shoes to begin to drop, for someone to spout heresy or advocate a new morality. Even though it was quickly evident that there are as many sinners and eccentrics in Orthodoxy as any place else, it never happened.

At my first Antiochian clergy conference the theme was pastoral ministry, which could have taken some odd turns, but then I listened in wonder as the parish clergy began to respond, as the teachings of the Scriptures and the Fathers just flowed out of their mouths and no one contradicted them. The Orthodox Church has its problems, but Father Tom spoke the truth.

Episcopalians and other western denominations are arguing now over who Jesus is and whether those in homosexual relationships should be bishops. Orthodox are arguing over the titles of bishops and what color we should paint the front doors. The faith really is established here and doesn't need me to defend it. Here God controls the Church; I don't have to do it. Here God saves people; I don't have to do it. I have learned to trust people again. Again I have "let a thousand flowers grow" and this time very few weeds have come up. I just do my pastoral work (not far different than when I was an Anglican) and try to save my soul, and then I watch Orthodoxy take root in people and change them and me for the better. Protestant teaching was that God did it all and my works didn't matter, but I felt as if I had to do everything. Now that I'm Orthodox where the teaching is that good works are necessary for salvation, I feel as if God is doing it all!

So I began to relax and become myself again. I am again positive minded about the Church and happy and enjoying life. (Orthodoxy, which can look so forbidding and rigid and solemn from the outside, is so warm and cozy on the inside.) I feel I'm growing spiritually again. I am more at peace inside than ever in my life. I've got the "old Father Bill back." My body tells me I'm twenty years older, but in my heart and soul I feel twenty years younger.

2) I got my mind back, for better and for worse. Late in my Anglican days I realized that I was at the point where I could think only defensively about the faith, forever lining up arguments against opponents. Which meant I wasn't really thinking; I was just trying to score points. During war or as in much of American politics today, with sides lined up in bitterly opposed camps, real thinking ceases. All people do is just react and throw rocks at each other.

Orthodoxy does not suppress free inquiry. Now that I'm Orthodox and don't have to fight the old battles any more and am able to actually think again, I find I have more questions than I did before. It feels as if I understand God and the faith less well than I did. I think this is: 1) because I have discovered (not to my pleasure) that much of what I once took for strong faith and deep conviction was just stubbornness: "I'll be damned (literally!) if I'm going to let 'them' tell me Jesus isn't the Son of God." 2) because Orthodoxy is showing me how unfathomably great God really is, opening up to me depths of faith and life and theology that I never even knew existed. I find it hard now to speak about God—no words seem even remotely adequate—except to say that he is Father, Son and Holy Spirit (and I don't know what that really means—the Fathers didn't pretend to know either; they only drew a fence around the Mystery) and that he is good and loves mankind.

Thank God Orthodoxy isn't based primarily on rational thinking. Reason for us is mostly apophatic, negative; it helps us to exclude wrong possibilities. The English language doesn't even have a word for what makes Orthodox believe: it is the νους (nous), the capacity of spiritual perception. We Orthodox believe not because we can figure God out and explain him in a systematic fashion, but because we experience and perceive him and his work in our lives in the Body of Christ, in the Church, in the worship, in the sacraments, in the people. God and his Kingdom are almost palpably present at Divine Liturgy. God reaches out to me continually through the people of the Church. I have a profound new sense of the Church as the Body of Christ. I can't begin to explain any of this, but I experience it daily.

All this has changed, for example, my preaching style. Once my sermons were designed to convince people of some theological or moral point. Now I often just tell the stories of the saints, and try to make the Scriptures and seasonal themes come alive, and instead of telling people what to think or what to do, now I usually just let them figure it out for themselves. Here I don't need to convince anyone of anything. I just try to lay Orthodoxy out for the people to see and experience for themselves. And they do. Maybe it's not because of my words at all.

3) Someone told me that after I became Orthodox the world outside would seem ever stranger to me. Yes and no. In light of Orthodox emphasis on persons, love, mercy, compassion, I'm torn by modern America, where there is so much personal kindness and a wonderful ability to integrate newcomers into our society, mixed with such a spirit of nastiness,* and we ignore so many who are poor, sick, homeless, hungry, unborn. In light of Orthodox emphasis on truth, the amount and effectiveness of propaganda and lying and willful disregard for facts—look at politics and advertising and the internet—sometimes tempts me to despair. So does the raw power of money in America today, considering how much Christ taught about the dangers of greed.

But for the most part I don't think we Orthodox should condemn the world (Jesus didn't: John 3:17—and remember what the first century world was like). Rather we should love the world (God did: John 3:16) and try to find what is good in it and draw it into the Kingdom. Our job is to believe and live our faith positively, not to dump on those who don't. Orthodoxy gives us solid ground from which to think creatively about the world, its faults and its virtues—because despite our ethnic appearance, the Orthodox Church is not "of the world." Orthodoxy does not fit into contemporary American religious and political categories. Orthodoxy is neither liberal nor conservative nor middle of the road. We come from somewhere else. We are ancient, international, multi-cultural, in fundamental matters supra-cultural. We are a colony of heaven, living on earth but rooted in the Tradition of the eternal Church, the Gospel of Jesus Christ.

To my surprise in some ways the world looks better to me now that I'm Orthodox. Orthodoxy has made me more open minded and tolerant

---

*   I also remember when men were expected to be humble, respectful and courteous, not macho blowhards.

(dare I say "liberal"?), for two reasons: 1) partly because the Orthodox Church has exposed this Anglo-Welsh-Irish-German-American to people of other cultures. Believe it or not, twenty years ago Greeks and Slavs seemed exotic to me, and I knew nothing of Arabs and their ways. Now they're all my friends and I've learned much from them. And, to my surprise, I have not been poor as a church mouse but have had money to travel and see new things. There are other and sometimes better ways of seeing and doing things than my old Anglo-American ways. 2) partly because Orthodoxy teaches that the Holy Spirit is "present in all places, filling all things," that Christ is God "filling all things . . . boundless." Orthodox don't believe that you have to be Orthodox in this life to be saved. So Orthodoxy has led me to view people not so much according to whether they're Orthodox or Christian or American or even religious, but according to whether they bring love, goodness, truth, beauty, joy, kindness into the world. If they do, God's Holy Spirit is there and Christ is at work in them, whether they know it or not. I'm learning that God can work through people I disagree with, even disapprove of. "Many who are first will be last, and the last first." [Mt. 20:16]

On the other hand, and maybe to contradict myself, I find that being Orthodox has made me less sympathetic to other kinds of Christians. Are they getting odder, or is it just that I now have a higher standard of comparison? Orthodoxy is so broad, so full, so deep, so rich, so fulfilling in its faith and life, so organic, so unitive, so "put together," and these things seem so self-evident and natural to me now, that I get upset with Christians who diminish and narrow and compromise God and Christ and the Church or make them seem ludicrous. I think much of American Christianity today, both liberal and conservative, is just embarrassing, and it hinders people from coming to the real Jesus Christ. Being Orthodox has also made me less tolerant of ideologues who set up human political and economic systems, whether of the right or the left, and then treat them as absolutes, as if they're divine revelation. Only one thing is absolute: God.

4) I was going to conclude by saying that after twenty years I have "got over" Anglicanism, never think about it any more. "That was then, this is now." Wrong. I recently had occasion to go back to my old Episcopal church. How things had changed. For 21 years I had worked to teach the Bible and the Fathers and to build up an "Anglo-Catholic" parish, trying to be Orthodox in a non-Orthodox setting. Now the building was bare, the style was casual (guitars *twang twang* at a funeral!), no incense or Eucharistic vestments, the late-middle-aged priest wore an earring for heaven sake (not literally), and his sermon made no mention of God, Jesus Christ, the resurrection or eternal life. The Episcopal Church is no

longer mine to criticize, but it really upset me. I had bad dreams about it. But then I thought: that was exactly why I left Anglicanism. I saw that I was spinning my wheels, building on sand, nothing I was doing would last. Bring in a new priest or bishop and a whole new religion often comes in—and so it did.

Here it is different. My successor at Saint Nicholas, Cedarburg, will have his own style and skills and strengths and weaknesses. By God's mercy he may be better organized and move faster and have more energy than this old man. But I know he will be Orthodox. He will believe and teach the same Orthodox faith, he will celebrate the same Orthodox services in the same way, and the tradition of Saint Nicholas Church, which is simply the Orthodox Tradition, will continue. Here we have built something that will last. And so when my time comes I will die a happy man, feeling I have accomplished something. Thank God and thank the Orthodox Church—and thank you.

But not yet, please, Lord. If it may be permitted, I would like to enjoy Orthodoxy and the people of Saint Nicholas Church and my wife and family and (Oh, why not speak the truth . . . ?) my *perfect* grandchildren for a while longer. Maybe long enough to write a paper entitled "Thirty Years Later"?

Chapter Two

Genuine

Disingenuine among religious brings images in my imagination of the effete middle aged clergyman in a high liturgical tradition, raised in a wealthy family whose expectation is that their children make them proud by becoming doctors, lawyers and clergyman. Such a stereotype is the opposite of Fr. Bill.

In the second selection of this chapter, "2009 Trip Report," Father internally questions himself regarding his "professionalism." Few would fault Father for "taking a break" on sabbatical, but he wouldn't have anything to do with that. Why? Because Fr. Bill is genuine. "Taking a break" for Father is bandying about on Patmos and Crete in civilian clothes while continuing to derive great spiritual pleasure from worship and spiritual reading on sabbatical. (How about meditating on The Revelation on the beach?) Clearly there isn't any occasion for Fr. Bill to take a break from Orthodoxy.

The integration of Orthodoxy into the daily life of Greece is symbolic of the integration of Orthodoxy into the everyday life of this priest. He can't help but to compare our life here in the States with Greece. Perhaps on one of these sabbaticals Father will simply just not come back!

Part of genuine Orthodoxy is a vibrant life of faith and experience with the living saints. Again and again Father demonstrates this with St. Nektarios and St. Nicholas. For him the saints are alive, real and immanent, even in the mundane events of our lives. "Orthodoxy is not a doctrine. It is a way of life," Father writes in the first selection, "2007 Trip Report."

As stated earlier, it is impossible to separate out one trait in these given selections. The trait of Fr. Bill's that is consistent with his personality and appears repeatedly is knowledgeable. How does one become knowledgeable? By reading lots and lots of books!! A separate chapter (Four divided into three parts) is devoted to this conspicuous quality.

If Father was ever controversial it could perhaps have been in the area of politics. Though Father is not political by nature nor was he ever "political" in his homilies, some were perhaps offended by comments that Father made that were interpreted as being overly critical of the United States. (Father did not hide his fondness for European living.) Many at St. Nicholas are familiar with his political views. However, it has always been the position of Fr. Bill to speak politically as it relates to the functioning of the Church and the moral issues that affect the lives of people. This was made abundantly clear in an email sent to the editor (James) in response to questions about this issue. There was never a time that politics ever came close to taking priority over Orthodox living and spirituality. While Father could enjoy a good political discussion he firmly addressed overemotional situations (usually leading up to a presidential election) in the church that potentially threatened the unity and peace of the church.

2006 TRIP REPORT

I've got to tell you about my trip. I keep going to Greece. As you know, I have a particular love for Greece and particularly Crete, I think mostly because I first really discovered Orthodoxy there in 1985—can it be 21 years ago already? On this trip I partly just recovered from Holy Week and Pascha but I also checked out a lot of churches and monasteries and ancient ruins. First I went again to visit the island of Aegina and Saint Nektarios, and I have another Saint Nektarios story to tell. Every time I go there something surprising happens.

This time I was a day late visiting Aegina because my suitcase didn't arrive in Athens when I did and I spent most of a day tracking it down. So a day late I visited the shrine, lit candles, and prayed for you all. Many of you gave generously for candles, and when the candle-watcher lady saw me put 50 Euro in the slot, she practically grabbed the prayer list out of my hands so the nuns could pray over it; they got their money's worth, more than 400 names! But nothing unusual had happened. There were many pilgrims and the chapels are small, so I decided to go outside and sit on a bench and watch it all. A voice from beside me on the bench said, "Are you an American?" I turned and there sat Khouria Catherine Heers and her husband Father Gregory, and their son who is now Father Peter, a priest in the Church of Greece getting his doctorate from the University of Thessaloniki—old friends from my Episcopalian days in Milwaukee 35 years ago. I know them all well. I remember when Peter was born. They turned Orthodox (Antiochian Archdiocese) soon after we did, so we've been in touch all these years. And there they sat beside me on a bench in front of Saint Nektarios. The nuns gave us a free lunch, and we spent the rest of the afternoon together. So he did it again. Surely one of these times Saint Nektarios' surprise for me will be no surprise. But not thus far.

I visited some really interesting places on Crete. At a beautiful little women's monastery on the hill above Rethymnon, a sweet nun gave me a tour and again something to eat. I visited some nearly abandoned monasteries way up in the mountains. Preveli is a men's monastery newly active again, wonderfully situated on a cliff above the Libyan Sea. The first weekend I went to Vespers and Liturgy there. It's isolated, nobody lives for miles around, but about 25 or 30 people showed up including 3 young families. For 12 days I wandered in and out of monasteries and churches and ancient ruins. (That was in the mornings, afternoons I hit the beach.) I visited the ruins of Saint Titus Cathedral where the apostle Titus presumably was, where Saint Andrew of Crete (he of the long Lenten canon) was once Archbishop. I visited Kalyviani, a large women's monastery, this one not isolated, just off a main trunk road. As I drove up to it early one morning, through the gate I saw what looked like not a monastery but a village: a wide street lined with flowering trees, people and cars coming and going, the church off to the side. The nuns have there an orphanage, an old folks home, a school, a conference center and I don't know what all else; it was just bustling.

It is a treat to go from place to place, the countryside covered with little chapels, all the towns with many Orthodox churches, most of them well kept with good iconography. The morning I arrived on Crete I visited a city church which was nearly full—on the Friday after Pascha—celebrating the feast of the Theotokos of the Lifegiving Spring. The second Sunday I went to Liturgy in a town of about 1,000 people, which had a big Orthodox school and complex at one end of town, and a large beautifully appointed downtown church which was packed. I could hardly get in. Mostly men on the right, women on the left but not entirely. For example, there was a cute young teenage couple in front of me flirting with each other all through Liturgy. This small town church had 3 priests and a young deacon—all with shortish hair and beards. A number of women wore . . . slacks, in a Greek country village! (Don't confuse hair and dress fashions with the essence of Orthodoxy.) There was a memorial afterwards; the woman who I think had lost her husband fainted dead away Mediterranean style, and as the priest chanted on everyone gathered around her, and a man who must have been the town doctor (He had a very competent air.) came and gave her a glass of water, and she roused. Then there were large trays of kolyva afterwards for everyone. Once again Orthodoxy was very much alive. Are established state churches a bad idea? Do they necessarily go dead? Well, in the western world that seems to be the case. But from what I have seen, not in the east.

As I flew home I got to thinking what a remarkable thing we have going on here at Saint Nicholas, what an interesting experiment we are conducting here. Let me give some background to that thought before I make it. Christianity, Orthodox Christianity, has two chief sources: Middle Eastern and Greek. Our faith came out of the Middle East. All the Old Testament figures, Christ and his Mother and all the apostles were Middle Easterners. The Bible is a Middle Eastern document. In order to understand it and them we need to have a Middle Eastern mindset. Take something as basic as the image of Christ the Good Shepherd. I've told you this before: in the western world shepherds drive their sheep from behind, with sheep dogs rounding them up, barking at their heels. It conjures up an image of clergy whose job as shepherds is to drive lay people on. But in the east shepherds go first, leading their sheep, and because they know and trust the shepherd, the sheep willingly follow. "The Lord is my shepherd: he *leads* me beside still waters." That is a very different approach. Sunday before last as I headed for the monastery, there was a large flock of sheep blocking the road, and I thought: Ah! I'll get to see shepherding eastern style. What I actually got was a guy in a pickup truck pushing them from behind. Oh well . . . Anyway the first source of Christianity is Middle Eastern.

The second source is Greece. From the first century on, Christianity was channeled through Greek culture and language. The New Testament was written in Greek. Most of the early Church fathers were culturally Greek. Christian doctrine was formulated in terms taken from Greek philosophy. The words we English speakers still use to describe our faith are mostly taken directly from the Greek without translation: Christ, Theotokos, Trinity, Person, Bible, Baptism, Eucharist, Liturgy and many more. The second source of Christianity is Greek.

Now here we are in America, trying to develop an expression of Orthodoxy which is both genuinely Orthodox, true to our Orthodox roots, but which is also understandable in terms of American culture. Most Orthodox churches in America are mono-ethnic in one form or another, chiefly composed of Middle Easterners or Greeks or Serbs or Russians or whatever—with only a few members who don't fit ethnically into the pattern. There are also an increasing number of new American congregations which tend to be composed chiefly of converts, with only a few members of native Orthodox background. The first sort of old world ethnic congregations easily preserve their Orthodox roots, but it is hard for them to relate to American culture. The convert congregations relate easily to America, but they find it difficult to get the authentic feel of Orthodoxy. We converts often know lots of facts and figures about Orthodoxy, but Orthodoxy is more than facts and figures. There is an Orthodox culture, an Orthodox feel, an Orthodox style, a way of life that you can't get out of the books, and that is what is hard for convert churches to get into. That's why I like to visit around in an old-world Orthodox country to try to get the feel of the church there.

But my point is, here at Saint Nicholas we have something unusual going on. From the beginning we have had a wonderful combination of people from old world Orthodox ethnic backgrounds and people who are converts, in more or less equal numbers. I don't mean to put people into pigeonholes; not everybody fits. But generally speaking at Saint Nicholas we have people from three cultural backgrounds: Middle Easterners, Greeks and converts. People who represent and have a natural feel for the two major sources of Orthodoxy, and people who culturally have long-term family roots in American culture. And we also have a few of the Slavic tradition, too; I don't want to forget you. Maybe in time we'll have more representatives of this venerable Orthodox tradition too. But what we are developing here is a combination of original Orthodox Christian roots and American ethnic roots, trying to be true both to the authentic spirit of Orthodoxy and also genuinely American. At Saint Nicholas we have all the resources to do this. How to do it? How to integrate all this? I don't know. I'm a convert; I don't have all the answers; I'm still learning. But together we seem to be doing it. And what we're working out, I think, is the future of Orthodoxy in America: American Orthodoxy. Saint Nicholas Church is not unique in this, but we are unusual. Think of the other Orthodox churches you know. How many can you name that have this balance of cradle Orthodox and convert Orthodox? Saint Nicholas Church, Cedarburg, is a special place with a special vocation. That is what I flew home thinking about.

2007 TRAVEL REPORT

It was a great trip. Khouria Dianna and I were together for a week on Crete, then she came back for her niece's graduation in Oregon, and I took the ferry to the island of Patmos where the apostle John the Evangelist and Theologian spent a few years in enforced exile about the year 90 and wrote his book of The Revelation. Some have asked: why do you keep going to Greece? Nothing against the rest of the world or against home—I love traveling anywhere and I'm happy here—but Greece, Crete to be exact, is where I first really discovered Orthodoxy at a conference in 1985, so I have a sentimental attachment. But more than that: I had been on sabbatical that summer. Tom Grossman who then was vestry chairman at our old Episcopal Church had arranged it (so Tom is "godfather" of Saint Nicholas Church). The family and I did Western Europe for a month; then they flew back from Rome, and I took the overnight ferry to Greece. Early next morning I looked out the porthole and saw the outline of the first Greek islands in the mist and said, "That's it. This is my place." And it is. I have no idea why. My theory is that one of my great great great great great great great great great grandmothers was more than friends with a Greek soldier from the imperial army. It feels like Greece is in my genes. By the time the conference was over I knew I loved Greece and suspected I needed to be Orthodox.

Why Patmos? Because a few years ago Mike Huber gave me a book, *Patmos—a Place of Healing for the Soul* by Peter France, an English skeptic who was baptized there by Bishop Kallistos Ware. Ever since I read it I've wanted to go. So I had a week on Patmos, a lovely small island (you can get there only by ferry) on the eastern frontier of Greece. On a clear day you can see Turkey, the coast of Asia. (There are many negative things one can say about Turkey, but I could pick up classical music from there [more than you can do in Milwaukee these days] and old American music: I spent my last evening on Patmos packing and listening to Nat King Cole from Turkey!) Greece is 98% Orthodox, but some don't practice it. Patmos, on the other hand, is a place where Orthodoxy is very much lived. With a population of about 2500 (less than 1/4 the people in Cedarburg) Patmos has about 500 Orthodox churches and chapels—some nice town and village churches, but most are family chapels. In Greece families often build private chapels. The small local military base has an Orthodox chapel. The exclusive resort

Porto Scoutari has an Orthodox chapel. All of these have services from time to time—but when? where? I came across a few in progress. But when the bells ring, you look around and can see 8 or 10 churches, and which one is it? By the time you find out it's usually too late. On Sunday I decided I would drive about and visit every church I saw—well, some I decided not to climb up to. Most were open, all had candles burning: they were being used. And for those who say Orthodoxy is not evangelistic enough, on the waterfront on Patmos is the Orthodox Information and Cultural Center with good video displays in many languages. At the entrance is an excellent presentation on Orthodox environmentalism, a major concern of Ecumenical Patriarch Bartholomaios, as it should be for all of us.

Little Patmos has 2 large monasteries—Evangelismos women's monastery on the west coast with about 45 nuns (I went there for Sunday services) and Saint John's Monastery on the top of the island with about 25 monks and a magnificent museum—and another small women's monastery and a number of hermits back in the hills who do not give out their addresses. I try to imagine all this in, say, the east side of Cedarburg which has about the same population. I can't. Everywhere you look there goes a monk driving a pickup truck or a priest walking by. One morning I saw a priest and his flock of about 20 leaving a church after Liturgy, heading down the street, no doubt to go to the kafenion, the coffee shop—just like home! Orthodoxy is the same wherever you go. It really is. It still amazes me. As I came into Sunday Matins I thought: why is the priest censing at the wrong place? But he wasn't. They had started earlier than I thought, and it was the usual censing at the Song of Mary, just as we do. Some of the music was different, and it was in Greek of course; otherwise it was our Matins and Liturgy.

The Orthodox Church is integral to the life of Patmos. So has this turned the people into a bunch of hard-nosed religious fanatics? Not at all. There is a sweetness, a gentleness, a grace that pervades the place. You can feel it. The lady who ran my hotel (a German who moved to Patmos) wrote in her book about the island: "While the Greek Orthodox Church plays an important but not all-dominating role in the life of its adherents, it disapproves of any religious fanaticism—its views are far too human." Yes! Orthodoxy is humane. Also, the book says there is no reported thievery on Patmos (except for construction materials . . . no explanation given!), no reported violent crime, and the last murders took place during World War II, over 60 years ago, committed by German Nazis not by Patmians. There is no great wealth on the island, no great poverty, and it is considered tasteless for those who have money to show it ostentatiously. (Take me back . . .)

One evening walking on a back street I came on the Byzantine Tekne (arts, crafts) store with wonderful things, including many original icons. One icon of John the Apostle, Saint John the Theologian, Aghios Ioannis o Theologos as he is on the icons, caught my eye. It showed him an old man, his face filled with wisdom and knowledge and pain (he had been driven out of his homeland, he was exiled to Patmos), but above all with love. They say that in his great old age they would carry John to church, and he would say only, "Little children, love one another." I asked the price, gasped (it is original), left and thought about it, came back, left and thought about it some more—and decided if I didn't buy it I would always regret it. I had the money, thanks to you all—money you have given me for house blessings and weddings and the like—so taking your money I bought it and would like to give this icon to Saint Nicholas Church in memory of our dear Deacon John McQuide who knew and loved his patron John so very much. In personality Deacon John was like his patron. Both were sons of thunder ("boanerges"—the nickname Jesus gave to young John and his brother James), and both also were filled with love. Deacon John, dear friend Jack: may your memory be eternal. The young man who runs the shop makes incense for all the churches on Patmos (he must be rich!) and for monasteries on Mount Athos. I obviously was showing an unnatural interest in incense, for he asked me, "Are you a priest?" (I've told you I travel incognito—I need a break.) I said, "Yes." So he gave me the names of his family to be remembered at Divine Liturgy. When you hear "Anastasia, Anastasios, Vasiliki, Zoe, Nikolaos and Vasilis" this morning, that's them. I also brought back three kilos of that elegant incense. Today's is made from a gardenia, phouses, which grows only on Patmos. I also brought the latest from Mount Athos: here—elasticized prayer ropes—one size fits all! The Orthodox Church has finally entered the elastic age!

While I was on Patmos I obviously spent all my time in church, so my great tan must be a miracle of some sort—yes? No. Afternoons I found this little beach away from town—usually had it to myself—and I read. My spiritual project was to ponder the Gospel and Epistles of John and the book of The Revelation and see if I could understand them any better on Patmos where John was. I have always found John's Gospel and Epistles beautiful but difficult, and his Revelation fascinating but impossible. So many questions: how did a fisherman write the fine Greek of the Gospel and the epistles? Is the Gospel history or theological commentary? Jesus' sayings in John often seem to me to be filled with non sequiturs, so different from the other Gospels. As for The Revelation, how did the same man write this in such inelegant Greek? And how did the man who in his Gospel and epistles stressed love ("love one another . . . greater love has no man . . . if you don't love your brother whom you have seen, how can you love God whom you have not seen?")—how in the book of The Revelation could he write so enthusiastically of the wrath of God? And how ever to interpret the details? Some have said it was a different John who wrote The Revelation, but the earliest tradition seems to be that it was all the work of John the Apostle. The Church in the East was very slow to accept The Revelation; though we consider it canonical, to this day we Orthodox never read it in church. So on my little beach I read it all and pondered it, and I would like to report: it didn't help, except in one respect.

I visited the cave of the Apocalypse where John had his revelation, dictating it to his scribe Prochoros. It's a little hole in the wall; it would be dank in winter. I can see John in old age having arthritis unable to write, and there probably weren't many scribes on a small island, and maybe Prochoros didn't write good Greek. But as for the content of The Revelation, I tried to imagine the beautiful blue waters of the Aegean turning to blood and the stars falling out of that gorgeous sparkling night sky and God pouring out his wrath upon that sweet island—and I didn't even want to think about it. I believe The Revelation was written for its own time: it's about the Church's triumph over imperial persecution; it refers to then-current events which 1st century people knew about but are now long forgotten. What if anything does it prophesy for the 21st century? I have no idea. My guess is: nothing. I agree with an early bishop (I forget who) whose people were getting excited by the book of The Revelation, and he told them (this is a loose translation): "Cool it. Nobody has ever understood it; nobody will till the Second Coming. It will only confuse you."

So back to Athens and a visit to the island of Aegina and the relics of Saint Nektarios. I've told you that on each previous visit he has done something I can only call "cute" for me. I told him this time that I wanted no little signs please, just a happy visit. Actually his trick this time was on Patmos. I was way out at my little beach, nobody around, climbed up to the car and went through all my bags: no car key. I went through all my bags again carefully: no car key. I began to panic, so without forethought, not even saying please, I blurted out, **"Saint Nektarios, I need my key!!"** I then reached into a bag and instantly pulled out the key; it was right on top. It had not been right on top a moment before. As for my visit to the shrine: Tony and Chris Wood had been there some years ago. Tony came back trying to put it into words. Words can't express it, but he inspired me to go. Whatever time of year, whatever time of day, there is a sense of light and peace and great joy and happiness. It overwhelms me. I always cry—happy tears. As pilgrims came and went I had time to intercede for the 562 (but who's counting?) names you gave me to pray for, plus everyone from Saint Nicholas which brought it to over 760. A woman took the list so the nuns could pray for all of them. I had time to pray the Jesus Prayer for about half an hour. It felt like only a few minutes. The feeling of Saint Nektarios hangs over me for days. It's still with me. I'm still a little weepy.

As I got onto the bus for the Athens airport on Friday morning, the bus driver was wearing a prayer rope. Along the way I looked up and saw a church with someone going in to pray. Later I looked up again and saw another church with someone coming out after prayer. At the airport right down from McDonald's where they serve (no kidding) Chicken Mythos, there was the airport's Orthodox chapel. Orthodoxy integrated with life. What can I say? On BBC while I was there, I heard a debate between Christopher Hitchens (a sharp, clever atheist conservative with whom I disagree about most things) and the Anglican dean of something-or-other (who was entirely innocuous) over whether God exists and whether religion is a good thing or a bad thing. (Actually I agree with Hitchens that religion can be a bad thing, and I could give you many contemporary examples, both Christian and non-Christian.) But the answer to the question is not in intellectual debates: the answer is in the living of it. There is more true religion in lighting a candle and saying a prayer, or in venerating an icon, or in hugging someone, or in giving money to the poor, or in my experiences with Saint Nektarios, than there is in all the philosophical debates in the world. Right theology is essential, but true religion is found not in words but in life. Orthodoxy is not a doctrine. It is a way of life: Orthodoxy integrated with life, Orthodoxy integrated with society, Orthodoxy integrated with culture.

So I have come back to (what seems to me to be) our increasingly unfocused, disoriented, disintegrated American culture, renewed again, rejuvenated in Orthodox life. Greece and Saint Nektarios have come through again. And I have come back to you, and that is a joy. Because what I saw there is also to some extent here for the Orthodox Church is here. Orthodoxy and its people are my rock. If I didn't have it I honestly do not know what I'd do.

2009 TRIP REPORT

This year's trip report is not very exciting. This time I have no cute Saint Nektarios stories. I asked him—and the Lord too, of course—before we left for a safe trip, I lit candles here before our trip and there during our travels and asked him to guard us as we traveled. Everything went smoothly, and here we are safe and sound at home. That's the way it should be. If I'd done that for my other trips, things would have gone better, and Saint Nektarios wouldn't have had to do special tricks to get me through.

On my visit to Saint Nektarios (five weeks ago already) I stayed in Aegina town in the hotel where Bishop Nektarios used to stay when he rode in on his donkey for supplies. The bells of Saint Nicholas Church next door rang the hours and half hours just as ours do. In the evening I sat on the big pier on the waterfront watching all the boats, large and small coming and going and the sun setting over the islands and the Peloponnesus mainland to the west, and thinking there's no place more beautiful than this in the entire world. At the end of the pier was a chapel of Saint Nicholas, patron of seafarers, staffed like most chapels by widows. Many people were going in and out. I also went in and lit a candle. There were teenagers all over: two boys preening themselves using the windows of the chapel for a mirror! When they saw me smiling at them they laughed and ran off after some girls.

The monastery where Saint Nektarios' relics are is out in the country on a hill above the main road. I love the place: every time I'm there it has the same happy, peaceful, sweet feel. As always there were many pilgrims praying, coming and going, buses parked in the lot down below. In two days I paid three visits to Saint Nektarios, had time to pray for each of you by name and for your needs, lit candles for all with special needs, prayed the 500 names you gave me and then gave them to the nuns for their prayers. I tried to visit two nearby women's monasteries where I could hear the bells ringing and the semantrons clacking, but they didn't welcome visitors. Have I told you that Greece, which has a population of about Wisconsin and Minnesota combined, has over 1000 Orthodox monasteries? In Greece there is almost always a church or chapel in sight. I drove up a hill above Saint Nektarios to a chapel where I was alone, absolute quiet except for the wind and the birds; I could see boats far away coming and going out of the port of Athens. On the chapel was a bell and on the bell was a rope and on the rope was my hand: I couldn't resist. I rang it—it was loud!—and then drove away slowly trying to look innocent. Who? Me? I've learned enough in Zoe's Greek class so I could understand the priest who wanted a ride back to the limani/port and we were even able to talk a little. Thanks, Zoe.

Otherwise it was a much needed R & R vacation. I was very tired after Pascha, hadn't really felt well all winter with that flu that just didn't want to give up. So for the remaining 28 days (Khouria Dianna joined me the last two weeks.), I slept a lot, ate, drank retsina, went to the beach (had some gorgeous big beaches almost to myself), explored a little, and read almost 4000 pages (but who's counting?). Besides my daily prayers and Bible readings I read three religious books by the old English author G.K. Chesterton, a book Marina gave me about a Greek guy who got involved in the occult before returning to the faith—do not mess with the occult!—Mary Stewart's four super books on the Arthurian saga, President Obama's two books, the poems of the Greek poet C.P. Cavafy and a book by a Brit who walked the length of Crete. On the trip over they inspected my suitcase, probably wondering what that big mass of stuff was; I bet they were surprised to find that it was all books!

But I went to church on Sundays and on Saints Constantine and Helen. I tried to go on Ascension but couldn't find a Liturgy. Three of my four Sunday experiences were good, the first not so much. On May 10 I was at the little town of Kandanos in southwest Crete. It is a lovely building. In all these churches, picture an old fashioned iconostasis, Christ presiding on high from the dome, the walls covered with murals, most women on the left, most men on the right. At Kandanos all women but one wore black. Greek widows usually wear black, but they couldn't all have been widows. The only reason I can imagine was that the Nazis shot all the men and boys of the town, and for a long time all that was left was women in mourning dressed in black, and maybe it became the custom. All during Liturgy men came in, went up front and lit candles, and then 90% of them walked out. There was a continual undercurrent of conversation. I left early.

On May 17 I went to church at Akoumia in south central Crete, a village squeezed on the side of a hill, so much that you had to enter church from a side door in the middle on the right. The candle stand was in the middle as you came in, cantors front right where also stood a very holy looking old priest, men front left, all women strictly segregated in back. The church was full, the people reverent, at the sermon the people's eyes were glued to the priest; you could see he loved them and they loved him. It was a good experience. An hour and a half seemed like a few minutes. I grew up in a country village in Ohio. It would have been like this if it had been Orthodox.

On May 24 I was at Kalyviani women's monastery out in the country. From the highway you drive up this long wide road, then walk through an arched gate onto a wide street with blooming trees on both sides and birds singing, past the orphanage and the school and the conference center, an active monastery with 30 or 40 nuns, a happy feel to it. Finally you come to the big church on the right. I arrived for the Matins Gospel; the place was already fairly full: girls from the orphanage, some Downs syndrome people, many men as well as women, and people just kept coming. At the Great Entrance nuns ushered people further front so more could get in. It got really claustrophobic: a good problem!

On May 31 Khouria Dianna and I were at Spili, a town of about 700 people, a handsome church with three priests and a young deacon, a superb male cantor and a good female cantor, the Liturgy done well, correct but not fussy. Much felt familiar: we have green plants all around our church; they have two large trees by the pillars up front. The church 3/4 full, maybe 120 people. In summer it's Matins at 7:30, Liturgy at 8:30, but like us they can't get Matins done in an hour so Liturgy began about 10 minutes late. At the Great Doxology the bells rang, the lights came up. Parents lifted up children so they could kiss the icons, people wandered in late—just like home. Some things were different. The deacon read the Gospel from a lectern hanging way up there; that would be fun. At all the churches I've attended on Crete, the people participated verbally very little; most days only children receive Holy Communion. Our way is better on these things. But otherwise services are virtually the same. It still amazes me to walk into an Orthodox church 6000 miles from home, and even without knowing the language well, immediately I can tell exactly where they are in the service. Orthodoxy has an amazing uniformity. And as near as I can tell, the Church is still alive and well in Greece, as opposed to Western Europe where not many go to church any more.

What else? Old country Greek churches are less formal then we are. I'm not recommending, just observing. But I never saw an acolyte vestment. At the Great Entrance at the monastery two people carried candles: a nun and a teenage boy wearing a purple soccer shirt with a big 731 on the back! In four Sundays I saw only two or three men in suits. Even at the monastery women had no head coverings and some wore slacks. Many clergy now have short hair and short beards. All the churches I've visited in Greece have had chairs for people to sit. Some American Orthodox try to imitate old-country Orthodoxy as it used to be years ago, not as it is now. How should *we* dress for church? There are no eternal rules. 1500 years ago all men wore robes like mine to church. That changed. The basic rule is: dress so as not to call attention to yourself according to the customs of your culture. Dress so that people will look at God, not at you.

A good thing the trip did for my spiritual life is this: an occupational hazard of being a clergyman is that I get paid for going to church. This can cause me to question my motives. Sometimes I worry: am I here because I love God or because it's my job? So when I go on vacation I wear my civvies, no one knows I'm a priest, no one's watching, I have no role to fulfill—and thank God, when I woke every morning I wanted to say my prayers, and on Sundays I could feel the Church drawing me. I wanted to be at Liturgy. I love the Church. I love to worship the Lord. This is not just my job, this is my life. So after four weeks I was eager to come back to you all; and I was also not ready to leave. I still wake up hearing and smelling Greece.

One more thing: I return home to hear that something dreadful is happening to America, we're going socialistic, losing our freedom, government will now control every aspect of our lives and we'll become a horror like Europe. Like *Europe*?! Do these people know anything about Europe? European governments are democratically elected just like ours. In some ways they interfere in peoples' lives less than ours does and allow more freedom than we have. Europe specializes in free enterprise, small businesses. America has been taken over by the big guys, big farms, big business, big franchise operations; it's hard to make it in this country anymore unless you join up with one of the big guys and do what they tell you. Europe is filled with small privately owned businesses, "mom and pop" operations. For four weeks on Crete I saw not one franchise store except for auto dealers and petrol stations, till the last day we found a Starbucks—and immediately went in of course! But otherwise it's all small independent businesses which encourage initiative, creativity, responsibility the way it used to be here. There was no Motel 6 or Hilton for me to stay at, so I stayed at four fine little locally-owned places each with its own individual style.

I wish we would become as "horrible" as Europe. Europe where there is great public transportation, where the elderly and those without cars can get around, where nobody goes bankrupt because they get sick and have no health coverage. Christ commanded us to care for the sick. This is a moral issue. Did you know that Germany and France spend far less per person than we do on health care, cover everybody and 80% of the people say that they have good health care? Germany has had universal health care since 1883. Europe has a crime and murder rate far lower than ours. Most of Western Europe now has a standard of living higher than ours. Secular Western Europe has an abortion rate lower than ours. Furthermore, after centuries of wars Europeans seem to have discovered how to stop making war. Consider: since 1950 America has been involved in wars in Korea, Viet Nam, Grenada, Panama, Bosnia, Afghanistan and Iraq twice. Did I miss any? If I count right 22 years out of 59 the US has been at war. Since 1950 Greece has been involved in no wars, 59 years of peace. Now America is a good place and Europe is not paradise; they have their own problems to deal with. You choose what political or economic system you prefer.

I'm just presenting facts. But you know that untruth drives me nuts, and when I come back from Europe, I cannot figure out how people in this country can believe all this stuff about Europe that is just not true. There. I said it and I'm glad.

Chapter Three

Intermediary

The term "intermediary" reflects the basic function of the priest as recorded from time immemorial. Not just Orthodox, but even pagan religions have viewed the priest in this manner. The priest, as intermediary stands in the gap between God (or the gods) and man, between heaven and earth. Thus when Christ came as God Incarnate He fulfilled the highest function of this office.

But for this work I choose a less liturgical application of this term, but, none the less, one that has spiritual depth and application. Fr. Bill had a unique way of bringing his experience of the Divine and Holy from ancient lands, cultures and saints in such a meaningful way as to be a spiritual blessing and benefit to those who listened. His experience with St. Nektarios can't be underappreciated as the reader has likely experienced in the above selections. Therefore two separate homilies repeat the story of St. Nektarios with personal application and benefit to the reader. I would ask that the reader be patient here. Some of the stories of Fr. Bill's experiences with St. Nektarios are repeated three times in this volume—each with different details and a slightly different flavor which makes it intriguing. I personally *never* tire of reading these over and over again.

It also brings up the difficulty of miracles in the church and the world according to Orthodox account and experience. As a Protestant convert I still occasionally battle the inner skeptic in my brain that insists that these stories at best are the sentimental imaginations of desperate and unsophisticated people. Thus it is continually refreshing and renewing to have St. Nektarios, a recent saint where documentation of his miracles is repeated and convincing, even in a modern, skeptical world.

At times even Fr. Bill would seem to imply that some stories of the saints perhaps were just that—embellished legend. Whether that is true or not in some cases the experiences of St. Nektarios stand as a solid testimony to the activity of God and the saints in our personal lives.

But wherever there is the skeptic there is the opposite as well—the gullible hysteric who would believe anything without sufficient evidence and reliability. Fr. Bill stands as a fine example of reason and balance when it comes to this concern. Recently when a fantastic story was being disseminated throughout the Orthodox community in the US Father took his usual cautious approach. As it turned out the story was false—an overzealous attempt to prove that modern day miracles exist in the US not just in traditional Orthodox lands.

2002 TRIP REPORT: Part 2—Saint Nektarios

After I left Mount Athos I took the train to Athens and prepared to visit the burial place of Saint Nektarios. I had heard of him for years and someone even gave me that little icon of him, which has been on our wall, and I have used oil from his shrine occasionally for anointing, but I didn't really know much about him. I became intrigued by Saint Nektarios two years ago after Tony and Chris Wood brought me a book about him, which touched me deeply. Nektarios was a turn-of-the-previous-century bishop from Alexandria who had a tough life. His patriarch took a disliking to him and stirred up a lot of trouble for him even after he went to Greece. He lived a life of great patience and forbearance and finally founded a monastery for women on Aegina, an island not far from Athens. But his life was nothing extraordinary—until he died in 1921. The man in the hospital bed next to him was immediately healed. Then there followed a series of miraculous healings—the story gave me the chills. The healings have continued. He seems to have a special concern for cancer patients. Anyway, I felt drawn to go to Aegina. So I took the train down to Athens, and Tuesday September 24 was my day to visit Aegina. It turned out to be a wonderful, amazing day. And I made a new friend, a very dependable friend with a sense of humor: his name is Nektarios.

I was taking the boat to Crete that night, so I left my backpack at my hotel in Athens, took the Metro to Piraeus, the port of Athens, and planned to catch the 9 o'clock boat to Aegina, about a one hour journey. However, I had some business to tend to, and I missed the 9 o'clock boat. No problem. I had been assured that boats ran every hour. But not that day: no 10 o'clock boat, the next one was at 11. I wondered if I should give it up. Will there be time to do this? I didn't know the island. I didn't know where the shrine of Saint Nektarios was or how to get there or how long all this would take. Would there be time to do all this and get back to Piraeus, back to the hotel for my suitcase and back to Piraeus again in time to make my evening boat? But I so much wanted to go. So I said "Agios Nektarios, Saint Nektarios, I'm coming to visit you. You've got to work this out and get me back in time." Well . . . !

Sitting at the front of the boat was a young priest. I assumed he was going to visit Saint Nektarios, and I assumed he was Greek. Maybe I could follow him or he could tell me what to do. So I went up and asked "Do you speak English?" He said, "Not very well." So I began to mutter in my primitive Greek, and he said "I speak Greek even less." It turned out he was Russian, a priest monk from Trinity Saint Sergius Monastery outside Moscow, Father Kallistratos, a very pleasant and pious young man of 28. He also had just been to the Holy Mountain, and had climbed to the top of Mount Athos (about 6500 feet) by night so he could celebrate Liturgy at the little chapel up there at dawn. And he was indeed going to visit Saint Nektarios, for the second time. He was to be picked up by a friend, a retired Greek man, who would take him out to the shrine, and he said "Please come along." Thank you, Saint Nektarios.

So I got a free ride to the shrine of Saint Nektarios and a tour and explanation of what it was all about from the inside—things I would never have figured out by myself. It is a beautiful, light-filled airy place up in the hills, by the way, with a great sense of peace about it. When I came before Saint Nektarios' tomb I was just overwhelmed. I can't explain it—I started to cry. There was a woman clinging to the tomb with both arms and crying the whole time I was there. I don't know who she was or what her trouble was, but . . . oh, pray for her, whoever she is. God knows. Then I lit candles for us and prayed for all the people whose names you had given me and for others too. It was then that Father Kallistratos said, "Would you like your names to be put on the Proskimidi list? Just give it to that woman there." Oh yes. So I did, and so we have been prayed for at Divine Liturgy before Saint Nektarios. Again, something I never could have arranged by myself. Thank you, Saint Nektarios. I met some of the nuns and saw the house where Nektarios lived. Father Kallistratos stood there and sang his hymn to the Theotokos in Russian, and I stood there frustrated because I couldn't remember it in English.

Father Kallistratos is also much devoted to Saint Nicholas. He says every second church in Russia is dedicated to Nicholas, and he was pleased to know that ours also is Saint Nicholas Church. He was traveling next to Bari in southern Italy where the body of Saint Nicholas is. There is a Russian priest there who has permission to celebrate Liturgy at the tomb of Saint Nicholas, and Father Kallistratos was going to do the same. He said he would pray for us, so . . . we have been prayed for at Divine Liturgy at the tomb of our patron. Thank you, Saint Nektarios.

Father Kallistratos was staying, so I moved on. I checked out the gift shop and bought a new icon and went down the hill and checked out the big Saint Nektarios church which is being built. Then I thought: maybe I should start thinking about getting back to the boat. I didn't know anything about the busses, so I went down to the road to look for a bus. There stood a couple about my age and a young woman, so I said "Pou einai to leoforio pros Aegina?"—my pigeon Greek for "Where is the bus to Aegina?" The man answered "We speak English." It was a Greek-Canadian family from Montreal, and he said "Why don't we get a taxi?" So we did. On the way in he asked what my line of work was (I was in civvies playing the tourist), and I told him, and when we got there he wouldn't let me pay. So I also got a free ride *back* from the shrine of Saint Nektarios. Thank you, Saint Nektarios.

It was about a half hour before the next boat, so I said to myself, How about a snack? I walked into an ice cream shop, and they had all kinds: vanilla, strawberry, pistachio, chicago. What kind of ice cream, I asked, is chicago? "Oh, very good," said the waiter, "very good." I said I'd take it. What was chicago ice cream? It was two scoops of chocolate with chocolate fudge on top! Thank you, Saint Nektarios. Now the saint had really won my heart!

And so I took the boat back to Piraeus, and you know what time it was when I got there? It was not yet 3 p.m. The whole trip had taken less than 4 hours! I asked for a quick trip, and St. Nektarios gave me a quick trip, headspinningly quick. I could hardly believe it, and I grinned for days. I got back to the hotel, got my suitcase, got back to Piraeus and had over three hours to kill before my boat left for Crete. Thank you, St. Nektarios.

Saint Nektarios is famous for curing diseases, but for me he is also my patron of travel, and I prayed to him all the way home. I feel I have met a saint who really knows how to come through when you ask him. "Saint Nektarios, pray for me," is now an integral part of my prayer life. Thank you, Saint Nektarios.

SAINT NEKTARIOS THE WONDERWORKER
Sunday November 9, 2008

Here is one of my special saints. Nektarios was from a poor family of the town of Selybria in Thrace (northeast Greece, then part of the Turkish empire) born in the mid 19th century. When he came of age he went to Constantinople to find work. There are stories even that early. It is told that he had no money for a ticket, but the boat refused to move till finally they let him aboard. It is said that there was a storm on the way, and when he let his cross down into the sea on a string (within it was a piece of the true Cross), the wind ceased, but he lost his cross. Later in the voyage there was a knocking beneath the ship. When they docked they found the cross stuck to the bottom of the ship. These stories might seem like legends, except they are nothing compared to what came later.

When Nektarios was 29 he became a monk on the island of Chios, then deacon and assistant to the Patriarch of Alexandria. Some clergy took a disliking to him, and he was sent away to study in Athens where he lived in poverty for a time. Then he was ordained priest and was made Bishop of Pentapolis on the island of Euboia. But his enemies from Egypt spread stories about him and he was removed from office. He became head of the School of Theology in Athens, but again his enemies dogged him. His whole life was lived under a cloud of accusations all of which proved untrue. Finally in 1910, weary of all this, he retired to the island of Aegina off Athens. At the request of some young women he established a women's monastery there. Again many criticized him.

Externally Saint Nektarios led not a very notable life. Maybe it was his difficulties that made him humble. Once a janitor who worked at the school fell ill and was about to lose his job. Lest that should happen, Bishop Nektarios did his work for him secretly, even cleaning the toilets every night, till he recovered. The story came out later. Once a notable visitor came to the monastery, saw an old man shabbily dressed, working in the gardens, to whom he said haughtily: Go find Bishop Nektarios. The old man said he would do so. The visitor was embarrassed to discover that the gardener was Bishop Nektarios.

But it was after he died that big things began to happen. In 1920 Bishop Nektarios' health failed, and he was taken to an infirmary in Athens where he died on November 9. As his body was being prepared, his shirt was placed on the bed next to him in which lay a man long paralyzed, who immediately stood up and began to walk. The room was filled with a sweet fragrance for many days after his death and has since become a chapel. Nektarios' body was taken to the monastery on Aegina for burial, while it continued to exude the fragrance. They buried him hastily, planning to provide a finer burial place in the spring. That winter Bishop Nektarios appeared frequently at night to his nuns as if alive. At first this startled them (no wonder!), but as time went on they began almost to take it for granted. He spoke with many of them and often counseled the abbess/gerontissa on how to run the monastery in his absence—if you can call that absence! In the spring they exhumed his body for better burial and found it perfectly preserved with myrrh-like substance running from his face, and again the fragrance which now filled the whole monastery. Lemon flowers which had been buried with him were still fresh, though they wilted after about 8 to 10 hours. A year and a half later according to custom they exhumed his body so the bones could be put in a vault, but still it was incorrupt and fragrant. After 10 years it was the same. After 20 years Nektarios' body had disintegrated. A woman who had gone to him for confessions was sad about this, till one night she looked up and saw Bishop Nektarios sitting there. He asked what was wrong, and she explained. He said: but I prayed for this, so that my relics could be taken all over the world. 33 years later in 1953 when Nektarios was formally declared a saint, again his grave was opened. This time the fragrance was so strong it could be smelled even on the road down below the monastery. At the time a bus passing by had a flat tire, and a young woman on the bus known for her profligate ways asked what the fragrance was. On being told she got off the bus, walked up the hill and became a nun.

Equally important are the multitude of miracles that have taken place away from his shrine. There are books full of them; the internet has many stories. They began when Saint Nektarios died and have never ceased, all over the world. He has been seen many times not only in the monastery but throughout Greece and the rest of the world. They say if people don't recognize him, he often identifies himself and tells them to take a few drops of the oil from the lamps which burn in his chapel and add it to their drinking water. He has cured many; or if not that then provides them a good death with little pain. In all this he is just continuing in the tradition of healing established by Christ the Good Physician, passed down through his apostles. Nektarios has become one of the most popular of modern saints. His relics still lie at the monastery on Aegina, and every time I've visited there have been many pilgrims. It is a peaceful, happy, light filled place even on dark days. There's a sweetness that pervades the place. I love it there.

Now let me tell you of my experiences with Saint Nektarios, how I've come to know and love him. I know you've heard all this before, but I like to talk about him, so please humor me. It began 7 or 8 years ago when Tony and Chris Wood came back from Greece, and Tony (*may his memory be eternal*) brought me a book about Saint Nektarios and told me what a wonderful place his shrine was. He said he just couldn't get it into words. I read the book, and when I came to the part where the miracles began I got the happy chills and I knew I had to go there.

A few years later I did. I had just left Mount Athos, was in Athens for a day and was to take a ship to Crete that evening. I had planned to go out to Saint Nektarios for the day, but I got moving slowly, arrived to the dock late, missed the 9 o'clock boat. They canceled the 10 o'clock boat, and there I sat on a bench waiting. I hadn't even brought a map or a guide book to tell me how to find his shrine on Aegina. So for the first time, definitely not the last, I called on Nektarios: Saint Nektarios, Αγιος Νεκτάριος, help. If you want me to visit you you'll have to work it out. As I boarded the 11 o'clock, I saw a young monk and thought maybe he's going to Saint Nektarios. I tried to ask him in Greek. He replied in English that his Greek wasn't good either. He turned out to be a Russian monk from Trinity Saint Sergios Monastery, and he said: a friend is meeting me at the dock, so why not come along? We'll give you a ride to Saint Nektarios.

Once we got there they took me through the place and showed me everything, even inside the monastery. I stood before the icon which inspired Saint Nektarios to write his hymn "Rejoice, O unwedded bride." I said, not for the last time: thank you Saint Nektarios. After a while I thought: I don't know the way back to town or how long it will take to get there, so I wandered down to a road—the wrong place to catch a bus, as I know now. There was a family, so I tried again to ask in Greek: που είναι το λεοφορίο--where's the bus? The man answered in English: let's get a taxi. They were a Greek Canadian family from Montreal. (By the way, I was not wearing clerical garb, so they weren't just being nice to a priest.) The man got the taxi and paid my way back to Aegina town. Thank you, Saint Nektarios. I had time before the boat left, so I thought I'd get a snack. Ice cream! The shop had pistachio, strawberry, vanilla and *Chicago*. What's Chicago, I asked? Ah, very good, very good, the waiter said, so I ordered it. Turns out they got the word wrong. It was not Chicago but σοχολάτα, two scoops of chocolate with chocolate syrup! You know my passion for chocolate. I said: thank you, thank you, Saint Nektarios! I got back to Athens with hours to spare, and I grinned for a week. That was my introduction to Saint Nektarios.

I had to go back again. Since then every time I go back something unusual happens. The second time, a year later, he appeared to arrange my transportation again. I left my hotel at 7:15, had to take metro trains to get to Piraeus, the port of Athens, and figured I'd catch the 9 o'clock boat. First metro stop, there was my connection waiting for me; second stop, again my connection was waiting. I got to Piraeus at 8, assuming I'd missed the 8 o'clock boat, walked slowly to the dock, there was the boat still waiting. I got a ticket, the attendant said: hurry they're about to leave. I got on the boat, they slammed the gate behind me and at 8:05 I was off to Aegina. Thank you again, Saint Nektarios!

On my third visit, I got to the shrine, said my prayers and sat down on a bench to watch the pilgrims come and go. A woman's voice beside me asked: are you an American? There sat old friends from Wisconsin, a former Anglican priest and his wife whom I've known for 30 years, both of them now Orthodox, and also their son who is now an Orthodox priest in Greece. We spent the rest of the afternoon together. Now what were the chances of that? Thank you, Saint Nektarios.

Fourth visit, it was evening when I arrived, dark and beginning to rain, though inside the place still felt as light-filled as on the sunniest of Greek days. The light there is of a different sort. As I took the boat back to the mainland there was sharp lightning in the north. I caught a taxi back to the hotel. I had no sooner got inside than the storm hit: thunder, lightning, so much rain it closed the roads and poured into the lobby of the hotel. Had it hit 4 hours earlier I would not have been able to get to Aegina. 30 minutes earlier and I would not have made it back to the hotel. Thank you, Saint Nektarios.

The next year, at the beginning of the trip I said to Saint Nektarios: look, I'm not coming here for thrills. I just love visiting you. No little tricks this time, please. So the trick came elsewhere, on the island of Patmos. Instead of visiting churches that day, I was at a beach way out and away all by myself. In the evening, I went to get into my car and . . . no key. I looked through both bags, I looked through all my pockets, I went through everything twice. No key. Without planning it I said—I demanded—very uncourteously: Saint Nektarios, find my key! I reached into my bag . . . and there it was sitting right on top. It had **not** been there a moment before—I swear it hadn't. Thank you, Saint Nektarios. My visit to Saint Nektarios on Aegina a week later was uneventful.

My sixth trip was last May. Khouria Dianna and I were in Toronto, where they expect you to pick up your luggage and transfer it to the next terminal. We went to collect our suitcases: they were not there. We went to the baggage office: no one had any idea where they were. Why don't you try Olympic Airlines in the other terminal? Maybe they sent them there. So we took the train to Olympic: no luggage. They said: they must be back in the other terminal, so we took the train back. Still no luggage.

Finally I remembered what to do. The year before, Zoe Ganos and I, coming back from Archdiocese Convention in Montreal, got stranded at O'Hare airport late at night: nothing open, no car available, no way out. I fumed and fretted and fussed and finally called Khouria Dianna who drove down and rescued us at 2 a.m. Afterwards I thought: haven't you learned anything? Why didn't you ask Saint Nektarios? He would have worked it out. Your wife could have avoided a four hour trip in the middle of the night. So when our luggage was lost in Toronto I finally remembered to say: Saint Nektarios, help! We went back to Olympic, but there was still no luggage. We tried to relax. About 20 minutes before boarding time, someone came to us with a message: your luggage has arrived. Thank you, Saint Nektarios.

Later on the same trip I was driving alone on Crete, way south to the isolated village Kali Limenas, Fair Havens, where in Acts 27 it says Saint Paul had been shipwrecked. I arrived and looked at my gas/petrol gauge which showed about 1/16 full—right down to the red mark and there was no gas station. I figured what can I do? So I said: Saint Nektarios, help! and did my exploring. Afterwards when I came back to the car and started it . . . the gas gauge read almost 1/3 full! I have no explanation for this whatsoever except: thank you, Saint Nektarios.

For most people Saint Nektarios provides healings and peaceful deaths. Why, for me, he arranges transportation and does funny tricks I have no idea. But apparently he does, and in the process I have developed a great devotion to him and affection for him. I have come to love him dearly; he makes me smile. And because of Saint Nektarios, when Tony was dying a few years ago, I knew what to say. I told him: Tony, just hang onto that feeling of Saint Nektarios—the peace, the light, the happiness you felt there, because that's where you're going; heaven will be like that. And when my time comes, I know who I'm going to turn to and what I'll hang onto. Thank you, Saint Nektarios.

2005 TRIP REPORT

I usually preach from the Bible or on the saints. Today may I do a travelogue? I returned last Monday after four weeks away, my longest trip since 1985. Then I left as an unhappy Anglican and came back nearly ready to be Orthodox. This time I left as a happy Orthodox, and I return as a happy Orthodox. It was a wonderful trip. In four weeks the first rude person I met was the young woman who tailgated me on I-43 last Wednesday. For one week Khouria Dianna and I drove through southern Spain. Then our son David joined us for a week in Switzerland.

They came home and I headed south to Bari, Italy where the relics of
our patron Saint Nicholas lie. Then after two weeks on the road I went
to Greece, my favorite place to "hang out" and visited the shrine of Saint
Nektarios before going to London last weekend for the 10th anniversary
celebration of the Antiochian deanery of Great Britain and Ireland.
Twelve years ago at the request of His Eminence Metropolitan PHILIP,
Father Peter Gillquist invited Khouria Dianna and me to go there to
speak to Anglicans who were seeking Orthodoxy. I have good news: they
found it!

Much of the trip wasn't made for religious reasons, but I saw a lot
of religion. We began in Spain where we visited architectural wonders
from the time of the Moors, Muslims who conquered Spain in the 9th
century and developed a high culture. You know, I assume, that Arabs
pioneered modern mathematics and science, and the Moors brought
them to Europe through Spain. Moorish culture was tolerant. Jews and
Christians paid high taxes, but we "people of the book" as the Muslims
call us were not forced to convert or leave, and in many places in Spain
Muslims, Christians and Jews lived and worked together in harmony.
Architecture tells a lot about a society. Moorish architecture was graceful
with intricate designs—light, airy, balanced, harmonious. Then the
Christians recaptured Spain, but these weren't the same Christians.
This was the Spanish Inquisition. Muslims had to convert or leave;
all Jews were driven out. For two centuries the Inquisition enforced
conformity—they were the fundamentalists of their time—and in the
interior of those light airy Moorish buildings the Roman Catholics built
dark heavy churches. In one I saw a morbid sculpture of the head of
John the Baptist, the flesh turning green and the arteries hanging out.
Most of the paintings were artificially emotional, many of saints looking
heavenward with enraptured expressions. One cathedral ceiling had
cherubs with fat bodies, harsh faces, heavy limbs, naked, looking as if
they might be about to do something unfortunate in the choir. As I say,
architecture says a lot about a culture.

But the modern Spanish people we met were uniformly kind and
helpful. Granted we saw only a little of Spain, but we observed little religion
being practiced. Statistics bear this out. The churches showed almost no
signs of piety—no one praying, few candles burning. At the cathedral in
Granada we found a small congregation at Saturday night Mass. Since
there was no Orthodox church we decided to go to Sunday morning
Mass. But on Sunday the place was locked; nothing happening. Khouria
Dianna suggested we go across the square to Saint Elizabeth's Church. It
also was locked; no one was there. That Sunday we didn't get to church.
In western Europe few people practice religion any more. An English

Orthodox priest told me that in his city, Lincoln, 3 to 4% of the people go to church, and in the suburbs it's about 1%. He says most English have no religious experience at all. He says kids on the street ask him, "What's that thing hanging around your neck?" He tells them, "That's a cross." What is growing rapidly is Islam. In some places in western Europe there are now more practicing Muslims than Christians.

Why this falling away from Christianity? I asked peoples' opinions. One English priest said, "It's because the English church is established." But the Church in Greece is also established, and as I will tell you Orthodoxy seems to be flourishing there. Someone said it's because of Christian divisions: each faction says, "This is the true faith," but each teaches something different, so people just give it up. But then how do you explain why in America, where Christians are more divided than anywhere else, about 2/3 of us go to church? Another person said it's because Christians, both left wing and right wing, are giving so much attention to politics that they have forgotten their wellspring: God and worship. That may be. A Greek theologian, John Romanides, says that western European irreligion is a justified rejection of a "terrorist" God. Perhaps he overstates the case, but he means that people are rightly rejecting the classical Protestant angry God who dangles sinners over hellfire or who predestines some to hell or who lets us off only if we sign on to a particular statement of faith. They are rejecting authoritarian religion and the dark oppressive God expressed in the art and architecture of Roman Catholic Spain. This is a good thing. These are a long way from our God whose "glory we see in the face of Jesus Christ," "who is good and loves mankind." Please don't misunderstand what I am about to say. I am a Christian. I believe in Jesus Christ. But while I was in Spain I kept thinking: if my only choices were Spanish Catholicism Inquisition-style or the Muslim Moors, I think I'd go with the Moors. There are kinds of Christianity which present such a false picture of our Lord Jesus Christ that I think they are worse than no Christianity at all. Thank God and thank the Orthodox Church that those are not my only choices.

I can tell you nothing about religion in Switzerland except that the bell at the local Catholic Church rang daily very early, very loud. (I wish our neighbors who complained about our bells could hear that one!) The reason I didn't check out the church was that David and I were too busy riding every train we could find. May I digress? May I tell you about public transportation in Europe? When I was a boy the United States led the world in this. We lost it. Europe has good roads; the bumpiest ride I had on the trip was I-94 coming back from O'Hare. Zurich, about the size of Milwaukee, has 2,500 passenger trains a day—fast, smooth, on time, well-used—and where the rails stop there are bus connections to every little village. Milwaukee has 16 passenger trains daily (a lot for this country), and as far as small towns are concerned, you can't get there from here. When I was a boy in small town Ohio Grandma couldn't drive, but I'd hear the bus stop, and Mom would say, "Grandma's here!" Now Grandma would be trapped at home. In Europe, people can still get around. Western Europe may not have much religion, but they have many people-oriented things I wish we had. (Shall I also mention free university education in many countries? and health care for all throughout the EU? and extensive time off work with pay for all new mothers? and four weeks vacation or more annually for all workers? and . . .)

So Khouria Dianna and David flew home. I took the train overnight to southern Italy and Saint Nicholas. It was a magical Sunday. His body lies in the crypt of the 11th century Roman Catholic San Nicola Basilica near the seafront. You know, I think, that merchants from Bari stole him from his home town Myra in Asia Minor in 1087. I arrived about 9 a.m. to find people in church! A sung Mass upstairs had a good crowd as did the high Mass later. But I went downstairs. Saint Nicholas' tomb is behind a screen, above ground with many candles burning and people praying. Bill Ohde IV asked what it felt like, and I struggled for words. It was holy, it was happy, with an almost palpable presence of the saint, the same Nicholas I have known and who has been leading us all these years. It was . . . I don't have words, but it was beautiful; it was alive, I'll never forget. I lit candles and prayed for each of you and your needs, and all the people you asked me to pray for.

Then I smelled incense. Behold, to the left of the tomb of Saint Nicholas is a little Orthodox chapel—in a Roman Catholic cathedral. What a wonderful thing! I wonder if we would be as generous. Divine Liturgy was celebrated beautifully in . . . Italian! The music was good. There were maybe 75 or 100 people present. Most of you know that for nearly 17 centuries the relics of Saint Nicholas have been exuding myrrh with healing properties. His body lies in this pool of myrrh. In 1925 the Roman Catholics analyzed it chemically (I think Orthodox wouldn't do that) and found it is like water but with no bacterial content. On the feasts of Saint Nicholas, a priest opens the tomb and removes some fresh myrrh. And *here it is*: myrrh from Saint Nicholas! A relic of Nicholas has been in our altar since our church was consecrated. Now we have this treasure! We'll use it for anointings on Saint Nicholas Day and when people are ill. Holy Nicholas, pray for us!

On to Greece, to the island of Paros in the Aegean. It is gorgeous! I poked around in villages. I relaxed, I was probably the only person on the beach reading theology! I visited churches. On Paros, Christianity is flourishing, and Orthodoxy is alive and well. On Holy Cross Day I went to Liturgy at what is called Ekatontapiliani Church ("100 doors" church—I didn't count them). The story is that in the 4th century Saint Helena, on her way to the Holy Land, visited the new little church on Paros and was so pleased by what she saw that she promised to build them a big church. Modern archaeological evidence indicates the church was indeed built in the 4th century. The older church became Saint Nicholas chapel and is still in use. So this is one of the oldest church buildings in the world in continuous use. And it is alive, filled on Holy Cross Day with approximately equal numbers of men and women—which is easy to tell because the men are mostly over *here* and the women mostly over *there*. Speaking of Bill Ohde, the man standing in front of me in church that day looked so much like Bill that when he turned around and it wasn't, I was almost surprised.

And I must tell this story. I've found that restaurants outside churches are usually good and not overly expensive. So on a Friday I was eating outdoors across from Ekatontapiliani. The only thing that looked good to me was beef stephado, so I justified myself. I said, "I'm on vacation, it's ok." As I began to eat the meat I realized that from my table I could see directly into the altar of this venerable church where people have been keeping the fast for 17 centuries. The only way I could get through the meal was to promise to fast on Saturday!

All over the island are churches. Every farm or house of any size has its own chapel. At one place I could stand and see seven churches at once. One day I came upon a young priest with a family doing a memorial service at their family chapel. Churches and chapels which in the towns are open and used, with candles burning and often the smell of incense wafting out into the narrow lanes, with men and women as they go by crossing themselves, many going in and out to light candles. If the church is of any size old people are stationed by the doors at all hours to monitor the candles—and with western European tourists standing outside wondering what in the world this is all about. Every morning when I turned on the radio, I could hear not a bunch of Bible thumpers but Orthodox services on three stations. Matins, Divine Liturgy, Vespers and Compline are broadcast daily, along with Orthodox teaching and commentary.

I began Sunday morning at a little monastery up in the hills, with about six monks, all of them aging (very different from Mount Athos with their young monks), a very holy looking old priest celebrating Divine Liturgy and about ten men and boys present. When the monastic prayers got too long for me I went down to Ekatontapiliani and found the crowd even bigger than before. I arrived late in Matins. In front of me were three typical teenage guys—not ultra-pious types—who were nevertheless there for Matins and the entire Liturgy, along with lots of families, many children. The services were celebrated with great devotion. Orthodoxy on Paros is alive, as it has been everywhere in Greece that I've visited. There is a genuine Orthodox revival going on there. Attendance is up especially among men and young people. Greece, with a population about that of Wisconsin and Minnesota combined, now has about 1000 monasteries.

While I was there I wondered, was this lovely experience of a popular lively Orthodoxy integrated with daily life the first breath of something that will spread out into the world? Or is it the last beautiful gasp of something that will fade in the face of modern secularism? I don't know, of course. I've concluded it really isn't important to know. All the matters is that we be faithful; the future is in God's hands. And it still impresses me that one can go to Orthodox services anywhere, and except for minor details they are the same. I think that is part of the power of Orthodoxy. Our message is not mixed. Our ways change little with the times. We know who we are. What you see here at Saint Nicholas is, in essence, what you get in the Orthodox Church wherever you go all over the world.

So back to Athens and an evening visit to Aegina and Saint Nektarios. You know that on my previous visits the saint had seemed to arrange my transportation. The first time I knew nothing about the place and I was running late, so I asked, "Aghios Nektarios, if you want me to visit you, please work this out." And I who was not wearing clerics (I love being incognito so nobody pays me special attention) was picked up by a visiting Russian monk who got me a ride there and gave me the special inside tour, and then a Greek Canadian family (again not knowing I was a priest) offered me a free ride back to the port. On my next visit, at three metro stops in a row there was a train waiting as I arrived. The 8 a.m. ferry to Aegina was running late, and so in less than half the time I had allotted there I was on my way to visit Saint Nektarios. Surely this great saint must have better things to do than be my private travel agent!

Nevertheless . . . this time it was evening when I got to Aegina. I took no chances, I got a taxi. The young taxi driver had the radio on and kept shaking his fist and yelling: "Ne!" ("Yes" in Greek). I asked, "What's happening?" "It's the Greek-Russian basketball game. Greece is winning!" But as a typical young Greek he was religious. As in most Greek taxis, there was a cross hanging over the dashboard (some have icons), and as we got to Saint Nektarios church he crossed himself. (I keep pointing out men who were showing their faith, because religion is so often assumed to be "women's work." (Not here it wasn't.) I hoped the place would be open. In fact I got there just in time for Vespers. There were pilgrims. A spirit of peace and joy filled the place as always. I prayed again for you all and those whose names you gave me. I lit many candles. A nun chased me out of the women's chapel and into the men's chapel (but nicely: "parakalo", "please"). I brought back more oil from the lamps that burn before his relics.

Then, as I rode the Flying Dolphin back to the mainland there was lightning in the north. I just got back to the hotel when the storm hit. Heavy lightning, heavy rain, the streets flooded, with water coming under the front doors of the hotel and into the lobby. If the storm had hit only a few hours earlier, I could not have made it out to Saint Nektarios; only a few minutes earlier, and I wouldn't have made it back to the hotel for a long time. Did Saint Nektarios do it again?

And then to London for the Antiochian deanery celebration at our cathedral, which is a former Anglican church. Father Michael Harper, the dean, had preached there 30 years ago when he was an Anglican priest. Now at the Divine Liturgy to his surprise he was made an archpriest in the Orthodox Church. English language Orthodoxy is taking hold, slowly but steadily. The deanery now has 14 or 15 churches, with not a thousand people yet, so the priests nearly all need to have secular jobs, but their spirit is upbeat and positive. About 200 people from all over England and even Ireland attended, some getting up long before dawn to make it—on the excellent British *high speed trains*. If they had to drive they probably couldn't have made it. Their Metropolitan Gabriel of Paris was there: a gentle, kindly man in his 80s, who fell downstairs a few years ago and has never recovered and is failing. He can just barely get around. After his good sermon he came back into the altar and sat down, panting in pain, and then he began to cry. Everyone thought it was because he knew it would be his last time with them. It was sad. But for me it was a happy fulfilling weekend, to see what Khouria Dianna and I helped to plant coming to fulfillment. An old deacon, a former Anglican, told me, "I can't remember just what your wife said, but whatever it was, it convinced me. When she said it, I knew I had to be Orthodox."

I love to travel. On the way home, I was already planning another trip. I also believe in the value of travel. Read the New Testament: see how early Christians were forever coming and going. "The Lord has made all nations of men to dwell on the face of the earth." To travel is to see other kinds of people whom God has made, other ways of doing things. On one hand it makes me value what I have. I am glad to come back home. You at Saint Nicholas are a treasure to me, and I missed you very much. On the other hand, traveling allows us to learn from others. I wish America were more open to what others have to teach us. There is so much we could learn, especially from some of the older cultures of the world. As we travel, we find out things we would never know otherwise. For example, now I know that Barney can speak Greek—with the same dippy voice he has in English! Travel makes us ask questions and think, not just take what we are and how we do it for granted. For example, with western Europe so irreligious and America so religious, why is their abortion rate lower than ours? Or again, since caring for the poor is absolutely central to Christian ethics, why do we Americans tolerate so much more poverty than the western Europeans do? I don't know, but now I want to try to find out.

So I have seen the world, and I am grateful. God willing, so long as I'm able I'm going to keep doing it. For "the spirit of the Lord has filled the whole world, and all things have knowledge of his voice." I want to see what he has been up to.

Chapter Four

Knowledgeable

If there is one trait of Fr. Bill's personality that stands out it would be knowledgeable. In a selection above we heard how Father joked about traveling overseas on sabbatical and imagining what those TSA agents at airport security think is in that one large suitcase—packed full of books!

On several occasions while visiting St. Nicholas, our Bishop Mark, one extremely knowledgeable in his own right, was stumped by several parishioners' questions. Referral to Fr. Bill brought immediate answers. During one epiphany season for house blessings Fr. Bill conducted a "stump the priest" campaign. To my knowledge Father was never unable to adequately address any question.

This could be heady stuff. The Orthodox Fathers write a great deal about the perils of knowledge. Any God-given gift of a trait of personality is subject to skewing ("twisting" as Fr. Bill would say) by the fall. "Knowledgeable" can easily become arrogance, pride or conceit. It is not difficult to find examples of this.

Not so with Fr. Bill. If there is one thing Father is impressed with about Orthodoxy (and there are many) it is the "Unknowable." To be Orthodox is to regain one's place in standing before God, the Unknowable, as creature. Father never made attempts to appear more knowledgeable than he was regarding things that are unknowable. His attitude was always a humble one. Yet we as parishioners are greatly benefited and blessed by his knowledge.

Reviewing the homilies of Fr. Bill "knowledgeable" breaks down into three distinct areas of application—Knowledgeable "In the World," "Not of the World" and "Within."

"Knowledgeable—In the World" is not restricted to "secular" matters. It also includes matters of religion from the nonOrthodox world. Being a convert priest and having many parishioners who are converts lent itself well to a series of homilies on the other Christian and nonChristian faiths. It is difficult to imagine an "ethnic bound" Orthodox priest in an ethnic parish delivering such a series of messages. Yet the reality of living in the United States presents this challenge—one the Orthodox Church has never been faced with in its entire existence. Certainly the Orthodox Church has always had to deal with splinter groups, some very formidable. But the number in the U.S. is now in the tens of thousands (!) and seemingly increasing daily. It takes an extremely knowledgeable priest to help his parishioners attempt to begin to sort through all of this.

The homily titled "Patriotism" is one of the finest examples of Fr. Bill's application of knowledge of the world around us. I would have titled this homily "True Freedom, Ethnicity and American Orthodoxy." It is one of his best examples of the power of critical reasoning combined with the priority of what is truly important in our world of Orthodoxy in the U.S.

The follow-up homily "The Da Vince Code" is a stimulating and fun ride at the intersection of Hollywood and Orthodoxy. This "homily" was actually an address at a public viewing/workshop of the movie at the theatre in Grafton, Wisconsin which included several other knowledgeable participants. At the time there was a great uproar over the film purporting to rewrite ancient history as it especially affected fourth century Orthodoxy and the First Ecumenical Council.

"Knowledgeable—Not of the World" relates to Orthodox matters of faith and practice and theology. The late psychiatrist M. Scott Peck used to jokingly thank the Roman Catholic Church for his lucrative professional practice. As a psychotherapist I can't count the number of times I've heard nominal or former Roman Catholic clients complain to me about how things were never explained to them. While I suspect the problem lay equally on both sides in these cases, such an accusation could never be justifiably leveled against Fr. Bill.

Father's series of homilies on the Liturgy is one every Orthodox person should read and regularly reread. Psychologically, the three most important words found in the Orthodox Liturgy are "Let us attend." Attention is a critical matter in both psychological and spiritual practice. The need for practice of attention and knowledgeable insight and participation in the Liturgy can't be over emphasized. I've selected three homilies from this series for the main body of this chapter. The remaining homilies in this series can be found in an Appendix at the end.

Fr. Bill's reliance upon the teachings of the Orthodox Fathers is ubiquitous. It is unmistakable that Father is not spouting off his own "creative," even ingenious personal thoughts on the matter when it comes to these critical aspects of Orthodox faith.

"Knowledgeable—Within" addresses the critical matter of the interior life as expertly described, clarified and passed down by those known as the Orthodox "neptic" Fathers. "Neptic" refers to that practice of attention that observes the workings and dynamics of the interior life, commonly referred to as the soul, heart, mind and/or "nous."

Therein lies an overlapping of the contemporary field of psychology with Orthodox spiritual practice. Though certainly never claiming to be a "psychologist," Father Bill does speak knowledgeably and accurately regarding occasional concerns of behavioral/psychological health and its interaction with Orthodox faith. The paramount example of this is Father's series of homilies on "The Seven Deadly Sins," especially the one on "Anger" included in this section. Of course I'm biased, but "Anger" is Father's best work on this integration between psychological workings and Orthodox spiritual practice.

In addition to "Pride" and "Envy," included in the main body of this chapter, "Lust" is also included in the Appendix. In "Lust" Father accurately acknowledges contemporary research facts regarding such behavioral health concerns as the genetic aspect of alcoholism.

There can be no doubt from these homilies that Fr. Bill is not just knowledgeable of the topics from an Orthodox perspective, but is also clearly experienced in neptic practice of his own life. Father's ability and willingness to be open and vulnerable about his own interior life goes strongly against the grain of his personality style which more typically tends toward distance and aloofness.

No doubt the reader will also notice Father's fondness once again for C.S. Lewis. Father has not been shy about using nonOrthodox (*not unOrthodox!*) sources to accurately convey Orthodox truth at times. In this way Father cannot be accused of judgmental narrow-mindedness that Father admits infects some in Orthodoxy. In the positive sense of the word, it could be stated that Fr. Bill has an "ecumenical" perspective. The first selection of this chapter regarding other faiths is a prime example of Father's love of peace combined with conviction about Orthodox faith.

In The World

ORTHODOXY AND OTHER FAITHS:
PART 1—Introduction
Sunday January 18, 2009

I was inspired to do this teaching series by our Saint Nicholas School director Marina Huff, who on these quiet Sundays between Epiphany and Great Lent has decided to cover this topic with our young people. Our youth grow up in a non-Orthodox world. Whether in school or in the media or wherever, they're exposed to many different kinds of Christianity as well as other religions and ideas. We can't protect them from this, nor should we. What they need is to learn about them from an Orthodox point of view, so they (1) will not be taken in by strange doctrines, (2) will not be threatened by them, (3) can learn to respect what is good in other people and their beliefs. So I decided to do the same for you adults, for exactly the same reasons.

Today an introduction: what is the general Orthodox approach to those who are not Orthodox Christians? Let's begin this way: (1) Orthodoxy teaches that Jesus Christ is the one way to salvation. Why? Because this was what he said. For example, *I am the way, the truth and the life; no one comes to the Father except by me.* (John 14:6) *No one knows the Father except the Son, and those to whom the Son chooses to reveal him.* (Matthew 11:27) (2) Orthodox also believe that non-Christians can be saved. Why? Because this was what Jesus said: He taught in Matthew 25 that at the judgment of the gentiles (the nations, the nonbelievers), those who did not believe but who had shown love and mercy to *the least of these my brethren*—the poor, the hungry, the lonely, the mistreated—will be taken into the Kingdom of heaven which has been prepared for them. In today's Gospel (Luke 17:12-19) it was the heretical Samaritan who pleased Christ. So Jesus Christ is the one way to salvation, and non-Christians can be saved. Is this contradictory? Orthodoxy which holds the fullness of the faith, which holds it all together, says: no, not at all. Both are true.

Yes, Christ is the only way to salvation. This is because God is salvation; fullness of life, eternal life is found only in God who is the only source of life. And Christ is God, so salvation is found only through him. But Christ is God, present everywhere, always. Christ is the Word, the Logos, the personal creative Reason who orders the entire universe, so that wherever there is truth, goodness, beauty, love, Christ our God is there. Orthodox believe there may be many who are now being saved by Christ but who are not yet aware of it, who may not know him until the end, but who then will say: yes, it was you I was seeking and serving all along—and Christ will usher these good people in. If Christ is truly God and if they are truly seeking that which is good and true, then sooner or later, in this world or the next, they must necessarily come to him who is the Source of these things. Surely God our Father will not condemn people because they grew up in a non-Christian culture and never got any farther. Christ said (quoting the prophet Isaiah) he came not to *break a broken reed or snuff out a smoldering wick* (Matthew 12:20), but rather to repair it, fan it into flame—for, as we hear at the end of almost every Orthodox service, God "is good and loves mankind."

So our emphasis on the divinity of Christ allows us Orthodox both to hold firm to our Orthodox faith in Jesus Christ as the unique, only begotten Son of God, the one way to salvation, and also to respect and honor what is good in other religions and other peoples, because we believe Christ God is working there too.

Do not be misled by two false approaches to this issue. One is the idea common among many conservative Christians that only Christians (or maybe only a certain kind of Christian) can be saved, who then denigrate others. You will hear it said that only those who have a particular sort of so-called "born again" conversion experience can be saved, or that in order to be saved one must make a commitment to Jesus Christ using a certain verbal formula. Khouria Dianna once heard a professor at Concordia University teach that all unbaptized people, even innocent babies, go to hell. I recently heard a preacher on TV say, "It don't bother me if people don't believe in Jesus, because I know they're going to burn for it!" (What ever happened to "love your neighbor as yourself"?!) You can even find a few Orthodox who think there is no truth outside the Orthodox Church. This is not authentic Orthodox teaching. (Those who believe in Christ and knowingly reject him, or knowingly reject what they believe to be true and good, are a different matter, but that judgment is up to God not us; we cannot see into other peoples' hearts and minds.) Beware of this narrow view of Christ which leads to putting down, blindly condemning other religions and peoples.

On the other hand, some liberal Christians take the opposite view. They say that since God is universal, since he works in all places and all peoples, then there is nothing unique about Jesus Christ and Christianity. Nothing is absolute; your truth is your truth, my truth is my truth, your lifestyle is your lifestyle, my lifestyle is my lifestyle, all is relative, everything is opinion. This is certainly not Orthodox Christian teaching. To repeat: we believe that salvation is only in Jesus Christ, who is the truth, who reveals the truth—and that's the truth.

Many today think it is ill-mannered and distasteful to say you believe anything to be true, for fear of offending someone who might disagree. I'm sorry, but this makes no sense at all. There is nothing arrogant or offensive about believing something to be true. Everybody believes what they believe to be true, or else they wouldn't believe it! And if they believe one thing to be true, this must mean they believe the opposite is not true. Someone who believes that God exists necessarily believes that atheism is not true. A Christian who believes Jesus is the Son of God must believe that Buddhists are in error about that. But that doesn't mean we should hate atheists or Buddhists (Christ explicitly commanded us to love all people, even our enemies.) or want to stretch them on the rack or condemn them to hell. When we find agnostics who love their families or Hindus who feed the poor, we should give thanks that Christ our God is working through them, whether they know it or not.

To disagree with people is not to put them down. At coffee hour after Liturgy, Tom Zompolas and Cal McIntyre sometimes almost come to blows over their views of economics. Do they therefore hate each other? No, they're friends; they respect each other and seem to enjoy their arguments. Beware of people who think they know it all, have all the truth and won't listen to others. None of us has all the truth. I believe Jesus Christ is the truth, but I certainly do not know all the truth that is in Jesus Christ. God can speak to me through people I disagree with and disapprove of.

In Old Testament times, according to the prophets, it was the pagan, unbelieving Assyrians and Babylonians who acted as God's agents to wake the Jews up to their own unfaithfulness. In America, we have lately gone through a phase where it has been fashionable to put down people whom we disagree with. I hope we're moving beyond that now, that we can stop yelling and start listening to each other again. Some of the people I have liked most have been those with whom I can have a good healthy disagreement and still be friends. At my last church, one woman and I disagreed about politics, and after Thursday morning Mass we sometimes really got into it. One time a new member who had never experienced this before sat and listened to us arguing, and his eyes got wider and wider as he thought, "We'll never see her again." Finally she said, "Gotta go now, have a good day, see you Sunday," and I said "'Bye," and his eyes got even wider. That was thirty years ago. I'm sure she and I still disagree with each other, but I've learned from her and respect her, and we're still friends. We still keep in touch.

The only sin which Christ said is unforgivable is to deny the work of the Holy Spirit. He said this after he had healed someone and the Pharisees had said it was the work of the devil. (Mark 3:29) So it is required of us to try to see the work of the Spirit, what is good and true, in people of other faiths or opinions, and not simply disagree with them or condemn them. I am altogether in favor of our youth learning about other denominations, religions and belief systems. I wish comparative religion were a required course in school. Religion has been central to human life, society, history, music, art and even the development of modern science, but most young people today are taught so little about it, for fear someone might be offended. How can we understand the world if we don't know religion? How can we understand why there are Muslim fundamentalists unless we know something about Islam? (We'll talk about that next time.) How can we understand America unless we understand the kind of classic liberal Protestant social teaching that is written into and assumed by our national Constitution?

So here in summary is, I think, the Orthodox approach to people of other faiths and beliefs: if Christ is the truth we have nothing to fear from the truth, no matter what its source, and from learning about others. This does not undercut our faith in Jesus Christ in any way. Indeed it is precisely because of our faith in Jesus Christ that we take this attitude. And as Orthodox Christians we can approach other peoples and their faiths (or lack thereof) from the solid foundation of a Church that is ancient, secure, stable, balanced, not threatened by any of them. Therefore we can be open-minded without losing our own faith, without being carried away by strange doctrines.

I recommend to you a little book, *Seeds of the Word: Orthodox Thinking on Other Religions* by John Garvey, book 2 of the Foundations series from St. Vladimir's Press.

Next week we'll go on to very briefly look at atheism, agnosticism and some non-Christian religions—how we agree and disagree with them. In the following weeks we'll consider in more detail the religions we deal with most of the time in this country: (1) Judaism and what the New Testament really says about the nation of Israel, especially in light of current events, (2) Roman Catholicism, and (3) the thousands of different denominations, independent groups and sects that have emerged out of the Protestant movement. I will try to be honest, fair and respectful. And at the end I hope we will all have a better understanding not only of other peoples' faiths, but of the truth and beauty of our own Orthodox faith, and of how our Lord Jesus Christ and Christianity are unique among the religions of the world.

ORTHODOXY AND OTHER FAITHS
PART 6—Modern Protestantism
Sunday February 22, 2009

Someone asked last week how could I speak about "one Orthodox Church," when we are divided into so many national and ethnic jurisdictions. Yes, we Orthodox in the new world need to get together institutionally. But while Protestant denominations and individuals disagree about the faith and revise their doctrines as they go along, Orthodoxy is united generation after generation in what matters most: the faith, the sacraments, the Christian life. We are in communion with each other. Orthodoxy has a miraculous unity, the gift of the Holy Spirit. I don't know how else to explain it.

I have given two weeks to Protestantism since it is so complex and disunited. Now we come to the complete fragmentation of the Protestant movement. Beginning in the late 19th century the major Protestant denominations (mainline Protestants, they are sometimes called, though they are now the minority) were much influenced by Biblical criticism, which meant simply investigation of the Bible, its origins and meanings, so that people could understand it better. Some good came out of that. But as time went on, almost every speculation was taken by someone as a serious possibility. The result was that great doubt about the Bible was planted in peoples' minds. Dr. Albert Schweitzer, a New Testament scholar, concluded that the Gospels tell nothing certain about Jesus, only "the barest whisper of the man." He lost faith, and so in order to do something worthwhile with his life, he became a doctor in the African jungle. A professor in the Methodist seminary I attended began by saying he would tear the New Testament apart so he could put it back together again. He did the first part very well, left us doubting everything; he forgot the second part. My faith was shaken till finally it occurred to me that if Matthew, Mark, Luke and John didn't get it right in the first century, chances were slim that Dr. Lundgren in Evanston, Illinois, nearly 2000 years later was going to figure it out.

This doubt about the Bible began in schools and seminaries. Bible, doctrine, worship and prayer were played down, often replaced by emphasis on social service. The Social Gospel as it was called is a good thing. God commands us to love our neighbors. But that is no substitute for loving God with all our heart, soul, mind and strength, which is the source of all good things. In time this doubt about the Bible worked its way into parish churches. It hit Methodists, Presbyterians and Congregationalists first; with Lutherans and Anglicans, who had retained some tradition despite themselves, it took longer. But when it hit it led, not surprisingly, to a considerable loss of members. In Britain today most Methodist and Presbyterian "chapels" are closed. Few go to church in Scandinavia or Germany. In America the Episcopal Church is typical. In 1965 it had 3.5 million members; today it has barely 2 million. What Protestants needed was the Tradition, the Fathers, the Liturgy to guide them in interpreting the Bible. But since they believed in Bible alone, when they lost their trust in the Bible their system fell apart. It's very sad.

Back to 1900. In reaction to this liberalizing some decided to "do another Martin Luther." They left the mainline denominations and tried to return to the fundamentals of early Christianity as they imagined it and called themselves fundamentalists. Fundamentalism is not ancient; it's a modern movement. Based on original Protestant principles they founded new churches based again on Bible alone, which they said must be interpreted strictly literally. But what did that mean? When Jesus said "I am the door," did he mean he swings on hinges? No fundamentalists took "This is my Body, This is my Blood" literally. "Woe to you who are rich . . . Hate your father and mother . . . Do not resist evil." Few fundamentalists took these literally.

Father Peter Gillquist tells how he and others left Campus Crusade and separated, each to build his own church on the basis of the Bible, but when they got together again they found their churches were all quite different. None of them had read the Bible the same way. So once again the Bible alone principle brought division. Using the social freedom available in modern society, Protestants now went off in a multitude of directions and founded a multitude of new churches. Some say miracles and speaking in tongues are essential, others that there have been no miracles since New Testament times. Some say to be saved one must have a born-again experience; others say that's not so, but you can guarantee salvation by saying you believe in Jesus Christ using a certain formula. Some are scholarly and stress teaching; others are more emotional. Some are bizarre with so-called spiritual gifts like fainting and uncontrolled laughter and barking like dogs. Most have abandoned liturgy and sacraments; worship services may be educational or just entertaining.

So we have the modern profusion of Bible churches, community churches, independent churches, Pentecostal and charismatic churches, and on and on. Some formed little denominations like the "Brook" churches around Milwaukee. Many have produced new breakaways. So today Milwaukee Protestantism has everything from mainline First United Methodist Church to Going Up Yonder Community Church to New Covenant Temple United Holy Church of America

Incorporated to Milwaukee Metropolitan Community Church which is for homosexuals. Recent changes in the Roman Catholic Church have added to the confusion. As I said last week, many Protestants long defined themselves in opposition to Rome. But if Rome changes what do you protest against? Many of these groups have grown, I think, because they offer something solid to live by; their doctrines are often taught as absolute truth. But in fact these churches also mutate. 50 years ago most Bible churches stressed conversion to Jesus; 25 years ago it was conservative political action. Now, led by people like Rick Warren, they're moving to the gospel of self-fulfillment. Who knows what they'll be next and who will break from them forming new churches believing who knows what?

Finally, four groups came out of Protestantism. Protestants don't claim them, but we should know about them because we hear so much about them. Unitarianism—so called because they disbelieve in the Trinity—as a denomination began in the 1700s in America. Today, even belief in God is optional. Unitarians draw on many religious traditions with the exception of traditional Christianity. Their original ideal was to believe in the religion of Jesus, not the religion about Jesus. How to separate the two I don't know, because the Jesus who taught good things also claimed to be Messiah and said he had all authority in heaven and earth. A Unitarian pastor once told me he prayed. I said, "Good. I wondered what you did in church if you didn't pray." He said, "Oh, by myself, not in church! Once I prayed in church, and a group came to me and said, don't do that again."

Mormonism, the Church of Jesus Christ of Latter Day Saints, began in the 1820s in New York state when Joseph Smith claimed he had a visit from the Angel Moroni who brought him some golden tablets on which was written in Middle Hebrew (an otherwise unknown language) the Book of Mormon, telling the story of people in America from 2700 BC to 420 AD. It says that Christ after his Ascension, knowing the apostles would mess it up, visited America and revealed the true faith to people here. This was recorded by the prophet Mormon. The evidence for this? Joseph Smith said so. No one else saw the tablets. He dictated the Book of Mormon from behind a curtain. One man was allowed to touch (but not see) them within a bag. Then the tablets were taken away by the angel. It's rather like the origins of Islam, so different from Christ's revelation which was witnessed by many.

To Mormons the Book of Mormon has the same authority as the Bible. It says that God the Father was once a man, who became God, but he does not have absolute power; he still has a body and now lives on his own planet. (This is obviously not the God whom we worship.)

Mormons believe Jesus and the Holy Spirit (who also has a body) are not divine but will become gods with their own planets, as will we all. Because the Book of Mormon allowed polygamy they were driven out of New York, Ohio, Illinois and Missouri and settled in Utah. In 1890 a new revelation from God forbade polygamy. The Book of Mormon says black people are inferior to whites; blacks were not allowed to take part in temple ceremonies until 1978 when a new revelation gave equality to blacks. Mormonism today is one of the fastest growing religions in the United States and in the world. Two pleasant young women once came to our door to convert us to Mormonism. I said, "I will listen to you if you let me ask you two questions." I asked, nicely, if they believed the things they just told me. They answered, "Yes, we do." I asked nicely, "Why do you believe this?" They said, "We just do." I said, "But please give me a reason." They turned and left.

In the 1870s in Pennsylvania Charles Russell founded the Jehovah's Witnesses, part of the Adventist movement who expect the imminent return of Christ, also called Millennialists because they expect a 1000 year reign of Christ on earth. Jehovah's Witnesses predicted Christ's return specifically in 1914, 1925 (accompanied by the resurrection of the Old Testament patriarchs) and 1978. They believe that Jesus is not divine, that his kingdom was established in heaven in 1918, that Jesus and the Archangel Michael are the same person, that Jesus died not on a cross (which is pagan) but on a wooden stake. They believe only Jehovah's Witnesses will go to heaven, and only 144,000 of them, and only those 144,000 receive Communion; all others will remain on earth. Jehovah's Witnesses do not celebrate birthdays or holidays, do not salute flags or sing national anthems or serve in the military or receive blood transfusions, based on Acts 15:28-29 where the first Apostolic Council told converts from paganism to abstain from blood so as not to offend Jewish converts. Where do they get all this? From the Bible alone as they read it; but they have also rewritten the New Testament, removing references to the divinity of Christ.

Christian Science (not Scientology, which is a very different thing) was founded by Mary Baker Eddy in Boston in the late 1800s. She wrote a book *Science and Health*, which is yet another one true interpretation of the Bible. It says that only goodness, truth, spirit, life and health are real; evil, sin, falsehood, sickness, pain, death and matter are illusions. Once you truly know these things do not exist, they have no power over you, so the key is to set your mind straight. Jesus is considered divine, but Christian Scientists do not believe in the Incarnation because they do not believe in the reality of bodies. There are grains of truth in Christian Science. The Church believes in spiritual healing; and once we believe

Christ conquered death, death loses much of its power over us. But pain and death are real. What is the difference whether something hurts or only feels like it hurts?

Loyal Christian Scientists do not go to doctors since sickness does not exist. Mark Twain said that if Christian Science kept growing it would have to be outlawed. Imagine without vaccinations how disease would spread. Once I visited the Christian Science church in Cedarburg. The very friendly people told us how once they knew pain, sickness and matter were not real, they felt better. Afterwards they asked if we had questions. I asked, "Do you really believe your body doesn't exist?" "Oh, yes." I asked, "Do you eat?" Their answer: "I guess if we believed fully we wouldn't." Then they invited us out for ice cream! My head spun for a week. Obviously they use words in a way the rest of us don't. Christian Science never releases membership figures, but they seem to be declining rapidly. And they must believe in matter in some sense. The small group of Christian Scientists left in Iowa City is asking our Saint Raphael Mission over $500,000 material dollars for their building.

Why do people believe these odd things? We can only speculate. Is it because they find a sense of fellowship, community, belonging? Is it the desire to be different? Saint Paul warned about people who have "itching ears," who won't listen to sound doctrine but will believe anything new and kicky. Is it just modern individualism which encourages spiritual pride, the notion that things are true because I think they are? If I stood here this morning and told you the Church has been wrong for 20 centuries but now I have discovered the Truth, how would you react? . . . But that's because you're Orthodox.

Orthodoxy requires spiritual humility. We know we did not invent Orthodoxy; we know Orthodoxy has been passed down ("traditioned") to us from Christ and the apostles, generation after generation in the Church. We know that our job is not to reinvent it or rework it, but to receive it humbly and pass it on untarnished to the next generation. Brothers and sisters, have sympathy for people in these other religions and for western Christians in general today. It is hard when truth keeps changing on you, when what was Gospel truth suddenly becomes false. In the Protestant denominations and their breakaways are many good people who seek God, many who love Jesus as best they can, and do many good works. Remember we will be judged not by which church we belonged to, but by whether we fed, clothed, and visited the least of Christ's brethren. "Many who are first will be last and the last first." Nevertheless, I find myself more sympathetic to non-Christians and non-believers than to those who use the name Christian but who pervert the Gospel and diminish Christ and his Church or make them seem ludicrous. There is much in modern "Christianity" that drives people away from Christ. I don't find it surprising that the number of unbelievers is now increasing rapidly in America.

Finally, how should we live as Orthodox Christians in a society which is religiously torn in all directions? I don't think it's so hard.

1) Be educated. Ignorance is dangerous. Know who we are; know who they are. 2) Be charitable. Seek what is good in all religions and all people. 3) Be wary. There are foolish dangerous teachings out there. 4) Think. If any religion or system tells you, "Don't ask questions, just believe it," *don't believe it.* If you have to check your mind at the church door, don't go in. Use your common sense. How likely is it that Joseph Smith finally got it right in 1820 or Charles Russell in 1879 or my Methodist New Testament professor in 1960, or Martin Luther in 1519, while 2000 years of unbroken consistent Orthodox Tradition is wrong? What are the odds? 5) Just be Orthodox. Live the Orthodox life, follow Christ; worship, pray, learn, confess, feast, fast, love, give to charity, forgive—and I think you'll find Orthodoxy has such quality and balance, such breadth and depth, such knowledge about God and man and life and death, and leads to so many good things, that you and your children will not be much tempted to turn to strange doctrines.

JUSTIFICATION AND THE HOLY CROSS

Sunday after the Exaltation of the Holy Cross: September 17, 2006

EPISTLE: Galatians 2:16-20

When I talk about this epistle, I always concentrate on retranslating and redefining terms, because the translation used by western Christians is incorrect and because Orthodox think some western definitions of sin and justification are wrong. We Orthodox who live in the western world are affected by this. Since we have no official Orthodox English New Testament, we often read Protestant or Roman Catholic translations (as we did this morning), and these days because of the fundamentalist revival, the Protestant understanding of justification by faith is just "in the air." Therefore, every year I try to explain this passage in an Orthodox way. This gets a bit complex. Hang in there with me.

The classic western (especially Protestant) understanding is as follows: *We are sinners—that is, we have broken God's law. God the righteous Judge is therefore angry at us and his just punishment is death and hell. Paul says we cannot be saved, cannot get to heaven by works of the law—that is, by doing good things—because we can't please God, no matter how hard we try. So how can we avoid hell and go to heaven? Only because Christ came and, because he was perfect, he could pay the penalty of our sins by his suffering on the Cross. Thus we are justified—that is, we are declared innocent by God, even though we're really guilty. And so we can go to heaven, even though we are still unworthy sinners.* In the Orthodox view, the preceding (except for the part about Christ coming to save us) is almost entirely wrong. It misunderstands the Bible and the Gospel, not least because it expresses our relationship with God chiefly in legal terms.

First, in the New Testament the word "sin" (hamartia) is not a legal term; it does not mean "lawbreaking." It's an archery, term which means "missing the mark." The mark is God and God's will—to love him with all my heart, soul, mind and strength, and to love my neighbor as myself. Hitting the mark means that I become good, holy, pure and righteous. Mankind's problem is not that we have broken rules and therefore God must punish us by killing us; it is rather that we are separated from God and his will, and because God is life, we therefore die.

Second, regarding the notion that on the Cross Christ paid the legal penalty of our sins, thereby assuaging the anger of God: there is no such teaching in the New Testament. Yes, God is our Judge. And Christ said once that he gave his life as a "ransom for sin" (Matthew 20:28 and Mark 10:45)—but ransoms are paid not to the judge but to the kidnapper. This saying means that Jesus chose to accept human death which was the result of our sins and "paid the devil his due." When Saint Paul says elsewhere that we "were bought with a price" (I Corinthians 6:20, 7:23) he is speaking figuratively. The Father is not a legal authority who impersonally dispenses penalties. Christ did not die to satisfy justice or to placate an angry God. The Good News, the Gospel, is, above all, that God is our merciful Father who is good and loves mankind. Jesus did not teach us to pray "Our Judge who art in heaven . . ." He taught us to pray to God as Abba (Daddy in Aramaic), to have faith in God as our loving Father. If we think of God as chiefly a judge, we'll never understand the Gospel. So let's go back to this passage and look at it not in a legal context, but in light of the Father's love for us and our place as his children in his family, the Church. And let's also translate it right.

I want to concentrate on one sentence from this Epistle because many western Christians misunderstand it in three ways, some in four—and it goes to the heart of Christian faith and life. In most western translations, Saint Paul writes: "We are justified not by the works of the law but by faith in Jesus Christ." Here are the points of confusion:

(1) The word which western Bibles translate as "justify" (a Roman legal term meaning to be *declared* just—that is, innocent) usually means something different in the original Greek. The Greek word is *dikaio*. In Orthodox usage it means "to be *made* righteous," to "righteousify." (There isn't a good English word for it, but "justify" is the wrong word.) It does not mean that we are let off the hook, declared legally innocent even though we are guilty. It means that we are to become truly innocent, to actually be remade into good and holy persons, acceptable to God and worthy of heaven. So what Saint Paul actually says here is: "We are made righteous . . ."

(2) " . . . not by the works of the Law." Most Protestants take this to mean that there is no good work (action) we can do which is sufficient to please God and save our souls. But in context Paul is speaking not of all laws but only of the Old Testament Law, which is his big issue with the Galatians. Paul is saying only that Old Testament religious rules are inadequate to save us, to make us perfect, filled with love of God and man. Only Christ can do that. So, thus far Saint Paul says: "We are made righteous not by keeping the [Old Testament] Law . . ."

(3) " . . . but by faith." What is faith? Some Protestants say this means correct belief, others that it means an internal attitude of trust in God. Classic Protestantism teaches that we are saved by "faith alone," that is, by our inner faith in Christ alone and that our actions have nothing to do with it. This also is not true to the Scriptures. Christ taught: "not everyone who says to me, 'Lord, Lord', will enter the Kingdom of heaven, but he who does the will of my Father in heaven." (Matthew 7:21) When Christ was asked by the rich young ruler what he must do to attain eternal life, the Lord told him what to do (keep the commandments, give his possessions to the poor), not what he should believe. (Matthew 19, Mark 10, Luke 18) Orthodox follow the teaching of the Brother of the Lord (James 2:26): "Faith without works is dead." Genuine trust in God involves correct mental belief, correct spiritual attitude, correct bodily actions—our whole being, integrated and given over to God. So, "We are justified not by the works of the [Old Testament] Law but by faith . . ."

(4) " . . . in Jesus Christ". That is a mistranslation. Saint Jerome, who long ago translated the New Testament into Latin, made a major mistake. The original Greek says we are made righteous not "by faith *in* Jesus Christ" but rather "by the faith *of* Jesus Christ"—not by our poor weak faith but by *his* faith. After Father Peter Gillquist became Orthodox he was asked by an evangelical friend, "So what do you believe now? Are we saved by our faith or by our works?" Father Peter answered, "No. We are saved neither by our faith nor by our works. We are saved by Jesus

Christ." To think we are saved by our own faith makes faith into a kind of work: if only I can work up enough faith in Christ I'll be saved. No, we are saved by the faith of Jesus Christ. So, here is the passage translated and understood correctly: "We are made righteous not by the works of the [Old Testament] Law but by the faith of Jesus Christ."

What is this "faith of Jesus Christ"? What faith did Jesus have? Here is where the Holy Cross (which we celebrate today) comes in. The Cross is our central image of the faith of Jesus Christ. The Cross is the sign of his faithful obedience to God the Father. The night before he died he prayed, "Father, take this cup away from me. Nevertheless not my will but thine be done." (Matthew 26:39) He went to the Cross in faithful obedience to the will of God. The Holy Cross is the ultimate sign of his love, his faithfulness to us. "Greater love has no man than that he should give up his life for his friends." (John 15:13) The Cross is the sign of God's power, the victory that faith leads to. He said, "When I am lifted up from the cross I will draw all men to myself"—as indeed he has. [Jn. 12:32] Jesus Christ has had more power, more influence, more followers by far than anyone else in human history. That is the faith with which he went to the Cross—the faith of Jesus Christ. This is then the Christian faith, the Church's faith which we receive from Jesus Christ. And this—faithful obedience to God, faithful love of God and man, faithful trust in God's victory—is what can make us righteous.

How do I get this faith of Jesus Christ, that faith he showed as he died on the Cross? Not by trying to work it up within myself, but rather from Jesus Christ himself. He pours it into us. In today's Epistle Paul continues: "I have been crucified with Christ. It is no longer I who live but Christ lives in me, and the life I live in the flesh I live by the faith of the Son of God who gave himself for me." (Here again the western translation reads inaccurately "by faith *in* the Son of God.") Paul is speaking here chiefly of Holy Baptism and the Holy Eucharist. He teaches elsewhere (e.g. Colossians 2:12) that it is in Baptism that we died and were buried with Christ. In Baptism we were joined to Christ, so that we become part of his Body the Church, so that he lives in us and we in him. Therefore we already live with Christ on the other side of death; we already have eternal life.

Likewise, in the Divine Liturgy, Christ the Word of God enters into our minds and hearts through the reading of the Gospel. In the Holy Eucharist, Christ bodily comes and lives in me, pours his life into me. So we get the faith of Jesus Christ chiefly through the Church, where Christ comes to me in a multitude of ways. Therefore Paul can say: I am still a sinner, my life is still off mark, I am not yet a righteous man, I still have a long way to go. But the cure is that, because I am in the Church, Jesus

Christ actually lives within me. His power, his faith, his goodness, his very life are at work within me. All I have to do is learn to cooperate fully with what he is doing, so that it is no longer I who live but Christ fully living in me. And so he will make me righteous.

Gospel: Mark 8:34—9:1

Here is the way to cooperate with Christ. "Take up your cross and follow me." Is this a call to masochism, to pain? Some people think so. No. Christ suffered on the Cross, but suffering was not what the Cross was all about. That is why our Orthodox hymns and crucifixes don't dwell on his agony. It wasn't till maybe the 10th century that Orthodox crucifixes even showed him dead on the Cross or gave any indication that it hurt. Instead they showed him alive and ruling from the Cross. And still our crucifixes show him not in agony but with a rather satisfied expression on his face, as if to say, "I've finished it! I've done it!" The way of the Cross is the way of faithful obedience to God, the way of Love, the way to Victory. If that requires suffering, so be it. If not, thank God.

Jesus says the way of the Cross is the way to save our lives. It is by hanging onto our old life, which is off the mark, which is not centered on God, that we can lose our lives. That is the life we need to deny and get rid of, again not because an angry God will punish us if we don't, but because God is life and if we're not with God we go dead. We may gain the whole world, but if we lose God and finally die, what's the point? But God is life. If we do whatever it takes to stay united with him: if we faithfully follow the way of the Cross—obey him, love, have faith and keep trusting—we will gain our lives. In the end death will not get us.

Jesus said, "Assuredly, I say to you, there are some standing here who will not taste death till they see the Kingdom of God present with power." Christ is not speaking of his Second Coming someday in the future—though he taught that. He is talking about now. The key word here is *see*. Jesus the King, the obedient servant of the Father was standing before them—and they did not yet see that in him the Kingdom of God was already present with power. By his cross and resurrection he would open their eyes. Christ is still present among us with power. He is present within you with power. In just a few minutes, you will receive his presence and power within you in Holy Communion. "Receive the Body of Christ, taste the fountain of immortality." And with his presence he will pour his own faith into you, and give you power to faithfully walk the way of the Cross and save your life forever.

PATRIOTISM
July 5, 2009

On this Independence Day weekend, what is the Orthodox view of patriotism? We're for it. Patriotism is a good thing—loving, treasuring one's homeland and people, a sense of belonging, our own way of doing things, our particular gifts from God. And we Americans have much to be grateful to God for, much to be patriotic about, things we easily take for granted: 1) Political stability—over 250 years with huge changes in society but no revolutions and only 1 civil war. America's founding fathers were brilliant in this regard. 2) Our freedoms—elected government, freedom of worship, of speech, assembly, the press. 3) America's capacity to receive people from all over the world and incorporate them—my ancestors a few generations ago and some of you here today.

I am reading the Journal of Father Alexander Schmemann. In it he tells how he and his wife Juliana came to America as immigrants, she not speaking a word of English, and 25 years later she was made head of one of New York's most prestigious schools for girls. He wrote, "The American dream is still alive!" Actually in my heart I think I'm an upper Midwest patriot. This is where the people I love are, this is where things feel right to me. Every time I go south of I-70, all the country music 24 hours a day about drives me batty! Up here, despite the winters, is where I belong. Orthodoxy has always formed a close identity with society and culture so that the faith is connected with life, not just with Sunday morning. In Greece, go into a bank or post office and there are icons on the walls, Orthodoxy is taught in school, it's on the radio—that sort of thing. The nation, with its sharply defined boundaries, actually is a fairly modern development in world history. Things were much more flexible in ancient times. But Orthodoxy has identified itself with nations too; that's why we have the Bulgarian Orthodox Church, the Serbian Orthodox Church and so on.

However, patriotism can be dangerous. Father Schmemann also wrote in his Journal that one of the worst things that ever happened to Orthodoxy was its *identification* with nations so people cannot distinguish between the two, like some American evangelicals or those who think that to be really Orthodox you've got to be Greek or Russian or whatever. When we were first looking at Orthodoxy 25 years ago a Ukrainian woman, a good friend (*memory eternal, Helen!*) asked me: why do you want to be Orthodox? You're not Ukrainian. A friend of mine once visited a Greek church (not in Milwaukee), interested in Orthodoxy, and the priest told him: I'm glad you visited. Now go back to your own church where you belong. This attitude is officially called phyletism—the belief that Orthodoxy is limited to a particular tribe or culture. It was condemned as a heresy at a pan-Orthodox council in Constantinople in 1872. Orthodoxy is for all the world, all cultures and nations and peoples. Orthodoxy is wider, broader, deeper, higher, wiser than any one nation or culture, not to be identified with any one nation or culture.

Today's Gospel reading, Matthew 8:5-13, fortuitously speaks to this. The Jews were and are intensely nationalistic. But who is it in today's reading that has faith greater than any found in Israel? It is a Roman centurion, a commander of the occupying forces. How often Jesus made foreigners the heroes: the Good Samaritan, the Samaritan leper who alone returned to be give thanks for his healing, and so on. "I tell you," said Jesus "many will come from east and west and sit down with Abraham, Isaac and Jacob in kingdom of heaven, but the sons of Kingdom [the Jews, or us if we are unfaithful] will be cast out into the darkness." As John the Baptist said, don't brag that you're sons of Abraham. "If God needs sons of Abraham, he can raise them up out of these stones." And likewise if God needs Americans . . . or if he needs Orthodox, for that matter.

The biggest danger of phyletism is that it limits Orthodoxy to one national way of looking at things. It narrows the Gospel. Today's Epistle Romans 6:18-23, for example, speaks to the issue of freedom. Saint Paul says sin can enslave us. We Americans especially value our political freedoms. We Christians are grateful for religious freedom here in this country. We can begin to think that these alone can make us truly free. No, there is an even more important kind of freedom, freedom from sin. In John 8, Jesus said to the Jews, "You shall know the truth and the truth shall set you free." The Jews said: how can you say that? We are Abraham's descendants. We're not slaves to anyone. They said this not because they had political freedom (They didn't; Rome ruled.) but because they had religious freedom. They could practice their religion freely, and they thought that made them truly free. Jesus answered, "I tell you, whoever commits sin is a slave to sin." If greed, lust, anger, hatred, drink, drugs, whatever controls you, you are not free. You can vote at every election and pray in every school, but you're still a slave. In fact one can have no political freedom, no religious freedom and still be free on the inside, free from sin. Christ came to set us free from sin—the ultimate and most important freedom.

American Orthodox are not much tempted by the heresy of phyletism. This is not an Orthodox country. And despite the myth believed by Protestant evangelicals, America did not have a Christian foundation in the classical sense of that word. At the time of the American revolution less than 30% of Americans had any formal religious affiliation. Only a few of America's founders believed in the divinity of Christ. Most were deists, who believed for the most part that God created the world but withdrew and now we're in charge. In today's terms they were religious liberals. George Washington was an Anglican who never received Communion. Thomas Jefferson rewrote the Gospels leaving out all miracles. Ben Franklin believed each solar system had its own god. America's founders were brilliant men. Look at what they created. (Goodness and wisdom and intelligence are not limited to Orthodox or to Christians.) They believed in the value of religion in general, but they very specifically established no particular religion, including Christianity.

So as Orthodox Christians how should we relate to America? We should incorporate what is good here. The Spirit of God fills the whole world. There are good things in all cultures, all people. The Orthodox Church has always moved into new lands and has taken what is good in the culture and brought it into the Church. Orthodox have not made African natives dress like Scottish Presbyterians, nor do American Orthodox need to dress like Russian peasants. Alaskan pagans had spirit houses in their cemeteries to honor their dead, and in native Alaskan Orthodox cemeteries today the spirit houses remain to honor their Orthodox dead. But Orthodoxy rejects those things in cultures which do not conform to the faith. If the natives are polygamous, they become monogamous when they become Orthodox. If Americans have loose sexual mores (as judging by the political news, apparently we do), they become strict when they become Orthodox.

Already some good American things are being pulled into the Orthodox Church. America is a democratic populist culture. Power is of the people. Americans like to participate. This is helping American Orthodoxy to recover some ancient Orthodox things that have been lost or underplayed such as worship in the language of the people, peoples' participation in worship, open icon screens so people don't feel cut off, Parish Councils and national Conventions, designed so that lay people can take their proper place in the running of the Church, so that the Church doesn't become a clerical preserve. All these are part of authentic Orthodoxy. Orthodox theology is clear that the Holy Spirit dwells in all our people, not just in the clergy. America is helping Orthodoxy recover that.

There are things in American culture that we do not want to pull into the Church. Two examples: 1) Arrogance. Many Americans both conservative and liberal take it for granted that we are right, everybody else is wrong and our job is to tell them how to do it. I have told you before that once I watched an American secretary of state on Greek TV telling the Greeks what they must do and how they must do it, and I could see the Greeks gently rolling their eyes. Whatever she said they were not going to do it. Arrogance is destructive—and since we Orthodox believe we are the original and authentic Church we are tempted by this kind of triumphalism. We need to reject it. It will drive people away—or, worse, it will attract proud, arrogant people. The Orthodox virtue is humility. 2) The modern American attitude towards money. It is taken for granted in our culture that the purpose of life is to get rich, make bigger profits, accumulate as much stuff as possible. Money comes first. In Orthodoxy this is called the sin of greed. American Orthodox are very tempted by this—to think that the measure of our success as a church is big budgets, big buildings, big money. This is not compatible with Orthodoxy. Thank God that he has provided us here at Saint Nicholas with the money we need but not much more.

Our mission here is not to make Orthodoxy American. Our mission is to make *Americans* Orthodox—gently, patiently, not arrogantly, to make authentic Orthodoxy available so Americans can enter into it. And we are growing. By the grace of God it is happening. I believe the Orthodox Church has arrived in America at just the right time and that Orthodox from the old countries, whether they know it or not, have come here by the hand of God, for the purpose of God.

Our mission is to make *America* Orthodox. The Orthodox Church has always been concerned not only with saving souls but with the conversion of cultures, creating Orthodox societies. In the Roman Empire 2000 years ago we were a small minority but growing, and you know what happened. Today we are a small minority in America but growing. In time by the grace of God, who knows what may happen? For the sake of America I hope so. For all nations, all cultures, all societies come and go—this is no secret—and we are blessed to live here, now. But they all fade away in the end, even the best of them, even the most stable of them—while the Church, by the promise and grace of our Lord Jesus Christ, will endure forever. The gates of death will never prevail against her, and in her and her ways is true national security.

THE DA VINCI CODE:
CONSTANTINE AND THE FIRST ECUMENICAL COUNCIL
Written in 2006 for a forum sponsored by Saint Nicholas Church

Dan Brown and Tom Hanks and Ron Howard say: don't take this so seriously. *The Da Vinci Code* is just a story; it's fiction. No, it is a mix of fact and fiction, and it doesn't distinguish between the two. As if someone wrote a story about the American Revolution and had the British win, or about the election of 2000 and had the Supreme Court rule in favor of Gore. These would be interesting speculations, and we would know how to separate fact from fantasy. But with *The Da Vinci Code* unless you know early Church history well, how do you tell truth from fiction? So people wonder. Might it have happened as *The Divine Code* says? And since this goes to the heart of the Christian faith, this is serious.

Can we know what really happened in ancient times? Granted, history is not entirely objective; events are seen through the eyes of people, and three people can describe the same event three different ways. However, there is historical evidence. We do possess ancient documents, and often we can tell when something is just being made up. Let me tell you first that I am not a professional scholar, just an old parish priest (if you professors wish to correct me after I'm done, please do), so the following is a sort of term paper. I've taken a small section (4 pages) from *The Da Vinci Code*—what [fictional character] Leigh Teabing says about the emperor Constantine and the Council of Nicaea—and will try to tell you what is accurate and what is not. I have some working knowledge of this. Every May 21 we Orthodox celebrate the feast of Saints Constantine & Helen, and on the Sunday after Ascension we commemorate the Fathers of the First Ecumenical Council. So we begin: Teabing says many things dogmatically. Some of them are true. I will quote the text exactly.

1) *The Bible as we know it today was collated by the pagan Roman emperor Constantine the Great.*

Not true. More than a century before Constantine, Christians had accepted most New Testament books without much controversy. Constantine had nothing to do with it.

2) Constantine *was a lifelong pagan who was baptized on his deathbed, too weak to protest.*

This is a blend of fact and fancy. Constantine was baptized not long before his death. Does that mean he was a pagan? No. At the time Christians sometimes postponed baptism for fear of committing major sin afterwards. That was a misunderstanding of baptism; it doesn't mean he was a pagan. Perhaps he wanted to be emperor to all the people. It is recorded that he visited pagan temples, just as an American Christian president might visit a mosque or synagogue. There is no evidence that as emperor Constantine participated in pagan worship; notably, after he conquered Rome he did not offer the customary pagan sacrifices.

Constantine's mother Helen was a Christian; she raised him after his father emperor Constantius divorced her. Constantine said he was converted to Christ by a vision of the cross inscribed with the words "*In this sign conquer.*" Even before that Christian priests traveled with his army. There is no evidence that he was baptized because he was "too weak to protest." Rather it was written that he welcomed baptism and for the rest of his life wore not imperial robes but only his white baptismal garment.

3) *In Constantine's day, Rome's official religion was sun worship—the cult of Sol Invictus, or the Invincible Sun and Constantine was its head priest.*

Romans worshipped many gods. Emperor Aurelian dedicated the Roman temple of Sol Invictus on December 25, 274. Constantine may have worshipped Sol early in his life. He allowed images of the sun to remain on Roman coins; he retained the imperial title Pontifex Maximus, high priest of the cult of Sol Invictus. Perhaps for reasons of political expediency? But Christians also used sun and light language about Christ, so this may have been his way of "transitioning" the empire into Christianity.

4) *Christians and pagans began warring, and the conflict grew to such proportions that it threatened to render Rome in two. Constantine . . . in 325 AD decided to unify Rome under a single religion, Christianity . . . [As] a very good businessman . . . He could see that Christianity was on the rise, and he simply backed the winning horse.*

Actually there had been tension between Christianity and paganism for three centuries. In the early 4th century the pagan emperors tried to exterminate the Church. Constantine ended this persecution by his Edict of Milan in 312, and began to give preferential treatment to Christians. But no, before Constantine Christianity was in danger of being wiped out. It was Constantine who made it the "winning horse."

5) *Constantine [brilliantly] converted the sun-worshipping pagans to Christianity. By fusing pagan symbols, dates and rituals into the growing Christian tradition, he created a kind of hybrid religion that was acceptable to both parties. The vestiges of pagan religion in Christian symbology are undeniable. Egyptian sun disks became the halos of Christian saints. Pictograms of Isis [nursing Horus] became the blueprint for our modern images of the Virgin Mary nursing Baby Jesus. And virtually all the elements of the Catholic ritual—the miter, the altar, the doxology, and communion, the act of "'God'-eating"—were taken directly from earlier pagan mystery religions . . . Nothing in Christianity is original. The pre-Christian God Mithras . . . was born on December 25, died, was buried in a rock tomb, and then resurrected in three days. By the way, December*

25 was also the birthday of Osiris, Adonis and Dionysus. The newborn Krishna was presented with gold, frankincense and myrrh.

Yes, there were many pagan antecedents to Christianity. How could there not be? Jesus was not the first baby to be born or carried by a mother. Christians took pagan art and converted it; Orthodox iconography developed directly out of Egyptian funerary art. When Christ instituted the Holy Eucharist he drew on pagan totem religion, in which people identify with a particular animal, sacrifice and eat it, receiving its life force into themselves: "Whoever eats my flesh dwells in me and I in him." [John 6:56] There are pagan gods who die and rise, symbolizing nature's annual cycle. In the 4th or 5th century Christians chose to celebrate Jesus' birth on December 25 near the winter solstice, a day previously used for pagan gods of light.

Teabing has a few inaccuracies. For example, Osiris' birthday was July 14 not December 25, and no Hindu text that I can find says Krishna received gold, frankincense and myrrh. But Teabing is right about Christ and Christianity being built on pagan foundations, as well as Jewish. This is not a new discovery. Where he's wrong is saying this was Constantine's invention. Also contrary to Teabing, there is something original in Christianity. As C.S. Lewis put it, in Christ "the myths became fact." In the myths gods lived once upon a time, nobody could really say when or where. Christians believe that the one God really became incarnate, actually died and rose in Palestine in the time of Augustus Caesar, and there were eyewitnesses. That is original to Christianity.

6) *Even Christianity's weekly holy day was stolen from the pagans. Originally . . . Christianity honored the Jewish Sabbath of Saturday, but Constantine shifted it to coincide with the pagan's veneration day of the sun . . . Sunday.*

Yes, Constantine made Sunday the imperial day off. For the rest, no. It is well documented that from the beginning Christians worshipped on Sunday to celebrate Christ's resurrection—sometimes on Saturday night following the Old Testament pattern where days begin at sunset: "there was evening and morning, a first day." We Orthodox still begin the day at sunset; many Christians keep eves of Sundays and feasts. The linguistic evidence that Christians worship on Sunday because of Christ not the sun, is that in Greek the first day of the week is called not Sunday but Kyriake, Lord's Day.

7) *At [the Council of Nicaea] many aspects of Christianity were debated and voted upon—the date of Easter, the role of the bishops, the administration of the sacraments, and, of course the divinity of Jesus . . . until that moment in history,*

Jesus was viewed by his followers as a mortal prophet . . . , a great and powerful man, but a man nonetheless. A mortal. Jesus' establishment as 'the Son of God' was officially proposed and voted on by the Council of Nicaea. A relatively close vote at that.

Here we have documentary evidence, five eye-witness accounts of the Council of Nicaea (the First Ecumenical Council). We have the Council's decisions; we know many details. To be precise, the bishops voted on what words to use to express the divinity of Jesus. The rest of what Teabing says is entirely false. Till the fourth century Jesus' divinity was not controversial among Christians. There are many clear references to it in the New Testament and the early Fathers long before Constantine. It was not Christ's divinity that some doubted but rather his humanity. The gnostic gospels (so-called) claimed that Jesus was divine but not fully human. Gnostics believed matter is unworthy and that Christ certainly did not take *flesh* . . . Saint John is typical in warning against those who deny that Christ came "in the flesh." [1John 4:2] The first notable follower of Jesus to say that he was a created being was Arius in the fourth century, and even he didn't say that Jesus was only a man, only a prophet. He appears to have believed that Jesus became divine, rather like one of the pagan gods, and was adopted by the Father at some point. In response the bishops approved the first part of what we call the Nicene Creed: Christ is *"God of God, light of light, begotten not made, of one essence with the Father . . . who for us men and for our salvation was incarnate and made man."* These words were not invented by Constantine. Except for the new term *essence* (homo-ousios) they were taken from an old Palestinian creed. Finally, was the vote close? Of the 318 (some say 348) bishops at Nicaea, 2 voted against it, Theonas of Marmaric and Secundus of Ptolemais. Was that a relatively close vote? Enough said.

8) *Because Constantine upgraded Jesus' status almost four centuries after Jesus' death, thousands of documents already existed chronicling his life as a mortal man. To rewrite the history books, Constantine knew he would need a bold stroke . . . Constantine commissioned and fashioned a new Bible, which omitted those gospels that spoke of Christ's human traits and embellished those gospels that made him godlike. The earlier gospels were outlawed, gathered up and burned.*

This also is entirely untrue. We know of no documents before Constantine that said Jesus was only a man. Constantine did not commission a new Bible, nor so far as we know did he authorize book burning. The book burning was done by his pagan predecessors who tried to destroy all Christian documents. Did Constantine insist on the divinity of Christ? No. The evidence suggests that Constantine did not grasp what the theological dispute was all about. All he seems to have wanted was that Christians stop fighting. In fact he later fell under Arian influence himself. He exiled Saint Athanasius of Alexandria, the most prominent defender of Christ's divinity, and he was baptized by an Arian bishop who denied Christ's full divinity. This passage is totally inaccurate.

9) *Establishing Christ's divinity was critical to the further unification of the Roman empire and to the new Vatican power base. By officially endorsing Jesus as the Son of God, Constantine turned Jesus into a deity who existed beyond the scope of the human world, an entity whose power was unchallengable. This not only precluded further pagan challenges to Christianity, but now the followers of Christ were able to redeem themselves only via the established sacred channel—the Roman Catholic Church.*

These references to the Vatican and the Roman Catholic Church are off the wall wrong. Constantine had already moved his capital out of Rome to Constantinople, now Istanbul. The Nicene Council was held not in Rome but in the east, near Constantinople, and of the 318 or so bishops who attended only 5 came from the Latin west. Pope Sylvester of Rome sent only 2 priests, no bishops, so he didn't even have a vote. The decisions at the Council were made by eastern bishops, and eastern Christianity has never been under the jurisdiction of Rome. Rome's only connection to the Council was that they endorsed its decisions. To say the Council was a Vatican power grab is just absurd. And in fact there was a further pagan challenge to Christianity: Constantine's nephew the emperor Julian the Apostate tried unsuccessfully to reestablish paganism in the empire.

10) *Constantine took advantage of Christ's substantial influence and importance. And in doing so he shaped the face of Christianity as we know it today.*

True, maybe not in the way Teabing thinks. Constantine did use Christ and the Church to unite his empire. But there is much evidence that he sincerely believed in Christ. We Orthodox see Constantine as a truly great man who ended the persecution of the Church and allowed the bishops freedom to clarify and hand down to us the original faith of the Church. In that sense, indeed *he shaped the face of Christianity as we know it today.* That is why, despite his many failings, we Orthodox call him Saint Constantine. But he certainly did not create Christianity as we know it today.

There, I hope I have demonstrated that these four pages of *The Da Vinci Code* are a mix of fact and fiction—an undifferentiated and I would say devious blend of truths and utter falsehoods. Now extend this into the remaining 485 pages. All I can say is if after this you trust the information in this book or find the theories convincing . . . I've got a bridge I want to sell you.

Not Of the World

PASCHA NIGHT AND DOUBTING THOMAS
Sunday after Pascha 2007
Gospel: John 20:19-31

These resurrection stories are so powerful, so beautiful, so radiant, so sweet. I just love hearing them and going over them every year. They never grow old.

It was Pascha night. Early that morning the women had gone to Jesus' tomb and came hurrying back saying that his body was gone and they had seen a vision of angels, or was it an angel? Or was it a young man dressed in white saying He is not here? He is risen. The apostles wouldn't believe it; the women must be hysterical with grief or something—typical male reaction? But this was very hard to believe. Then Mary Magdalene came saying she had seen Jesus in the garden. Again they would not believe it. But later in the day he had appeared to Peter; we don't know the details of that appearance, but now finally they accepted what the women had told them. Now that night they were in the upper room at the house of John Mark's mother, excited beyond belief, but still afraid of the authorities, the doors locked, when there had come a knock at the door. It was Luke and Cleopas all out of breath. They had run in from Emmaus about seven miles northwest of Jerusalem. They said they had been walking home and had met this man whom they didn't recognize who walked with them, who explained how the Messiah had to die and rise again. He had appeared to be going further, but they invited him in for supper. He had taken bread and blessed it, and "our eyes were opened and we recognized him"—and he vanished, he was just gone. The other disciples said: yes, we know. He is risen.

As they spoke, suddenly Jesus stood in the midst of them and said, "Peace to you." It's the traditional greeting: shalom, salim, peace, contentment, all good things, fullness of life to you. But that was not quite the apostles' first reaction. Luke says that even though they now believed he was risen, still they couldn't believe it. And though they loved him and trusted him, still they were very frightened. After all, the day before yesterday they had seen him hanging dead, lying dead. Luke says their first reaction was that they were seeing a ghost, and that Jesus dealt with this very matter of factly: "Why are you troubled?" he asked. "Why do you doubt? Look at my hands and my feet; it is I myself. Touch me, see for yourself: a ghost does not have flesh and bones as you see I have." And he showed them his hands and his feet, the hands and feet that they had seen nailed to the cross. Luke says they "still did not believe for joy," it was too good to be true, they couldn't take it in. Little wonder. So Jesus again very matter of factly said, "Do you have anything here to eat?" So they gave him a piece of broiled fish and some honeycomb, and he ate. He was alive, body and soul. With this they knew it was real and their hearts and minds began to settle down, and he reminded them, "These are the things I told you while I was still with you." [Luke 24:44]

Stop for a moment. Here he stands with them talking about the old days when he had still been with them; ordinary words and concepts obviously could not cope with what was happening here. And then he began "to teach them all the things in the Scriptures, the Law, the Prophets, the Psalms concerning himself, how it was necessary for him to suffer and rise from the dead and that repentance and remission of sins must now be preached in his name to all nations, beginning from Jerusalem. Behold you have been witnesses of these things." [Luke 24:44-48]

In our Gospel today from John the story is the same. The doors are shut. Jesus suddenly stands in their midst saying "Peace be with you," and he sends them out into the world proclaiming remission of sins. John as usual fills in some additional details. He picks it up with the apostles already glad to see the Lord. Then Jesus says again, "Peace to you. As the Father has sent me, so I send you." Then he breathed on them. In most languages the words for breath, wind and spirit (three words in English) are the same word: Πνεύμα/Pneuma in Greek, Spiritus in Latin both mean spirit, breath and wind. So in the Orthodox baptismal service the priest begins by breathing on the candidate. In the great blessing of water at Baptism and on Epiphany the priest breathes on the water to convey the Holy Spirit of God. On Pentecost the Holy Spirit came upon the apostles like a rushing mighty wind. Just as the Holy Spirit, God's holy wind blew over the face of the waters at creation, so Jesus breathed on the disciples and said, "Receive the Holy Spirit." This in later terms was their ordination, their commissioning. In ordination services the bishop lays his hands upon the candidate saying, "Let us pray for him that the grace of the All-holy Spirit may come upon him."

"Receive the Holy Spirit. If you forgive sins of any they are forgiven, if you retain the sins of any they are retained." In some traditions this is taken as the granting to the apostles, and thereby to bishops and priests the legal authority to take away the penalty of sin, and also the legal authority to refuse to forgive sins. In the Roman Catholic form of absolution the priest says, "By the authority granted me I absolve you of all your sins."

Protestants who also usually have a legal approach to sins tend to ignore this passage as if it doesn't exist. They don't know what to do with it. The Orthodox approach is to come at it less legalistically. We do not see sin and forgiveness as chiefly a legal problem. In the traditional Orthodox form of absolution the priest begins by saying, "I have no power on earth to forgive sins, only God does." But the Orthodox priest does have authority to declare to you that if you are repentant God forgives you.

I have said before that I wish we could get rid of the English word *sin*. It carries all sorts of baggage with it about personal and legal guilt and penalties. There's little of this in the New Testament where (as I've told you many times) the word αμαρτία (hamartia) means simply missing the mark. To say I have committed a sin means that I have not hit the mark of loving God with all my heart, soul, mind and strength; I have not loved my neighbor as myself—for whatever reason, whether intentionally or not I have failed. In New Testament Greek, to remit something simply means to take it away; it does not necessarily imply legal authority or power. So now let's look at this passage using non-legal terms. Follow me closely here. Jesus gives the apostles the power of the Holy Spirit and sends them out into the world saying: if you take away anyone's "missing the mark" . . . That's a double negative in English, so let's say it positively: if you get anyone back on the mark again, they will be back on the mark. You are the ones who have been closest to me, my chosen witnesses to my life, death and resurrection. Now I send you out to set the world right again. And I give you the power of the Holy Spirit to enable you to do it. If you get the world back on the mark, if you bring people back to God, it will truly be done. But if you fail to do it, it will not be done, because only you can do it; only you have witnessed these things. Christ gives the apostles and bishops and priests not a narrow legal power; he gives them an all-encompassing job to be done—to bring the world back to God, back to love of God and love of man. That is what this passage means retranslated out of legalese.

Now the second part of the story. Thomas was not with them when Jesus came. The others told him, "We have seen the Lord." Thomas said, "Unless I see the prints of the nails in his hands, unless I touch them, put my finger into the wounds of his side, I will not believe." Was Thomas being stubborn, faithless? No more than the rest of them had been only 12 hours before when the women first came with the good news. I think it's unfair that Thomas alone got stuck with the name Doubting Thomas. They all had doubted earlier in the day—and why not? How easy is it to believe that someone has walked out of his own tomb? Thomas certainly had believed before. When Christ was about to go into Judea to raise Lazarus, Thomas had said, "Let us go that we also may die with him." But John also tells us that Thomas wanted answers. On Thursday evening when Christ began to speak of his death—"you know where I am going and you know the way"—it was Thomas who said, it sounds almost in exasperation, "Lord, we do not know where you're going, so how can we know the way?"

The apostle Thomas is one of my heroes. He didn't settle for cheap easy faith. He wanted the truth. He wanted evidence. I say every year on this Sunday that the big problem in the world is not unbelief, not doubt; the big problem is gullibility. The fact is that people will believe almost anything on the flimsiest evidence or no evidence at all. "Communism will inevitably take over the world." "Nazism will reign for 1000 years." "The unregulated free market will never fail us." Why do people believe these things? What the world needs is more doubting Thomases who will say: show me the evidence or I won't believe. Why do people believe things? "Oh, I heard it on TV so it must be true" or "I saw it on the internet." I am still busy challenging some of the things you all send me on the internet which are just not true, and I'm doing it in honor of Saint Thomas who cared about the truth. As much as he must have wanted to believe Jesus was alive again—how wonderful it would be to believe it!—Thomas wanted evidence for himself or he would not believe. He wanted truth. More power to him and all like him!

Eight days later, today, the disciples were gathered again and Thomas was with them, the doors being shut, and again Jesus stood in their midst and said, "Peace be with you." He turned to Thomas. "Thomas, reach your finger here, see my hands, touch my hands and my side. Do not be unbelieving but believe." Note carefully, Jesus did not chastise Thomas for his unbelief. Rather he gave him what he asked for—the evidence. And so doubting Thomas became believing Thomas, the first person on earth to say aloud who Jesus is. Thomas cried, "My Lord and my God!" Jesus, accepting this title, continued, "Thomas, because you have seen me you have believed. Blessed, happy are those who have not seen yet have believed." That would be most of us, you and me. But how many have believed in Christ because we know there was this one apostle who refused to believe till he had the evidence. As one of our hymns says, "O blessed, happy unbelief of Thomas?"

And so in the reading from Acts 5:12-20, the apostles and their successors went out into the world proclaiming Jesus Christ and his saving death and resurrection, as he had commanded. No, they rode out into the world on the power of the Spirit. Robert Payne wrote in his book:

The Holy Fire that *they saw themselves . . . , they lived at white heat, when Christianity was still fresh as the morning dew, a thing that had come to birth only a few moments before. Lightning had struck and the earth trembled and . . . they saw the image of Christ God towering against the heavens . . . The face of Jesus had left shining on the air; almost they could see his face; and in his pathways they walked in fear and trembling. There was no haunting suspicion that divinity vanished from the earth when Christ ascended into heaven.*

What we feel briefly at midnight on Pascha they felt to the core of their being nonstop for the rest of their lives. They were men possessed, possessed by the presence of Christ their God and the Holy Spirit. And nothing could stop them. Still nothing stops them. You see, here we still are this morning celebrating his resurrection.

The Gospel concludes with my least favorite line in the Bible: "Jesus did many other signs in the presence of his disciples which are not written in this book." All the Gospel writers had to pick and choose among the stories they thought most likely to convince people that Jesus is the Christ, the Son of God. How I wish I knew the rest of the stories. I hope in heaven we will get to hear them all.

DIVINE LITURGY: The Preparation
Sundays of January and February, 2000

In this series, I won't say much about the history and origin of the Divine Liturgy. I simply want to go through the Liturgy section by section and explain the meaning of what we're doing. But before that, let's begin with some . . .

BASIC AND OFTEN UNASKED QUESTIONS ABOUT WORSHIP

1) **Where did the Divine Liturgy come from?** There were two chief sources. The first part of the Liturgy derives from the Jewish Synagogue service. If you visited a synagogue even today you'd see the similarity—psalms, prayers, Bible readings and a sermon. The latter part, the taking, blessing and consuming of bread and wine, came from our Lord Jesus Christ at the Last Supper when he commanded, "Take, eat . . . do this for the remembrance of me." This part of the Liturgy also has roots in the Jewish Passover Meal, Jewish temple sacrifices and even in pagan religious meals. The earliest fathers established the essentials of the Divine Liturgy. The Liturgy originally used in Jerusalem was attributed to Saint James, brother of the Lord, first Bishop there. There have been several Orthodox liturgical traditions, but our Byzantine Liturgy was standardized in the fourth century by Saint Basil the Great

and Saint John Chrysostom. Is Orthodox worship "unchanging"? Almost, but not quite. There is very slow organic development. However, our Divine Liturgy has changed scarcely at all since the early middle ages. Nor is there any move to revise it. Anything "new" that happens in Orthodox worship (such as more frequent Communions, or more peoples' participation) is really a return to more ancient practice.

2) **Why do we have fixed forms?** Why don't we change our worship around every few years, or even every Sunday, as many Christians do? It's because the forms of our worship services are like keys on a computer or on a piano. We could vary the location of piano keys (put low notes on the right and high notes on the left?), but the whole purpose of the keyboard is not to have novel experiences with the keys, but rather to use them to express yourself through music. It seems to me the big problem with computers is that somebody up there is forever upgrading the system, so we just begin to get it mastered, and whoops! They've changed it again, and we're back to stumbling over the technique. We spend too much of our time not using the computer but trying to figure out how to use it.

Orthodox forms of worship hold still so we can use them to worship God, so we won't be stumbling over them. Rather the forms are intended to become second nature to us, so that we can express ourselves through them without having to think about them—so that they become invisible, so to speak, and instead of seeing them we see God through them. Orthodox worship does have variety from day to day and season to season. Many variable hymns are sung by the choir or cantors, but the congregation's parts change almost not at all. And the forms of Orthodox worship are indeed fixed. The pastor doesn't pick out the Bible readings he likes. The deacon doesn't decide what he should pray for. The choir director doesn't select the hymns. This is so we will hear and pray the Gospel of Christ, the wisdom of the Church, the teachings of the fathers—not the Gospel of Father Bill, the wisdom of Deacon John, and the teachings of Sheila.

3) **Why are Orthodox services so long?** I once heard Father John Meyendorff answer that question. He said with a smile on his face, "Because Orthodox like it that way." Of course our services could be done more quickly and more efficiently. I hear that in

Spain the Mass is down to 11 minutes now! But Orthodox love to worship, Orthodox love to be with God. When you're doing something you love, when you're with someone you love, you don't hurry. You don't think of it as an obligation or a duty to get done with quickly. You linger over it. You try to prolong the experience.

4) **Why do we sing so much?** Jewish services were (and are) sung. Anciently, so far as we can see, no religion had said services. It never occurred to anyone to just stand before God or the gods and talk as to an ordinary person. God is holy. God is wonderful. Music expresses the mystery, the wonder, the joy of being in his presence. Besides, God has made us so that when we sing, we take in more oxygen and feel spiritually uplifted! Why at Saint Nicholas do we have the people (instead of just the choir) sing? This was early Church practice. The parts in our books now appointed to "the choir" were anciently sung by "the people." The word "Liturgy" can be translated "work of the people." The people need to work at it! The people stopped singing because over the years the music got so complicated they couldn't handle it. Now we're simplifying a bit and are recovering the peoples' participation. Our Antiochian Archdiocese is pushing hard for this. Good for them! And you at St. Nicholas are singing well. Good for you!

PART I—THE PREPARATION
(Antiochian Service Book, page 81ff)

Maybe some of you don't even know that there is a 30 minute service that takes place here before every Divine Liturgy, beginning even before Matins. Every Sunday at 8 a.m. Deacon John and I begin the service of Preparation for Divine Liturgy. (If anybody wants to join us, you're very welcome.) This is the most recent addition to the Divine Liturgy. It probably has ancient roots but its form became fixed probably in the 11th or 12th century. It consists of preparatory prayers, vesting of the clergy, and preparation of the Holy Gifts (the bread and wine) for consecration. I'll go into some detail about it, since few Orthodox (other than the clergy) are acquainted with it.

1) **The Kairon,** which means *the time.* Greek has two words for time. "Chronos" means "clock time"—as in "what time is it?" "Kairos" means the "appointed time"—as in "the time is at hand." Now is

our appointed time to begin our Liturgical journey beyond clock time, to transform clock time into the eternity of the Kingdom of God. The Kairon consists of prayers said before the icons. Standing outside the altar area, the priest and deacon prepare to enter the Holy Place. Then we go through the side doors, not using the royal doors which are reserved for more solemn moments. We kiss the altar and go into the sacristy to put on our vestments.

2. **The Vesting**. Why do clergy and acolytes wear vestments? They derive from men's Sunday dress clothes in the ancient world. The sticharion was the ancient equivalent of our modern pants and shirt sleeves. The phelonion is comparable to the modern suit coat. And when styles changed, the clergy and acolytes kept wearing the old style in church. Why? Well, just because they always had. Things don't change easily in the Orthodox Church. And so these vestments unite us to the ancient Church, with our history. But vestments also came to serve another purpose. They keep the individual priest or deacon or acolyte from distracting you during the service. Instead of looking at the priest and wondering why he's wearing that ugly suit or whatever, what you see is just "priest" looking like every other priest and "deacon" looking like every other deacon. Thus you may find it easier to concentrate on God instead of on us. The vestments also have taken on symbolic meanings, which I won't go into now. Then we return to the sanctuary, and after a symbolic washing of hands, we begin . . .

3. **The Prothesis** (Proskimidia). "Prothesis" means literally "the laying out of the bread." The Prosphora (Greek for "offering") is the holy bread for the Liturgy. It is a loaf, always leavened with yeast. Usually it is baked by someone from the congregation using an Orthodox recipe, though it may also be purchased from a bakery. Those who give the Prosphora always include a list of living and departed for whom they desire prayers. The priest now cuts out the center square from the Prosphora. This is called the Lamb. This is what will be consecrated to become the Body of Christ. Christ is the Lamb of God, the sacrifice, and in the prayers we identify this bread with Christ's Body given for us. The words are from the prophet Isaiah, "He was led as a sheep to the slaughter . . . his life was taken away from the earth . . ." and finally, "sacrificed is the Lamb of God who taketh away the sin of

the world, for the life of the world and its salvation." The priest places the Lamb in the center of the diskos (plate).

Then using the holy bread, he constructs an image of the Church. Christ in the center, then on the left, (on Christ's right, so to speak, since he is the King, facing us) we put a small triangular piece of bread symbolizing the Mother of God. Then on his left, nine particles are placed as we commemorate leaders of the seven categories of saints: holy angels, prophets, apostles, fathers, martyrs, ascetics, unmercenary physicians, then the saints of the day, and the author of the Liturgy (Saint Basil or Saint John Chrysostom).

Next, the priest places on the diskos a particle for each living person he wants to pray for, beginning always with the Metropolitan, then the Bishop who ordained him, and his sponsors in ordination and those whom he has sponsored, and then his own loved ones and friends, then those whom the deacon or anyone else present wishes to pray for, then those on the list given by those who provided the Prosphora, and then whoever has asked for prayers. And then (this is an advantage of having a small church) we add a particle for each member of Saint Nicholas Church and each former member, and others who support the congregation in whatever way. Each of you is there on the diskos every Sunday. And then we do the same for the departed: those Deacon John and I want to pray for, those on the Prosphora list, those whom we have been asked to pray for, and then all the departed members of this congregation. Last, at the very bottom, the priest places one particle for himself with the words, "Remember, O Lord, my unworthiness, and forgive all my offences, both voluntary and involuntary."

And finally with appropriate prayers we cover the holy bread with the asterix (a four-pronged cover) for protection, and likewise the chalice of wine and the bread with other veils for protection. We cense it all, and have a final prayer: "O God our God, who didst send forth the heavenly Bread, the food of the whole world, our Lord and God Jesus Christ, our Savior and Redeemer and Benefactor, blessing and sanctifying us: *Do thou thyself bless this Oblation and receive it upon thine altar above the heavens. Remember, as thou art good and lovest mankind, those who brought this offering and those for whom they brought it; and preserve us blameless in the celebration of thy holy Mysteries; for sanctified and glorified is thy most honorable and majestic name of the Father and of the Son and of the Holy Spirit, now and ever and unto ages of ages. Amen.*"

The Preparation is completed. The deacon cuts up the rest of the holy bread to be the Antidoron, the blessed bread which is distributed after Divine Liturgy. The priest tends to any last minute preparations for Liturgy, and we're ready to begin Matins at 8:30 a.m. At this point we're still at least an hour away from the beginning of Divine Liturgy. The Orthodox Church obviously intends us to do a lot of preparing!

The Service of Preparation teaches us two things: (1) Divine Liturgy and Holy Communion require serious preparation—however you do it. The Church intends the clergy to prepare by Vespers the evening before, the service of Preparation and then Matins, as well as by fasting and repentance, of course. Many lay people find all or part of this helpful in their preparation. Those who cannot come to these services need to make use of some of the Church's evening and morning prayers, and the Church's appointed prayers of preparation for Communion found in your Orthodox prayer book, and of course by fasting before Communion—and certainly by being at Divine Liturgy more or less on time. Barring emergency, you should be at Liturgy no later than the reading of the Holy Gospel. We are to prepare. The Church does not intend that we hurry in at the last minute and grab a little Holy Communion as if the Church were a fast food stand. This is the Heavenly Banquet. Don't treat it like McDonalds'.

(2) What we are offering to the Father through Christ is the whole Church, the whole Body of Christ. Specifically, there you are on the diskos every Sunday morning in your little particle of bread, being carried through the congregation at the Great Entrance, so that in your heart and mind and soul, you can consciously place yourself on the diskos. There you are every Sunday morning being carried to the altar, being offered to God and blessed and becoming the Body of Christ. There you are every Sunday morning receiving your life back renewed and made holy in Holy Communion. So when in a moment we come to the Great Entrance, I hope you can see, in light of this hidden rite of Preparation, that we are acting out something profound about what the whole Christian life is all about, and how it should be lived. I'll say more about this later in this series.

In the next instruction, we will begin to look at the first part of the public Divine Liturgy—the Pro-Anaphora, also called the Liturgy of the Catechumens and the Liturgy of the Word.*

---

*   [Ed. note: p. 172 in the Appendix]

The ANAPHORA of the DIVINE LITURGY OF SAINT BASIL
Lent 2007

PART II. The Story of our Salvation

The Thrice-holy Hymn has concluded. In the Anaphora Saint Basil now makes a seamless transition from the theme of God the Holy Trinity into the subject of Creation and Salvation, still addressing and praising the Father:

With these blessed powers, O Master who lovest mankind, we sinners also do cry aloud and say: Holy art thou, of a truth, and all-holy, and there are no bounds to the majesty of thy holiness, and just *are thou in all thy works, for in righteousness and true judgement hast thou ordered all things for us.*

I look at the world and at my life which are often such a mess and wonder: is this really true? Has God really ordered things right? Is he really *for us*, on our side? Listen to Saint Basil who now sums up the story of our salvation, all told in light of the Incarnation, Death and Resurrection of Jesus Christ.

God began by *fashioning*, creating us. We belong to him, he is in charge here. That's easy to forget in this modern world where we know so much and control so many things—or think we do. But it is God's electricity that we turn on; it is God's earth that we pollute; it is God's world, the reality that he created, that we study and learn about. All things originate in him. (How long it took him to create all things, whether six 24-hour days or twelve billion years is, I think, not worth arguing about, at least from a theological perspective. The Bible was not written to be a book of 21st century science.) What's important is that he created it, and he runs it. None of it belongs to us, including ourselves. God made us out of *the dust of the earth*. We exist by his grace alone. We are earthly. In the beginning God placed Adam and Eve in an earthly *paradise of plenty*. In Hebrew "Adam" means man, generic mankind; "Eve" means mother of all living. This is the story of mankind. The Garden of Eden is the natural innocent happiness, in union with God and nature that we once possessed.

But we were not only earthly. God also gave mankind a unique place in creation. He made us in his *image*, which means his spiritual image, since God by "nature" has no material body. Like God we can think, love, plan, imagine, even create in a way, using what he has given us. Like God we have freedom to choose, free will, so that we could grow up to be like him—filled with joy because we freely choose what is good. In his garden we were meant to grow into something greater. Like God we were made for eternity. He *promised us eternal life and the enjoyment of good things in keeping* his *commandments. But when* man *disobeyed thee, the true God, who had created him, and was led astray by the guile of the serpent, and rendered subject to death through his own transgressions . . .*

Why did God forbid Adam and Eve to eat from the tree of the knowledge of good and evil? Why do you forbid your eight-year-old to drive your car even though he wants to? I think that is the answer. We grabbed hold of knowledge before we were able to handle it. Why did we do it? Because someone tempted us—the serpent, Satan, the tough kid from the other side of the tracks. "Ha! So your dad won't let you drive? Chicken! *Do it.* You can be just like him." And so we did, and so we wrecked the car.

Where did the rotten kid, the serpent come from? That's another story that stands behind the Bible—the rebellion of Satan and his angels. What happens on that level of reality is mostly beyond our power to grasp. But out of this turning away from God and his will for us have come all the evils that have plagued the world ever since. Could God have stopped us from falling into sin? Yes. Why did he allow it to happen? We're not told. Could it have been otherwise? Apparently only if God had destroyed our free will, made us into automatons. But robots cannot share God's joy; robots can only obey. Let me stress that the preceding is speculation. Neither the Scriptures nor the Lord Jesus nor Saint Basil explain the existence of evil or the reason for our present condition. No human beings really understand these things.

Nevertheless, here we are, cast out of Eden, *banished . . . in thy righteous judgement . . . from paradise into this world.* You can't go home again. Just try to return to the natural innocent happiness you knew when you were two years old. It's impossible. Nor could mankind, so we were sent out into the world as we now know it, no longer innocent, no longer natural, no longer happy, no longer in union with God—and that must necessarily end in death, for God is Life. This was God's *righteous judgement*—that is, he judged that this was now the right way forward for us. So now we all are born into a world that is still God's world, his creation—it cannot exist except by his will—but which is occupied by an enemy, so to speak. The world is still good by nature; it is filled with people who are good by nature. We Orthodox reject the Reformation Protestant doctrine that mankind is utterly depraved, that there is nothing good in us. We are still God's good creation, but we are bent out of shape. Sin and evil have no existence by themselves; they are always good things twisted, contorted, distorted, turned away from God—and therefore dying, mortal. And so it is that nothing endures in this transient world, including us.

But God did not abandon us; he did not *forget the work of* his *hands* nor *turn away from the creature* he *had made.* This is obviously true, for we still exist; if he had turned away, we would no longer be. For a long time God worked mostly behind the scenes, but he was providing for us *the salvation of regeneration which is in thy Christ himself,* working through Christ even in pre-historic and pre-Christian times to save us, rescue us, restore us to life. He visited us in various ways *in his tender mercy.* He worked especially through the Jews to reveal his existence, his unity, his moral law, but also through other peoples. (Plato and Socrates sometimes appear in certain Orthodox icons.) God gave all mankind dreams of dyings and risings to new life and visions of other and better worlds. And *thou didst send forth prophets, thou didst perform mighty works by thy holy ones who, in every generation, were well pleasing to thee . . . the prophets . . . foretold . . . the salvation which was to come; thou didst give us the Law as an aid* to show us what we need to be and do if we are to live: "Thou shalt love the Lord thy God with all thy heart and soul and mind and strength . . . thou shalt love thy neighbor as thyself "—the summary of the Law and the Prophets. *Thou didst appoint guardian angels*—invisible presences guiding and guarding the world and us even when we are unaware of it.

And when the fullness of time was come, when the world was ready, when the time was right, *thou didst speak unto us through thy Son himself, through whom also thou madest the ages, who* is himself the true *image of God* (what we were created to be), who *upholds all things by the Word of his power, who* is *equal to thee, the God and Father.* Twenty centuries ago *he who was God before all ages . . . appeared on earth and dwelt with men . . . emptying himself* of his divine prerogatives, *taking on the form of a servant,* born of her whom we now call the *Theotokos,* the one who gave birth to God, and took on our lowly body so that he might remake us into *the image of his glory.* As Saint Athanasios wrote, "God became man so that man might become god." He became *a citizen of this world.* He gave us *commandments of salvation. He released us from the delusion of idols and brought us into knowledge of . . . the true God and Father.*

We Orthodox often focus only on the Passion and Resurrection of Christ. Don't forget his teachings. Listen to Jesus. Read the Gospels. Christ told us how to live, how to come to God and gain full abundant life. Beginning with the apostles, he gathered a new people to himself by Baptism, who in him would be *a royal priesthood:* a people who stand on the borderline between heaven and earth, restoring the world to God, bringing God into the world, *a holy nation,* a colony of heaven, an outpost of the Kingdom of God, the Church. And the center (though not the whole) of our priestly work is in the Divine Liturgy, where heaven and earth are so obviously united.

Having done all this, *he gave himself a ransom to death, whereby we were held, sold into bondage under sin.* Note: that is all Saint Basil says about the death of Christ. Here is where Orthodoxy differs profoundly from most of western Christianity. With us the Cross of Christ does not stand by itself; we hold it always in the context of God's whole plan for our salvation. Of course Christ suffered, but Saint Basil does not even mention it. There is here no sentimental appeal to how by my sins I made him hurt. Basil says nothing about Christ paying the price of our sins to satisfy the Father's demand for justice. The ransom he paid was *to death, to the devil,* not to God. Why did he die by execution? Because he is God, he is Life; he who is eternal could not die a "natural" death. Why did he choose to die? So he could enter into death, *and having descended into Hades through the cross . . . so that he might fill all things with himself,* so there is nowhere God is not, so that he could invade Hades, Sheol, the underworld, the devil's dark kingdom of death and set the prisoners free, so that he the Good Shepherd could rescue all his lost sheep.

Thereby . . . *he loosed the pains of death and rose again on the third day, making a way for all flesh unto the resurrection of the dead*—"I go to prepare a place for you . . . so that where I am you may be also" (John 14:2-3)—*for it was not possible that the Author of Life should be held by corruption.* So he became the *firstborn of those who have fallen asleep, the firstborn from the dead, the first in all things.* The resurrection—this is Saint Basil's emphasis; this is the Church's emphasis. This is why from the beginning Christians have worshiped on the first day of the week, Sunday, the day Jesus rose from death. And . . . *ascending into heaven, he sat down at the right hand of* the Father. Jesus Christ is God the Father's "right hand man."

. . . *and he shall come again to render to every man according to his works.* The world will not go on like this forever. We will not be allowed to go on like this always. Christ will come and set things right. Note: Saint Basil says that each of us will be judged not according to his faith, not according to his doctrines, not according to his spiritual experiences, not according to his religious affiliation, but *according to his works.* This was what Christ taught. True faith requires not just intellectual affirmation but an entire style of life. "Not everyone who says to me 'Lord, Lord' shall enter into the Kingdom of heaven, but he who does the will of my Father who is in heaven." (Matthew 7:21) "Inasmuch as you have done it to the least of these my brethren, you have done it to me." (Matthew 25:40) Did we finally love God with all our "heart, soul, mind and strength" and "our neighbor as ourselves?" That will tell the tale.

And that, according to Saint Basil the Great, is the story of our Salvation—all of which will now be made present to us, accessible to us, in the Divine Liturgy.

The ANAPHORA of the DIVINE LITURGY OF SAINT BASIL
Lent 2007

PART IV Conclusion:
The Cosmic Liturgy, Holy Communion

Last week we asked: what is the purpose of the Anaphora?* It is that we lift up our hearts into heaven and experience heaven on earth, earth raised up into heaven. You perceive, I am sure, that this is not a spatial thing. Even though we are lifted up to heaven during the Divine Liturgy, nevertheless we never leave Cedarburg, Wisconsin; we don't go hurtling up as in a space ship! Heaven is not literally up, not out there in the universe somewhere. We use the word "up" here as a figure, like climbing the ladder to success or moving up from fifth to sixth grade in school. Heaven is wherever God is, wherever God's will is done and we are with him. Christ is present both in heaven and on earth at the same time. If we were completely good and pure and holy here and now on earth, we would be in heaven here and now on earth. The Liturgy gives us a taste of this, of what could be and what by God's grace someday will be. In it we do not leave time but rather our time is transcended, swallowed up into eternity. Many experience this at Divine Liturgy.

The Divine Liturgy proceeds: we have laid aside all earthly cares. We have lifted up our selves and all whom we love to the Father through Christ in the holy bread. We have arrived in the Kingdom. We are at God's table at the heavenly banquet. We have offered it all to the Father: *Thine own of thine own we offer unto thee on behalf of all and for all.* And our offering of bread and wine is now seen to be the Body and Blood of Christ. It is radiant with his presence.

And now that we are in heaven, for a few minutes we get to play the part of saints—which, again, we will someday be by the grace of God, if we will have it. Now we become intercessors before the throne of God. All that we let go of at the Great Entrance, suddenly we get it all back

---

* [Ed. note: p. 183 in the Appendix]

again, but now in the presence of God without "earthly cares." We now dare to pray with all the saints:

> *forefathers, fathers, patriarchs, prophets, apostles, preachers, evangelists, martyrs, confessors, teachers and every righteous spirit which has completed this life in faith. Especially our all-holy, immaculate, most blessed and glorious Lady Theotokos and ever-virgin Mary.*

We pray for our beloved departed—no, we pray with *those who have fallen asleep before us,* for we are now with them in heaven. And standing like saints in heaven, we now look back to earth and intercede in confidence for everyone and everything there:

> *thy holy, catholic and apostolic Church . . . to the ends of the world, those who have set before thee these gifts, those who bear fruit and do good works in thy holy churches and who remember the poor, those in the deserts, the mountains and in caverns and pits of the earth, those who live in virginity* and *in asceticism, civil authorities, armed forces, the people here present and . . . those who are absent for reasonable cause,* the married, *infants, the young, the aged, the fainthearted,* those *wandering astray* and *vexed by unclean spirits,* those *who journey, widows, orphans, captives, the sick, those under judgement, those who love us and those who hate us, those . . . who have enjoined us . . . to pray for them, those whom we have not remembered, for this city and every city and countryside, our Metropolitan and our Bishop, the honorable presbytery, the diaconate in Christ and every priestly order*—the priest prays that *"my sins"* may not hinder *"the grace of thy Holy Spirit"*—for ourselves, for *temperate and healthful seasons,* for deliverance from *schisms* and *the ragings of hostile nations* and *uprisings of heresies . . .* Finally *receive us all into thy kingdom, showing us to be sons of the light and sons of the day; and grant unto us thy peace and thy love, O Lord our God.*

So much popular religion today is narrow and self-centered, mostly just about "me" and "my salvation," or it may be concerned with my fulfilling myself, or at best it may rise to the interests of our kind of people or our nation. But the Anaphora of Saint Basil is universal, all encompassing. It unites us with all people and all sorts of people on earth and in heaven, so that in the end we all may be received together into God's Kingdom, that all people and all things may be redeemed, renewed and lifted up into the Kingdom, that *with one mouth and one heart* we may *glorify and praise thine all-honorable and majestic name of the Father, and of the Son, and of the Holy Spirit, now and ever and unto ages of ages. Amen.* I don't mean to sound disrespectful, but my reaction to the cosmic sweep of Saint Basil's Anaphora is always: "Wow!"

Finally, just a few comments about Holy Communion. The Anaphora concludes and the preparation for Holy Communion begins with the Lord's Prayer, which also has universal concerns that we often forget: *Thy will be done on earth as it is in heaven.* The "Our Father" is a subject for another series of talks. But I should tell you that our English "Give us this day our *daily* bread" is a mistranslation of the Greek επιούσιον (*epiousion*). Of course we should pray for our daily material needs, but that is not what "epiousion" means; it means *supersubstantial*—above the things of this world, spiritual, heavenly. It means "Give us this day Christ who is the bread of eternal life. Give us Holy Communion today."

How often should we receive Holy Communion? Suffice it to say that Christ commanded us to *Take . . . eat . . . drink,* not just to observe. In the early Church, Christians normally received the Eucharist every Sunday. You know, I'm sure, that for many centuries Christians received Communion only once or twice a year. In some Orthodox churches and in many Protestant denominations this is still the case. There were many causes for this. Part of the reason was Saint Paul's warning that *whoever eats this bread or drinks this cup in an unworthy manner will be guilty of the body and blood of the Lord . . . and eats and drinks judgment to himself, not discerning the Lord's body.* (I Corinthians 11:27, 29) But Paul certainly did not mean that we should receive Communion only if we are morally worthy, without sin. In that case no one could ever receive except the Lord and his Mother!

Holy Communion is not a reward for good behavior; it is God's way of making us good. Worthy reception means that we should come to the Holy Eucharist in faith, aware of Christ's presence in the sacrament (the Body of Christ) and in the Church community (the Body of Christ), and with proper preparation. The form of preparation varies somewhat among Orthodox jurisdictions. In our practice, it should include pre-Communion prayers, penitence (sacramental confession is not required before each communion, but should be taken from time to time), fasting (usually from food and drink after midnight—or in the case of evening Communions, after lunch), attendance at the full Liturgy (or from the Gospel reading at the very latest)—and above all, a heart that has forgiven others and is truly seeking God and goodness.

The early Church assumed that her people would come to church prepared and so would receive Holy Communion regularly. I'm glad that for the most part we have gone back to early Church practice of frequent Communions. Personally I feel the need for frequent Communion. How often should you receive? That is for you and your spiritual advisor to decide. I say as often as possible, so long as you take care not to receive it casually, lest you receive it to your judgement—for it is "fire burning the unworthy."

In Holy Communion we eat and drink the Body and Blood of Christ. We have done this so often that we don't think what a very strange thing it is. But when Jesus first taught *I am the living bread which came down from heaven. If anyone eats this bread he will live forever . . . Unless you eat the flesh of the Son of Man and drink his blood, you have no life in you,* Saint John says many took offense and turned away from him. (John 6:30-69) What did he mean when he called the bread and wine his Body and Blood? One's Body is where one is. Blood is power and life. It means that Christ himself is our food and drink, that in Holy Communion Christ himself comes and dwells in us, that the power of Christ our God moves within us, so that our lives are no longer our own. He lives in us and we in him, so that now we are the Body and Blood of Christ, the presence and power of Christ in the world, and he now acts through us.

Can you see how the Holy Anaphora and Holy Communion give us an image of how our life in Christ works? We offer to God what he has given us, the ordinary things of our life and labor in the symbols of bread and wine. He takes them, and they become Christ's Body and Blood, his presence, his power, so that what we have given him is returned to us magnified infinitely. We give him the food and drink of this earth; he gives us the food and drink of eternity. We offer him our earthly lives, he gives us eternal life. So we receive our Sunday Holy Communion and carry the Kingdom of God out into our world, living the week that follows in the presence and power of Christ. Then we return the next Sunday to offer God a life that is, by his grace, holier and more acceptable, so that at every Liturgy we can make an even better offering. And so on and on into eternity.

Note that the Divine Liturgy contains formal entrances, but it has no formal exits—so that Sunday by Sunday, week by week, we enter further up, further into the Kingdom of heaven. And by the grace of God we will never leave, now and ever and unto ages of ages. Amen.

Within

THE SEVEN DEADLY SINS: Part 1—Pride
October 12, 2003

After I represented His Eminence Metropolitan PHILIP at the recent Episcopalian Convention, I complained about their preoccupation with disordered sexuality. I recently warned parents again about letting their kids watch the trash on TV. I then realized I might be leaving the misimpression that the only sins worth worrying about are sexual ones. The Church has long listed seven chief sins, of which lust is only one, and there are other kinds of lust besides sexual lust. Orthodox moral teaching tends to accentuate the positive. We usually try to inspire people towards loftier goals. However, I thought it might be instructive to approach the subject from the negative side for a change—thus this series of talks on the Seven Deadly Sins. Let's begin by defining some terms.

"Sin" in the New Testament (αμαρτία, hamartia) means "missing the mark." The mark we should try to hit is God, the Kingdom of God, the will of God. We may fail as we try to hit the mark or by failing to try, since there are sins of omission as well as sins of commission. The reason we examine our sins is not so we will wallow in guilt, but rather so we can get ourselves back on the mark—because sin is dangerous. Sin is like a disease of the spirit. Sin kills spiritually; sin destroys our souls. Unfortunately, we all know how this works. When we first fall into a particular sin we feel bad about it, but (haven't you noticed?) if we keep it up and it becomes a habit, it doesn't bother us so much any more. Our conscience begins to go numb; little by little our souls go dead. And that's how, if we're not careful, any of us can wind up doing dreadful things and finally losing our souls. Murderers started out just like everybody else, but progressively their consciences have gone numb, and murdering no longer troubles them. Sin kills our inner life. And if we let sin get control of us, then when we die physically, we have nothing left to take into the next world. That is why we refer to the seven deadly sins. Actually our little Antiochian Pocket Prayer Book (p. 28) titles them the Seven Grievous Sins, but I like the traditional term "deadly sins" better, because it's scarier.

These seven deadly sins are the interior, spiritual roots of external acts of sin. For example, because of greed one may steal or tell lies or even murder. Stealing is a symptom; greed is the disease that causes the symptom. So we need not only to control the external symptoms, but even more we need to cure the inner disease itself, to deal with the deadly sins. The following are the seven deadly sins and their definitions from the Pocket Prayer Book: 1) Pride: the lack of humility befitting a creature of God. 2) Greed: too great a desire for money or worldly goods. 3) Lust: impure and unworthy desire for something evil. 4) Anger: unworthy irritation and lack of self control. 5) Gluttony: the habit of eating or drinking too much. 6) Envy: jealousy of some other person's happiness. 7) Sloth: laziness that keeps us from doing our duty to God and man.

C.S. Lewis' *Mere Christianity* was, next to the Bible, the best selling Christian book of the 20th century. It is taken from a series of talks he gave on the BBC during World War II, and is about as orthodox as a book can be without being written by a member of the Orthodox Church. He wrote:

There is one vice of which no man in the world is free; which every one in the world loathes when he sees it in someone else; and of which hardly any people except Christians ever imagine that they are guilty themselves. I have heard people admit they are bad-tempered, or that they cannot keep their heads about girls or drink, or even that they are cowards. I do not think I have ever heard anyone who was not a Christian accuse himself of this vice. And at the same time I have very seldom met anyone who was not a Christian who showed the slightest mercy to it in others. There is no fault which makes a man more unpopular, and no fault which we are more unconscious of in ourselves. And the more we have it ourselves, the more we dislike it in others. The vice I am talking about is Pride or Self-Conceit; and the virtue opposite to it, in Christian morals, is called Humility . . . According to Christian teachers, the essential vice, the utmost evil, is Pride. Unchastity, anger, greed, drunkenness, and all that, are mere fleabites in comparison: it was through Pride that the devil became the devil. Pride leads to every other vice: it is the complete anti-God state of mind . . . . if you want to find out how proud you are the easiest way is to ask yourself, 'How much do I dislike it when other people snub me, or refuse to take any notice of me, or shove their oar in, or patronize me, or show off?' The point is that each person's pride is in competition with every one else's pride. It is because I wanted to be the big noise at the party that I am so annoyed at someone else being the big noise . . . Pride is essentially competitive—is competitive by its very nature—whilst the other vices are competitive only, so to speak, by accident. Pride gets no pleasure out of having something, only out of having more of it than the next man. We say that people are proud of being rich, or clever, or good looking, but they are not. They are proud of being richer, or cleverer, or better-looking than others. If everyone else became equally rich, or clever, or good looking there would be nothing to be proud about. It is the comparison that makes you proud: the pleasure of being above the rest . . . Greed may drive men into competition if there is not enough to go round; but the proud man, even when he has got more than he can possibly want, will try to get still more just to assert his power. What is it that makes a man with L10,000 a year anxious to get L20,000 a year? It is not the greed for more pleasure. L10,000 will give all the luxuries that any man can really enjoy. It is Pride—the wish to be richer than some other rich man, and (still more) the wish for power." (**Mere Christianity**, chapter 8)

Sometimes the word "pride" is used to mean taking satisfaction in something in the sense of being grateful for it: to "take pride" in a job well done or in one's children or in one's heritage. That is not what is condemned here, so long as we remember that all these things are gifts of God, not just our own doing. In the Christian Tradition, the Scriptures and the Fathers, the word "pride" means haughtiness, arrogance, lack of humility, particularly in relation to God. Pride is putting oneself in the place of God, trying to make oneself the center of reality. In the old movie Bedazzled (which still shows up on TV), a British short order cook (geeky Dudley Moore) sells his soul to the devil (handsome, suave Peter Cook). The movie is funny as can be and theologically very correct. The cook says to the devil (this is the approximate dialog), "It seems to me you had it pretty good up in heaven: how did you get thrown out?" The devil says, "I'll show you. I'll stand up on this pedestal and be God, and you praise me." So the cook stands below singing, "Holy holy holy, glory to you in the highest" and so on for some time. Finally he says to the devil on the pedestal, "I'm getting tired of this. Can we trade places?" And the devil says, "That's just how it happened." Pride says: "I'm tired of being a creature. I'm tired of being obedient. I want what I want. I want to be the center of things. I want it all to revolve around me. I want my own way. I want to be . . . God."

The Biblical teaching about pride is, so I read, unparalleled in other religions and ethical systems. The Fathers say that pride is the ultimate sin, the essence of sin, that all other sins, even the other six deadly sins, flow out of pride. Pride was the sin of Adam and Eve: The serpent said, "Eat of this [fruit] and you will be like God." (Genesis 3:12) Boasting and trusting in oneself or in anything human apart from God is condemned again and again. Ethnic pride is condemned: "Do not say to yourselves 'we have Abraham as our father'. God is able to raise up sons of Abraham from these stones." (Luke 2:8)

In the New Testament we find that God himself is not proud. God does not stand on his own dignity. He becomes incarnate—a fetus, an infant, a man. Like the father of the prodigal son, God humbly rushes out to forgive us. Saint Paul says that Christ "did not count equality with God a thing to be grasped, but rather emptied himself . . . even to death on a cross." (Philippians 2:5) Paul warns often against pride; he says that no one has grounds for bragging, "for by grace you have been saved . . . it is the gift of God . . . lest anyone should boast." (Ephesians 2:8-9) So far as I can see the only people Jesus condemned were the proud scribes and Pharisees who were so sure that they were right, that they were good. There are so many Biblical and patristic quotations against pride that I could go on for pages. The Song of Mary which we sing at Matins sums up the Christian attitude: [God] "has shown strength with his arm; he has scattered the proud in the imagination of their hearts. He has put down the mighty from their seat and has exalted the humble and meek." (Luke 1:51-52)

God does not tolerate human pride. "A man's pride brings him humiliation . . . pride goes before destruction, a haughty spirit before a fall." (Proverbs 16:18) I can think of no better place to observe this than in politics, year after year, in all parties and every political persuasion. Our political system seems to require candidates to be (or at least pretend to be) proud, arrogant: "I have all the answers, I know all the truth, and my opponents are stupid wicked fools." And when someone gets elected to high office, how often it goes to his head, and he really begins to believe it: "We are totally in the right. We make no mistakes; we admit no errors." No mere mortal can keep that up without destroying himself. You have observed many times what happens next. God intervenes. "Pride goes before . . . a fall."

Certainly there are arrogant Christian leaders too, but at least the Church's system doesn't encourage it. Before Holy Communion at every Divine Liturgy we pray: "I believe, O Lord, and I confess that thou art truly the Christ the Son of the Living God who came into the world to save sinners of whom I am chief." As he receives Holy Communion the priest says, "The precious and all-holy Body [Blood] of our Lord and God and Savior Jesus Christ is imparted unto me, the unworthy priest . . ." In the Liturgy of Saint Basil, the priest prays, "Be mindful also, O Lord, of my unworthiness according to the multitude of thy compassions; pardon my every transgression both voluntary and involuntary and withhold not, because of my sins, the grace of thy Holy Spirit from these gifts here spread forth." If I could find a politician with this attitude, I'd vote for him in a minute.

What is the cure for pride? Humility, which does not mean putting yourself down. It just means keeping perspective. "I am not God. I am not the center of the universe. I am weak. I do not have all the answers. I make mistakes. I am a sinner. All that I have and all that I am and all that I do come from God." Saint Maximos the Confessor wrote, "A man is proud only if he is ignorant both of divine help and of human weakness." (*Third Century of Various Texts*, #64)

What is the cure for pride? Saint John of the Ladder says "Some drive out empty pride by thinking to the end of their lives of their past misdeeds for which they were forgiven and which serve as a spur to humility. Others remembering the passion of Christ think of themselves as eternally in debt. Others . . . think of their daily lapses. Others come to possess this mother of graces by way of their continuous temptations, weaknesses and sins. There are some . . . who humble themselves in proportion to the gifts they receive from God and live with a sense of their unworthiness to have such wealth bestowed upon them, so that each day they think of themselves as sinking further into debt." (*The Ladder of Divine Ascent*, Step 25)

What is the cure for pride? Raise your standards. Why have the greatest saints not suffered from pride? Because the holier they got the more they saw God's holiness and what he calls us to. Because they had very high and lofty goals, they were not tempted to be proud even though their virtues were very great.

What is the cure for pride? Walk with God continually. If you are with God, how can you stand proud? But if you wander from God, then even humility can lead to sin. Then you will begin to say of yourself, "How very humble I have become. Why, I must be the humblest of men!" And behold, you will be proud of your humility, and pride will have you again. Saint John of the Ladder writes of a monk who once said to an older brother, "Forgive me, father, but I am not proud." "My son", said the wise old man, "what better proof of your pride could you have given than to claim that you were not proud?" (*The Ladder of Divine Ascent*, Step 23)

THE SEVEN DEADLY SINS: Part 4—Anger
November 2, 2003

Anger is defined in our Antiochian Pocket Prayer Book as "unworthy irritation and lack of self control." Consider four cases: (1) Long ago we had a family friend who was a very dignified soft-spoken woman—until she got behind the wheel of a car, when suddenly she became a demon from hell cutting off other drivers, insulting them, using words ladies did not use in those days. What caused her anger?

(2) While driving to and from church conferences I sometimes get outside the range of public radio, and to keep awake I turn on AM talk

radio—call-in shows, where there is such hostility! White American males are one of the most privileged groups of people in history. One would think they (we) might be grateful, magnanimous—but at least on the radio they seem so very angry. Why?

(3) Some women become very angry at those who wish to limit abortions in any way? Why? Some men get very angry at those who wish to limit their use of guns in any way. Why?

(4) When I was a young Episcopal priest, I did not think I was an angry man, but when we began Mass I often found myself becoming hostile. I would spend the service fighting in my mind: "If he says that to me, I'm going to say this to him," and so on. When Mass ended, the anger would be gone. What could explain this?

Anger really is a kind of lust. Lust, remember, is a compelling desire for something wrong like addictive substances, power or improper sex. People also speak of "lust for vengeance." I think anger is listed as a separate sin because it is more complex than the other lusts. Saint John of the Ladder quotes anger saying, "I come from many sources, and I have more than one father. My mothers are pride, greed . . . and lust, too. My father is named conceit. My daughters are remembrance of wrongs, hate, hostility and self-justification." (*The Ladder of Divine Ascent*, Step 8)

Anger may result from indulging in other sins. For example, modern consumer culture tells us that happiness comes from grabbing as many material things as we can—that is, by practicing the sin of greed. We hear in the media that we will be fulfilled by unfettered sex, the sin of lust. Our culture encourages us to "look out for #1," to believe that we deserve to have our every desire fulfilled, because "I'm worth it!"—which is the sin of false pride. Political idealists tell us that we have the ability to build the perfect world, or totally defeat evil and have complete worldly security—which is encouraging the sin of national false pride. And then when we get our expectations up and can't get all we desire, or when we do and we're still not fulfilled, we get frustrated and angry.

C.S. Lewis wrote in *Screwtape Letters* (chapter 21) that anger can be caused by a "false sense of ownership," the idea that my time is my own, my life is my own. I claim that this is "my body" or "my gun" or "my property," and nobody should interfere with my right to do what I want with what is mine. It's an absurd idea, since we did not create the world or time or even ourselves. Lewis says, "The more claims on life that [a man] can be induced to make, the more often he will feel injured, and as a result ill-tempered." Then I feel, when anyone or anything intrudes on what I want to do when I want to do it, I have a right to be aggrieved and angry. Does this explain the anger of talk radio hosts and of the pro-abortion lobby?

Being angry at other people may be caused by the spirit of false judgment. I assume that when I am slighted or people don't do right by me, they are doing this on purpose—while of course my motives are always pure as the driven snow! When I was a young priest I was sent into a church that had many problems. For reasons I won't go into, the people had good reason to be suspicious of clergy. How did I handle it? In my pride and naiveté, I took it all personally. I thought they were purposely out to get me, poor innocent me, and so I got angry—which gave some of them good reason to be angry at me in return. God can heal these things, and he did, but my spirit of judgment and anger did not help that situation. Over the years I have become convinced that most hurts and slights are unintentional. Usually people are preoccupied with and upset about their own problems, and we just happen to get in their way. When we take it personally and get angry, then they wonder why we're mad at them!

The Prayer Book calls anger "unworthy irritation"—but can there be "worthy irritation," justifiable anger? Yes. There can be "righteous anger" at injustice and evil, such as Christ showed when he cleansed the temple. Also, anger is often the natural result when people are mistreated. Children who are unloved or abused, the poor and needy who suffer because nobody cares, ordinary people cheated out of their savings by CEOs and financial manipulators, people who are tortured by oppressors—all these have good cause to be angry. One reason Psalm 69 is in the Bible is to show us how a mistreated man reacts. Listen to him: "I looked for pity but there was none; and for comforters but I found no one. They gave me poison for food, and for my thirst they gave me vinegar to drink." What is the result? Anger: "Let their own table . . . become a snare . . . let their eyes be darkened so that they cannot see . . . add to them punishment upon punishment . . . let them be blotted out of the book of the living . . ." Injustice causes anger. (This psalm is also a prophecy of another Man who would have no one to comfort him, who would be given vinegar to drink, but who did not get angry.)

Anger is always the result of lack of faith in God. Whatever its immediate cause, people get angry because they are not convinced that God can remedy the situation; they fear that it's hopeless. I'll say more about this later.

Ultimately anger like all sin is demonic. The devil plays on our weaknesses. But we can never say "the devil made me do it." We have free will. We give in to it. We let him have his way.

What are the results of anger? 1) We may lose our temper. Anger boils over, and we lash out and say things we should not say, things we probably do not really mean, but which can never be taken back. Even if we apologize, those words will hang in the minds of those who heard them, maybe forever. Even if they forgive us and get on with our common life, they will always wonder: which words did he mean most, the words of the apology or the words spoken in anger? The apostle James wrote: "The tongue is a fire, a world of iniquity . . . it is set on fire by hell . . . it is an unruly evil, full of deadly poison." (James 3:6) "My beloved brethren, let every man be swift to hear, slow to speak, slow to anger, for the wrath of man does not produce the righteousness of God." (James 1:19) Christ spoke forcefully on this: "Whoever is angry with his brother without a cause shall be in danger of judgment. Whoever says to his brother 'Raca!' [about the worst thing you could call somebody in Aramaic] shall be in danger of being taken to court, and whoever says 'You fool!' shall be in danger of hellfire." (Matthew 5:22)

2) Anger may result in a more calculated action called vengeance, which is forbidden to us. Christ commanded us to do good to our enemies. "'Vengeance is mine' says the Lord. 'I will repay.'" (Deuteronomy 32:35) Consider the Holy Land, now dominated by two religions that believe vengeance is a proper response. Many innocent Palestinians were driven from their homes and lands by Israelis. The occupation has gone on and on, so some Muslims strike back in vengeance. (This is not to justify terrorism. To understand something is not to favor it.) Israelis, angered at the deaths of innocent relatives and friends, respond in vengeance. (Again, to understand is not to condone.) Muslim Palestinians retaliate again, and so the anger ever increases.

3) We may hold anger within us and brood over grievances. "What's wrong?" "*Nothing.*" "Are you sure?" "I'm *fine*!!" Perhaps when the time is right we may produce the list: "I remember how you ignored my mother in 1973, and how you insulted my sister in 1985." These are signs that we never forgave, never got over the anger. Or hidden anger may come out indirectly, in our driving, for example. I still wonder what that otherwise nice lady driver was really angry about. If we do not act outwardly on our anger in any way, is it still a sin, still "missing the mark?" Yes. It is a sin against God who loves us, for anger is spiritual suicide. Anger held within us, not dealt with, is like a cancer eating away at us, killing our God-given souls. Such hidden anger does no harm to the person who hurt us. In fact it gives him more power over us, for it allows him to continue to make us miserable. That is why when people come to Confession, I usually ask: is there anyone you have not forgiven or are not prepared to forgive? If the answer is yes, we need to talk.

Therefore the Scriptures advise us again and again to rid ourselves of anger, to overcome it: "Put away anger, wrath, malice, blasphemy, filthy language out of your mouth." (Colossians 3:8) "He who is slow to anger is better than the mighty, and he who rules his spirit than he who conquers a city." (Proverbs 16:32) All well and good, but how can we do it?

What is the cure for anger? (1) We need to begin by trying to control the external symptoms, the loss of temper, the vengeful acts, because they do so much harm, get us into so much trouble. We need to plan how to hold our temper, because anger is a quick acting demon. Adultery takes time to arrange, but harsh words are often out of our mouth before we know it. Saint John of the Ladder (who has a lot to say about anger; he must have dealt with many angry monks, or was this a temptation he fought himself?) says, "The first step toward freedom from anger is to keep the lips silent when the heart is stirred." (Step 8) Plan ahead so you will know how to "sit on it," not lose control. Plan so that when you feel anger coming on you will, for example, say the Jesus Prayer ten times before you speak. Plan so that if you are still not in control you will cast out the demon. That is how I learned to handle my hostility at Mass years ago. When I felt it coming on, I would say to myself, "Satan, in the name of Jesus Christ, go to hell." And he did! I think it was purely demonic. After I cast it out, I wasn't angry with anyone.

The following suggestion may seem silly, but I think another plan would be to look into a mirror. On Mount Athos there are no mirrors lest the monks be tempted by vanity, but in this case a mirror might help avert sin. Sometime when you are about to explode, look at yourself: the bulging eyes, the distorted, misshapen face. Anger is so ugly. Do you really want people to see and remember you like that? Saint John of the Ladder says those overcome by anger look "pitiable". He also advises, "Singing in moderation can . . . ease a bad temper." (Step 8) Join the choir! I would also add: form the habit of good manners. It is bad manners to cut people off on the highway, to call them "raca" even to oneself while driving alone. The good habit of speaking and acting kindly to people can help control angry words and actions. If you fail—if anger wins out and you say or do something hurtful—as soon as you dare, apologize. Deal with it directly. Don't beat around the bush. Don't assume the other person knows it. Say, "I'm sorry." If you regularly lose your temper, you need help. Go to Confession, and lay it before God. Get a professional counselor, and find out what's gone wrong inside you.

2) However, even worse, for the angry person at least, is to hold the anger inside and not deal with it. We need to get it out. Do surgery on the soul-destroying cancer. Saint John of the Ladder wrote, "I have seen people delivered from [anger] by the very fact that they had flared up and then poured out their long-stored grievance, and in addition they got from their offender either some reparation or some explanation for what had caused [it]. Those who were silently harboring resentments . . .

were it seems to me more to be pitied than the men prone to explosions of temper." (Step 8)

However, this means that always we need to deal not just with the symptoms but with the disease, the root of the anger: (1) Pull back and think about it. The fathers speak of anger as a failure of rationality. Recall the causes of anger that we mentioned earlier. Don't just be angry. Instead ask: why am I angry? Then deal with that. Do this quickly, for anger builds on itself. Saint John Chrysostom wrote, "If you fail to master your anger on the first day, then on the next day and even sometimes for a whole year you will still be dragging it out. Anger causes us to suspect that words spoken in one sense were meant in another. And we will even do the same with gestures and every little thing." Saint Paul advises, "Let not the sun go down on your wrath." (Ephesians 4:26) Consider: do I want to feel like this forever, this burning misery to go on unto ages of ages? That would be hell. Indeed, hell consists of being consumed by our sins.

(2) Redirect your anger. Like all sin, anger is something good twisted out of shape. Saint Paul said, "Our enemy . . . is not flesh and blood, but . . . spiritual powers of wickedness in high places." (Ephesians 6:12) Saint John Chrysostom wrote, "Be angry with the devil . . . This is why God has armed us with anger." Turn your wrath upon Satan, the source of all evil.

(3) Transform your anger into love. Take the same energy you're devoting to anger and pray daily for those you are angry at; either they will change or your attitude will change or both. Stop judging their motives; we do not know why people act as they do. Forgive them, which does not mean to forget; it means not to pay them back. Do good to people, perform positive acts of charity, especially to those who have angered you. "Love your enemies. Do good to those who hate you, and pray for those who spitefully use you and persecute you." (Matthew 5:44)

(4) To overcome any sin, it is a great help to go to Confession regularly and to have a spiritual director, a competent and loving Orthodox spiritual father or mother, to help guide you.

(5) Work on your faith in God. Spend more time in worship and prayer and spiritual study.

C.S. Lewis says somewhere that while events cannot be changed, the meaning of events can be changed. For example, having an argument with your spouse is bad, but it can lead either to evil (greater alienation, divorce) or to good (increased understanding, forgiveness, deeper love, a better marriage), depending on what you do with it. Whatever caused your anger and the fact that you were angry cannot be changed. If you nurse it, brood on it, wallow in it, it can take you to hell. But if you allow

God and his love into it, he can use that same event, that same anger, to let you understand yourself and others better, overcome sin, grow stronger spiritually, and change you into a more loving, more forgiving, better and holier person. That which once made you angry can lead you to heaven. If we let him, God can change the meaning of events, untwist them and turn them all into good—if not in this world, then in the next. And if you have faith that God can do that and will do that, what in the world do you have to be angry about?

THE SEVEN DEADLY SINS: Part 6—Envy
November 16, 2003

Envy is defined in the Antiochian Pocket Prayer Book as "jealousy of some other person's happiness." Some distinguish between envy and jealousy. I will use them here as synonyms, but the derivations of the two words provide interesting insights. Envy originally meant to "look at someone with malice or resentment." 'Look how happy he is and I am not, how much he's got and I have not, and I hate it and I hate him.' Jealousy comes from a French word meaning "blinds" or "shutters," suggesting that jealousy is often a hidden sin. Envy secretly looks at others with resentment.

In my first talk, I said that the original sin was pride—trying to put oneself in the place of God, making oneself the center of the universe. However, some of the fathers say envy was the primal sin. Lucifer was jealous of God's power and authority, and envy twisted his mind, causing him to see God as the enemy who refused to "give the devil his due," and so he rebelled. Likewise one could say that envy was the sin of Adam and Eve. Satan asked: "Why should God have such freedom and knowledge, and you do not?" Then envy twisted their minds. They wanted to be like God and could not, so it seemed to them that God was their enemy, and they rebelled against him. Envy lay behind the crucifixion of Christ. Pontius Pilate tried hard to release Jesus because "he knew that [the chief priests and elders] had handed him over [to him] because of envy." (Matthew 27:18) Christ had power and popularity, serenity and confidence they did not possess, and which they wanted—and their envy twisted their minds, so that they could not see him clearly, and he seemed to them to be the enemy who had to be destroyed.

Remember, the seven deadly sins are all interior, the inner roots of outward acts of sin. Only one of the Ten Commandments, the last, deals exclusively with inner motivations: "Thou shalt not covet thy neighbor's wife, thy neighbor's house; nor his field nor his manservant nor his maid nor his ox nor his ass nor any of his cattle, nor whatever belongs to thy neighbor." (Exodus 20:7) Covetousness is a strong desire for something that is not ours, and it leads directly to (maybe it is really the same as) envy and jealousy.

Envy, like all sins, is something good that has been misshapen. The fact is that each of us is also someone good twisted out of shape. God created us and declared that we were very good, and we were—but now look at us. We are rightly dissatisfied with what we are and what we have. We were made for better than this. Granted, many of the things people become envious about are superficial: "Oh, if only I had a Mercedes like him." "If only I were shaped like her." But we should seek genuinely better things for ourselves—better health for the bodies God has given us, more knowledge and wisdom.

Some should try to provide better for themselves and their families, so as not to be a burden on others. There is nothing wrong with trying to look better, doing the best we can with what God gave us. Above all we should try to become people more virtuous and more holy than we are. Nor is admiration of others the same as envy; we all need heroes and heroines, people we look up to. I wish the modern world gave us more of them.

Where this goes wrong is when, instead of trying to improve ourselves, instead of imitating worthy people, we get focused only on their supposed superiority. That easily leads to envy. "Why does he deserve to have all those things which I do not?" "Why is she so smart and I am not?" Remember how envy distorts our perception. I begin to see the person I envy as an enemy who looks down on me, who thinks he's better than me. This can lead to anger with God: "Why does God love him more than me?" We begin to see God as the enemy—and then we are in deep trouble, for this is the same path taken by Lucifer.

Envy is a hard sin to deal with, for two reasons: (1) Because, as I said, it is often hidden, at least for a long time. It is hidden from others unless it results in some outward action, and even then they probably won't understand it was out of envy. Envy is often hidden even from ourselves, hidden within our own hearts. We know we are miserable, unhappy with life, but don't know why. Anger quickly leads to loss of temper, but envy often just lurks within us. Later we may realize that the hardness in our heart, our resentment of others, the distance between us and God have been caused by our envy.

(2) Because both the origins and effects of envy are complex. I said earlier that the various deadly sins are interconnected; one may lead to another and that one to yet another. This is particularly true in the case

of envy. Consider, for example, the interrelationship of envy and pride. The fathers say that pride, putting myself in the center, leads to envy of others, causing me to believe I deserve what they have. But in another way, envy seems the opposite of pride. Pride consists of looking down on others from my position of supposed superiority, while envy consists of looking up at others with malice from my position of supposed inferiority, so that I may think I am being very humble. Yet this also is pride, for in my envy I am wishing I were in the center of things, as they seem to be. The sins of greed and lust for various things also lead to envy, as we desire what others have for ourselves. On the other hand, envy may lead to greed, anger, hatred, acts of revenge, thievery, lust, even murder. Confusing? Yes. The sin of envy catches us in a maze from which it is hard to escape.

Even when it is never expressed outwardly but remains hidden, envy is still misery; it destroys the joy of living. Saint Basil the Great summed it up:

There is no other passion engendered in human souls more pernicious than envy. It does less harm to strangers, but is the chief homegrown evil for whoever possesses it. As rust eats away at iron, so envy eats away at the soul in which it lives. Envy is grief over a neighbor's wellbeing. Therefore the envious man never has a lack of sorrows and afflictions. What can be more pernicious than this disease? This is a corruption of life, a profanation of nature, enmity against what is given to us by God, opposition to God.

Worst of all, I think, envy is a dreadful waste of our lives. God gives each of us particular gifts to be used for his service and in the service of others, to be developed and employed and enjoyed by us with love and gratitude to him. Of course, you can always look and find someone richer than you, smarter or better looking or more spiritually gifted than you—but you can never look and find another you. God has made each of us unique, a never-to-be-repeated combination of gifts, talents, experiences and abilities. No one just like you has ever existed; nor will anyone just like you ever live again. And if you spend your life moping over what other people have and you do not have, you will waste the unique contribution that you and you alone can make to the Church and to the world. Don't throw away the gifts you have out of envy for those you do not have.

Therefore envy is condemned again and again in the Scriptures: "Envy is rottenness to the bones." (Proverbs 14:30) "Wrath is cruel and anger is a torrent, but who is able to stand before jealousy?" (Proverbs 27:4) In Galatians (5:21) Saint Paul lists envy as one of the works of the flesh (our fallen nature), placing envy right between heresy and murder;

you get the point. Saint James (3:16) says, "Where envy and self-seeking exist, confusion and everything evil are there." However, Saint Paul tells us also that envy can be overcome. He wrote to Titus (3:2, 3), "Once we lived in malice and envy, hateful and hating one another. But when the kindness and love of God our Savior toward man appeared . . . he saved us [from all this]." How then can we be rescued from envy?

(1) By the practice of thanksgiving. Every night before you go to sleep, thank God for the gifts he has given you that day. This can change your whole mindset. Don't forget to thank him for the things we so often take for granted: good health, the love of others, the fact that bombs are not going off outside our homes, the beauty we see around us every day, the gift of life, of existence. You might not have had any of these things. Instead of envying what others have, be grateful for what you have.

(2) Challenge your assumptions. Remember how envy distorts our perceptions. Do you know for a fact that those you are jealous of are happier, better off than you are? You do not; it may in fact be quite the opposite. For example, do you envy the rich? Consider that the rich person never knows who his friends are. He is never sure whether people give him attention because they love him or because of his money. Is that what you really want? The poor know they are not being loved for their money. Furthermore, many people appear to have a trouble-free, happy life when they do not. I sometimes look through our parish address list to see if I can find anyone who is not dealing with a major problem. Usually I cannot, and even though I'm their pastor I'm sure people have far more troubles than I know and are bravely bearing with them quietly. You may look at others with envy; perhaps if you knew the truth about their lives you would not.

3) Treat the person you envy like a fellow human being. Pray for him daily as one who needs God's grace and love just as you do, someone who, for all you know, may be envious of you and people like you. Pray, and either the other person will change or, in this case, more likely your attitude will change. Saint Thalassios wrote, "If you share secretly in the joy of someone you envy, you will be freed from your jealousy; [likewise] if you keep silent about the person you envy." (Third Century.57) Saint Paul advised, "Rejoice with those who rejoice and weep with them that weep." (Romans 12:15)

4) Work on your faith in God. Do you really believe what we say in the creed, that God is creator of all things? Do you believe that all good and perfect gifts come down from him? That he is your Father who loves you, who will never give bad things to those who ask him for good? Saint John Chrysostom wrote: "What do you envy, that your brother has received a . . . gift? But from whom did he receive it, tell me; was it not

from God? That means you are at enmity with him who gave it to him. God gives one thing to one, and another thing to another for his own good reasons." Envy is ultimate unfaith: belief that God does not know what he is doing or that he does not care.

5) If there is something missing in your life that is truly good and needful (not a million dollars or a facelift or your neighbor's wife), then go after it. Don't waste time secretly looking with malice at those who have it. Seek it for yourself. You need to do two things, in this order:

(a) Pray. Ask God for it. Hear the Apostle James (4:1-3): "You desire and you do not have. You murder and covet and cannot obtain. You fight and make war. Yet you do not have them because you do not ask. You ask and do not receive, because you ask wrongly, so that you may spend it on your pleasures." But if you desire something good, not just for your own pleasure but to serve God and man, then ask for it. Pray much, like the poor widow shouting at the judge's window, until he answers you—and then trust. God is almighty, he "is good and loves mankind," and he will give good things to those who ask him.

(b) Work. Orthodoxy does not teach that we should sit back and wait for God to hand us what we want. Our doctrine is synergy, cooperation with God. If someone has a garden and you want one, get to work and grow one. Use your God-given brains, have a plan, learn God's system for growing things. Then cooperate with him: plant the seeds at the right time, water them, wait patiently, pull out the weeds. That's how to get a harvest. Saint Maximos the Confessor says, particularly regarding envy of those we think are better than ourselves, "The person who out of jealousy envies those who practice the virtues is more than misguided, for the choice of believing and acting, and of receiving grace according to the measure of his faith clearly depends on him and not on anybody else." (*Third Century of Various Texts*.35)

And in the end if, after you prayed, worked and tried your hardest, God does not give you what you desire, then: Glory to God for all things! It must be that he has something better in mind for you, even if you don't understand his purposes yet. If you believe that, you will be able to put aside the envy, and love God and love your neighbor anyway. "Love suffers long and is kind. Love does not envy. Love does not pride itself, is not puffed up, does not behave rudely, does not seek its own, is not provoked, thinks no evil . . . bears all things, believes all things, hopes all things, endures all things . . . For now we see in a mirror dimly, but then face to face. Now I know in part, but then I shall know just as I also am known." (I Corinthians 13)

Chapter Five

Personable

Originally this chapter was titled "Humility" or "Humble," a better word to describe a trait of someone. And Fr. Bill is truly a humble person. It would be no mistake to give him that description.

But there are a plethora of spiritual/psychological land mines surrounding humility. In the previous selection on "Pride" the elder reproved the monk for stating that he was not proud. Similarly, if one were to claim humility this would be taken as a sure sign that the individual was not. It didn't take long for me to recognize in my early years in Orthodoxy that if one were to talk about one's own humility a certain, everlasting curse would be placed upon that individual. Or so my dramatic imagination would tell me at that time.

To avoid all this I've selected the character trait "personable" to describe Fr. Bill. It is not difficult finding evidence of this in his messages. Of course, to simply read the homily would be to miss all the verbal and nonverbal evidence of Father's personableness in his actual delivery of the homily.

"Personable" means the ability to relate to others as "real" people. Others know that they live on the same planet as he does. "Down to earth" has been a phrase I have not only repeatedly heard but have also used myself to describe Father. This is not a priest who takes himself or his job too seriously. Nor are there any airs of aloof professionalism or any subtle or direct psychological nuances that suggest aloofness or belonging to some higher class of people. Perhaps it is just as well to call this humble.

The reader will perfectly understand this from the first selection of Father's 2002 report on his trip overseas. His homilies at the funerals for our former Deacon John and St. Nicholas member Duane Newhouse are a wonderful blend of real human experience combined with spiritual truth and strength.

2002 TRIP REPORT: Part 1—Mount Athos

The first half of my trip to Greece was a pilgrimage to Mount Athos, then to Aegina, the burial place of Saint Nektarios. I am grateful to the Parish Council for giving me the extra time off for it. The last half of the trip was vacation, recovering from the first half. That's where I got my tan, and I'm not going to report on that.

Mount Athos, surely you know, is the thousand-year-old center of Orthodox monasticism, located in northern Greece on a long peninsula extending out into the Aegean Sea. Its actual title is Ἅγιον Ὄρος, Aghion Oros, the Holy Mountain—which refers both to the mountain itself and to the peninsula from which it rises. I especially wanted to visit because a man who became Orthodox here at Saint Nicholas—Wayne Bulloch, a former Episcopalian priest, now Hieromonk (Priestmonk) Barnabas at Karakallou Monastery—invited me to visit him.* This is definitely the most distant pastoral call I've ever made! So on Sunday September 14 I gathered names from you to be prayed for on Athos and before Saint Nektarios, and off I went.

I had a day's layover in Thessaloniki where I had to get a written permit to visit the Holy Mountain. Previously I had to get permission from His Eminence Metropolitan PHILIP and from the office of the Ecumenical Patriarch. One doesn't just wander onto Mount Athos. In Thessaloniki I had time to visit the Church of Saint Demetrios and venerate that Great Martyr, likewise Saint Gregory Palamas in his church. I wandered into the Church of the Martyrs Sophia and her daughters Faith, Hope and Charity on their feast day, September 17th. There was a continual long line of people of all sorts, young and old, male and female—a young man in motorcycle boots carrying his helmet, a young woman quite inappropriately dressed—waiting to venerate

---

*   [Ed. Note: The Priestmonk Barnabus fell asleep in the Lord in 2009.]

their icon, and I joined them. There is a spiritual revival going on in Greece which involves many young people and many men, and not just "churchy" types. As always in Greece, the churches are open, and there is a never-ending stream of people coming in and going out, saying their prayers, venerating the icons, lighting candles. What a shame we can't have that in this country any more—but Greece is a nearly crime-free society. By the way in Thessaloniki I found something which to me (I am a train fan) seemed just right. In the railways station is an Orthodox chapel with good icons and a candle stand so people can pray for a safe journey. Orthodoxy naturally integrated with life—something else we will never know in our society.

On Tuesday I had dressed in my "civvies", since I was just a tourist. On Wednesday I put on my priest's outfit. (In the old world, wherever they go priests wear a rassa (cassock) and a sort of "stovepipe" hat. Father Ted Trifon had graciously loaned me a hat.) At breakfast in the hotel there were three priests who said, "Come and sit with us." Were they Greeks as I thought? No, they were (as we would say) Antiochians! from Beirut, leading a group of 40 lay people on a tour of Greek holy places. "Who is your bishop? Basil?" "No, Demetri." "Oh yes, Demetri!" "We visited Metropolitan Philip last year." Truly Orthodoxy is a small world.

The Holy Mountain. Where to begin? I'll begin with: It's hard to get to—intentionally so. It requires a two hour bus ride to Ouranopolis, then a two hour boat ride to Daphne, the port of Athos, then a scary bus ride back and forth about 2000 feet up the face of a cliff on an unimproved road to Karyes the capitol of Athos, and then 30 minutes further in a van driven by a lunatic driver—a mad monk, very fast over a very primitive mountain road (but not long ago the only way in was on foot) to Karakallou Monastery and Father Barnabas.

The setting is *gorgeous,* on a slope perhaps 500 feet above the blue Aegean, the area densely wooded, with the 6500 foot Mount Athos hanging over it. The feel of it, especially at night, keeps coming back to me. The deep silence, with only a barely audible "whssh . . . whssh" coming from the sea, and the brilliance of the stars. The moon was full while I was there and the weather clear . . . and at night the sea and the landscape shimmering and Mount Athos almost luminous in the moonlight, and then the semantron (the rhythmic clacking of wood planks) echoing through the monastic enclosure calling us to prayer, and then the majestic ringing of the bells. It gave me the holy chills. It still does. It was ethereally beautiful.

When we arrived, I and the other guests were greeted in the traditional way—with a glass of water, some loukoumi (Turkish delight, but don't tell the Greeks), and a little glass of ouzo (licorice-flavored liquor). After the van ride, I especially needed that! And there was Father Barnabas, barely recognizable to me with his long white beard, who is happy and doing well and sends his love to all. He offers a round of Jesus Prayers for us every day. After I kissed the abbot's hand, he kissed mine, which I took as a warm welcome, since he is quite suspicious of priests with short hair and short beards! Athos also is having a spiritual revival, in nearly all the great monasteries and cells and sketes up and down the peninsula, with many young well-educated novices and monks. Twenty years ago Karakallou had about eight monks; today there are about forty. There are many pilgrims. The boats I took to and from Athos were standing room only.

I guess I was expecting the monastery to be dank and dark and kind of spooky. Instead Karakallou is immaculately kept and spotlessly clean. The Athonite monasteries are subsidized by the Greek government, and also by the EU (European Union) as part of Europe's cultural heritage. A sense of holy peace pervaded the place. The contrasts are striking: a 500-year-old building, but with good modern Western European plumbing (those who know Greece know to what I refer . . .) and central heating, the last thing I expected. However personal washing facilities are primitive and there is hot water only 2 days a week, and all cooking is done on an ancient wood stove. The third day on Athos, I tried to find a mirror. There are no mirrors! You get the point. One is to be concerned only with the interior life. The food is medieval Greek peasant fare (although they find snacks for the pilgrims)—a strict Great-Lenten fast on Mondays, Wednesdays and Fridays, never any meat, and fish only on major holy days. (I know this, because we had a holy day, and I helped Father Barnabas, who works in the kitchen, clean many, many little fishes by hand.) But there is a modern card phone right outside the monastery. I put in the card, pressed 13 numbers and Khouria Dianna said "hello" just like she was in the next room. On the boat I was watching a rather stern-looking old monk, who suddenly pulled out a cell phone and began an animated conversation! But the churches are lighted only by candles, and the services have scarcely changed a syllable or a ceremony in over a thousand years. The feel of ancient Byzantium just permeates the place, and life is lived on "Byzantine time," with the hours beginning at sunset. On the other hand, Father Barnabas needs a new laptop computer, since he has nearly worn out his old Mac. You put all this together. I don't think I can!

Why was I so impressed by how beautiful things were at night? Because on Athos one spends a lot of the night awake. My most distressing memory is of the Finnish guestmaster knocking on my door every morning at 3 a.m. saying, "Pater, the services are beginning.

Wake up." Actually he was being kind. The services had begun at 2 a.m. Orthros (Matins) commences at 3 a.m., and typically goes on till 5 or 5:30 except on Sundays and feasts when Matins is about three hours long. (I mentioned to Father Barnabas and Father Alexis, a young monk from Dover, Delaware, that our bishops had just put out a directive that we should celebrate complete Sunday Matins, leaving a full hour for it. They just smiled.) And then each day they go on to celebrate Divine Liturgy. For one holy day (Nativity of the Mother of God, old calendar), we had a 9 1/2 hour service, beginning at 11 p.m., concluding at 8:30 a.m. the next morning. I told Father Barnabas I didn't think this would fly back home. But what you all might go for is that at this long service, after the Entrance at Vespers (about 1 a.m.), a few monks remain in church to continue to service, while everyone else goes out to get a cup of coffee and a snack to keep them going till morning! The longest service they have is . . . 17 1/2 hours! But all this is with traditional old world Orthodox flexibility. Worshippers come and go as they need to. During the 9 1/2 hour service, Father Barnabas and I both went back to catch a couple hours' sleep.

All told, the ordinary non-festival, non-Lenten worship day totals about eight hours—about six hours leading up to dawn, and then Vespers and Compline in the evening. In addition each monk has his own duties for the upkeep of the monastery—kitchen work, cleaning, maintenance, gardening, whatever. It's a busy life. Sleep is from about 8 p.m. to 2 a.m., with a morning nap if there's time.

I found life on Mount Athos:

(1) Physically exhausting. The wake-up knock on my door came at 3 a.m., which was 7 p.m. Milwaukee time. I had both jet lag and Athos lag! I slept only in fits and spurts the whole time I was there.

(2) Spiritually exhilarating. Since I was a priest I was invited to sit up front with the monks and to do all the standings, sittings, leanings, venerations, bowings and prostrations with the monks. I managed not to embarrass either myself or the USA too badly. Orthodox worship is essentially the same wherever one goes, and even though I am not proficient in Greek, I could figure out what was going on, with the help of an occasional whisper or nudge from Father Barnabas or Father Alexis. I saw everything from the inside—the impressive level of the prayer life, the meticulously-performed services, the enthusiastic chanting, the candles illuminating the faces of the ancient icons and the faces of the monks as they chanted in the darkness and Christ the Pantocrator ruling over all from the dome, high above. The images keep coming back to me again and again.

(3) Excessive, at least for me. I thought I liked long services. Little did I know. This was too much for me. I'm glad Mount Athos is there and prospering, setting high standards for Orthodox worship, preserving the Tradition entirely, plumbing the spiritual depths, praying for us—and that is their work: prayer, worship. But I have no intention of imposing Athonite worship on you or on me. The first thing I did when I got back to Thessaloniki was cut my hair and trim my beard, just to make that point. Furthermore, on the bus back, I found myself sitting there in my priest's garb, inadvertently staring out the window at pretty women. I definitely would not like an all-male world.

One evening I had a conversation with a hermit. He lives alone in a cell up in the hills above Karakallou and comes down for Sundays and feasts. What is your image of a hermit? This one is a chemical engineer with a special interest in medical ethics. In his demeanor he reminded me somewhat of John Philosophos. He was Greek who had never taken the faith seriously until, while he was working in Montreal, living with a girl, he read a theology book by Vladimir Lossky. God touched him and then his girlfriend. He said they both repented and decided to become monastics. He lived at Karakallou for a while and then got the abbot's blessing to become a hermit. He said his big problem is that he's spiritually lazy. I think his definition of "lazy" must be different from mine. The evening after the 9 1/2 hour vigil he asked me what I thought of the services, and I answered honestly (never lie to a hermit . . .) "I think they are beautiful, but they are *very long*." He looked at me as if he thought I had holes in my head. What is wrong with you, priest? Why would anyone not want to worship God for 9 1/2 hours straight?

And that is my report on Mount Athos.

SERMON AT THE FUNERAL OF DEACON JOHN McQUIDE
May, 2002

Christ is risen.

Before talking about Deacon John, I want to say a special thank you to His Grace Bishop DEMETRI for being here today. His schedule is exceedingly busy, and it wasn't easy for him, and we are very grateful. Many years, O Master.

Where to begin with Deacon John? Christ is risen. That is where. He believed that and trusted in Christ with his whole heart. That was the key to his life.

I don't preach eulogies. I prefer to talk about the resurrection. But His Grace Bishop DEMETRI has spoken well on that subject, and I do want to say some things about Deacon John. His family and friends may wish to share some reminiscences after lunch downstairs, so I won't tread on that. Let me just tell some of my own personal memories. Saedna, I hope it's alright if I call him Jack, at least when I talk about the early days. That's how I knew him long before he became Deacon John, and he'll always be Jack to me.

I first met Jack McQuide in the spring of 1968, 34 years ago. I was an Episcopal priest, ordained only three years, and the Episcopal Bishop of Milwaukee wanted me to take a little mission in Mequon, Saint Boniface. Dianna and I had visited once, but Jack and Jane were away then, so they invited us to have dinner with them later. Jane fixed one of her delicious meals (she never seems to fail), and Jack was direct-spoken and feisty—he expressed his opinions with great vigor. On the way back to Chicago I said to Dianna, "I'll take the church, but I'm going to have trouble with that one." I was never so wrong in my life. I have never met anyone who has given me less trouble. Let me say it positively. I have never met anyone more loyal, more faithful, more willing to give of himself with enthusiasm, with love, with honesty, especially honesty. For 34 years he critiqued almost every one of my sermons with great honesty, whether I wanted to hear it or not. And it did me good.

We had an odd relationship. At first Jack was about 45, and I was about 30, and he seemed almost a father figure to me—except that on the other hand I was his priest and father confessor. Over the years we also became really good friends. During the fifteen or so years since his retirement, we worshipped together almost every day, and we talked about many things, especially the two most important things in his life: his faith and his family. We liked each other, we enjoyed each other, we loved each other. I feel somehow as if I've lost a father, a son and a brother all at once. I hardly know how to cope with all that.

I have so many memories: *34 years* of hearing Deacon John's confessions! I can't tell you the content of course, but I will tell you that I know Jack was a man who truly sought after God, truly loved God. He had his own struggles. Don't we all? But he did *struggle* to be good, to do what was right, to be closer to God. He chased after holiness; he was thirsty for it. One of his favorite psalms begins "As the deer thirsts for the waterbrooks, so longs my soul for you, O God." [Ps. 42] Those of us who knew him well saw how he grew in faith, in love, in compassion. I felt that especially since his ordination there was a particular sweetness that came over him.

At our old Episcopal Church I knew Jack as vestry member, assistant at Holy Communion, Sunday school teacher, and as a very eager stewardship chairman. I remember him talking for hours to a fellow newly in from the Church of England who just couldn't figure out why he needed to give money to the Church. Jack told him why in no uncertain terms—and he coughed up the money! Jack always was serious about prayer. He cared about the spiritual life. He prayed with discipline. After he retired he asked me what he should do with himself. I suggested he come to Evensong (the Anglican equivalent of Vespers) every night, and he did, and when we became Orthodox he kept it up. It was a rare day when he was not in church.

As I moved by fits and spurts towards Orthodoxy, Jack was one of the first who wanted to come along. Somehow through Psalm 103 /104, the opening psalm at Orthodox Vespers, he received a vision of how indescribably great God is. For a while he could hardly stop talking about it. That was what moved him towards Orthodoxy. He began here the same old way as Council member, then treasurer and chanter and choir member and teacher at Saint Nicholas School. But then a few years into the Mission, one Sunday I suggested that we could use a deacon. Three men responded. Jack followed through. He said he didn't really want to do it, but something kept telling him he should, and he thought it was God.

So at almost age 70, 45 years after he had done his last academic work, he started Saint Stephen's Course of Studies. He studied, he thought, he wrote. I watched his theological mind begin to focus, and his writing improve. Jack just ate up Orthodox theology, even the tough stuff. Finally on several exams, he got better grades than I did—I, the seminary graduate.

In the fall of 1995 the Archdiocese disapproved his request for ordination. I called His Grace Bishop ANTOUN and asked why? He said: "Father, be practical. Look at his age." I responded: "Saedna, I may be 57 and he may be 72, but he's younger than I am." (I never thought of Deacon John as old. He never acted it. It isn't two years ago at age 76, that he came to Saturday Vespers with a cut lip, because he had made a particular aggressive move at tennis and had slipped and hit the floor. Even these past months when his body was slowing down, the man himself never seemed old. His interest in life and his enthusiasm continued as always. Anyway, through lots of prayer and a little holy arguing, we convinced the Archdiocese that he should be ordained. And in the fall of 1995 he was, and what a wonderful deacon he was to me and to this congregation.

Deacon John's special gift was always prayer and worship. He assisted at services every day but Friday for seven years. And besides that, every Friday he got up at the crack of dawn to assist at the Gathering, the meal program down in the city. As time went on I tried to talk him into slowing down. He wouldn't have it. At that long Holy Thursday Twelve Gospels service last year, *all* of us sat down occasionally to rest—except Deacon John. He loved the Church's services. He loved to worship. He loved to praise his God.

On the holy cards for Deacon John's funeral are printed the opening and closing words of Psalm 103 (104), which meant so much to him and which I think sum up his life: "Bless the Lord, O my soul. O Lord my God, thou art very great; thou art clothed with honour and majesty"—and at the end, "I will sing unto the Lord as long as I live; I will sing praise to the Lord while I have my being." Deacon John sang to God as long as he lived on earth, and he is still singing to the Lord, still praising God, for he still has his being, he still lives. For "Christ has risen from the dead trampling down death by death, and upon those in the tombs bestowing life."

Christ is risen.

SERMON AT THE FUNERAL OF DUANE NEWHOUSE
June 25, 2005

Three days before Duane got sick Mary Beth told me about a woman she knows who still has children to raise, who was diagnosed with a possibly fatal disease, and how someone in the woman's family had calmly said to Mary Beth, "Well I hope it doesn't happen, but if does she'll be in a better place." And Mary Beth said, "That was the wrong reaction. The right reaction is to get angry. The right reaction is to say: This [. . . .]." I won't tell you the word Mary Beth used. She said, "I don't usually use that word, but I needed something strong." I thought at the time that this was an appropriate reaction. And that prompted me to say that when people die untimely deaths I find it hard to say anything at all. All the theology and helpful explanations of why bad things happen to good people seem so trite, so flat, so inadequate at times like this. As Mary Beth and I talked about this, we never imagined that only four weeks later . . .

And sure enough my first reaction when I heard that Duane had died was: I got mad. After all the prayers and so much love poured out for this man . . . We really did storm the gates of heaven. People all over the country were praying. His Grace Bishop MARK was praying for him. On Monday I was talking to a former member of Saint Nicholas who now lives in Denver, and I said, "By the way, would you please pray for . . .",

and she said, "Oh yes, for Duane Newhouse." We were praying above
all for God's will to be done, but we were surely praying that Duane
would recover and live to raise his family. After all that praying, after all
that love, why did God allow this? God is all powerful. God is all loving.
So why . . . ? My second reaction was: how in the world am I going to
preach this sermon, when I'm not at all pleased with this Management
decision?

Where is God in the midst of all this? I could give you all the good
theological, philosophical explanations for why God allows evil and
suffering and death to go on—and I believe them, I really do. But Duane
is still dead. Where is God *here, now?* The answer is: *there [pointing to the
crucifix behind the altar]*. There is God incarnate, God who took flesh and
dwelt among us. There is God loving us, God suffering along with us,
God dying with us, God with us in the midst of it all. The only answer
God has given us is himself, this image of himself, the sign that God loves
us, God cares. "Greater love has no man than that he should give his life
for his friends," he said. [John 15:13] This is the sign that God suffers
with us, suffers more than we do. And not just on the cross.

I remember my father who loved me and was a sensitive empathetic
man. (He has been gone more than forty years now.) When I was young
and got sick and was hurting, or when I was coughing and wheezing (I
had allergies bad when I was a boy), my father would hurt so much for
me that I'd tell him, "Dad, it's okay. You're hurting more than I am." But
he couldn't stop hurting, because he loved me. That's how God, who by
nature is beyond all suffering, is suffering with us today. He has taken on
our sorrows.

At times like this we Christians begin not with explanations and
justifications and trite sayings, but with Jesus Christ, the cross of Christ. I
once heard a Protestant pastor from India say that in his time he had seen
so much suffering, so much death, so much horror, that if it were not for
Jesus Christ he would be a complete skeptic about God, the goodness of
God. We Christians begin not with the evidence before us and all around
us, but with Jesus Christ, with God loving us, God suffering for us, God
dying with us.

Therefore, today we begin not with Duane's body lying here but with
Christ our God who is good and loves mankind. That is the "given". And
from there we work back to this. How could God who loves Duane and
who loves us have allowed this? The answer is: I don't know. We don't
know. But we do know that God is good, and that he has a purpose in
all this. And so after all our prayers that God's will be done, we have to
accept his decision. As I told the Newhouse family, we don't have to like

it, but we do need to trust God now—and especially we need to trust that God will work back from the future and will turn this around, turn it into good.

C.S. Lewis wrote that while events cannot be changed, their meaning can be changed. The worst thing possible, the death of God in the flesh, became the salvation of the world. God does not will death. We were not born to die. Saint Paul wrote that the last enemy to be conquered will be death. And Duane's death will be turned back into life. Indeed it is already happening. At Pascha we sing over and over "Christ is risen from the dead, trampling down death by death and upon those in the tombs bestowing life." That is in the present tense: "*bestowing* life" now. "Whoever lives and believes in me *has* eternal life" now. "The hour is coming and *now is* when the dead will hear the voice of the Son of God and live." [John 5:24, 25] Christ has already led us into death, through death and on into eternity.

So I want to talk about what is happening to Duane Newhouse now. One of the best ways to cope with the death of someone we love is to try to move beyond our grief. As Paul says in the funeral epistle, to "grieve, but not as those who have no hope." When my father died forty years ago, my first reaction was that I had left him behind in January 1965. It took me a while to reach the Christian conclusion: no, he had left me behind on earth. He was still alive. He had moved on ahead of me. In our services we usually refer not to the dead but to the "departed," because they're not dead. They've just moved on.

What is Duane Newhouse experiencing now? First he is alive. When we die we leave our bodies behind, but our souls still live. Jesus said there are no dead in God's sight, for "all live to him." In the book of The Revelation those who have died are at the heavenly altar praying for us on earth. And how many times have we Orthodox known the intercession and intervention of the saints who have gone before us in ways impossible to deny? So we can say that Duane still thinks, sees, prays, loves, lives. There are other senses beyond the bodily senses. There is life beyond this bodily life.

What was it like for Duane to die? To us his death looks like tragedy. To him his death was almost a non-event. I don't say that casually. I am repeating what Jesus said to Mary and Martha: "He who lives and believes in me will never know death," that is, will never experience non-existence, will simply pass from this life to that life. [John 11:26] That is why in the New Testament and in Orthodox usage, death is often called "falling asleep." That is not a euphemism. Dying in Christ consists of falling asleep here and waking up on the other side.

What it is like to live a bodiless existence is hard for us earthlings to imagine. We don't do it yet except in dreams. The difference is that dying is apparently more like waking up from a dream. At death we emerge from all the confusions and shadows of this world, all the things that have bound us down here. During his last month Duane was surely bound down. I wish we had been able to keep him here, but not like that. What a relief it must have been for him to rise up from the torments of all those tubes and machines, all that agitation, and be free again.

What is happening to Duane Newhouse now? Some Orthodox say that the departed remain close to us here on earth during the first forty days, and then proceed with their journey. It may be. Obviously some of the saints are still busy on earth many centuries after their death. But what we know about Duane is that he is still with Christ, still part of the Church which encompasses heaven and earth.

Remember how on Holy Friday night we process out of the church into the darkness, and walk under the epitaphion, passing through death with Christ? And how we find after we've done it, that we're back in church again? Duane is still in the Church, still praying for us as we pray for him; still loving us we still love him. He is proceeding further into the Kingdom of heaven, continuing a journey which he began when he was baptized. He is still "working out his salvation with fear and trembling," only he has moved ahead into the next phase, journeying towards the perfection to which God calls us. Everlasting life means, I think, that God gives us all the time we need to complete the journey, first in this life, then in the next—and how many more rooms there are in our Father's house Jesus didn't tell us, but he said there are many. Some of the fathers suggested that it is a never-ending journey, that maybe we never stop growing in knowledge and love of God and of each other—forever "further up and further in" into the glory.

So, we who are grieving, let us try hard to look up, look ahead, look out. This will be easier to do later. Today grief still overwhelms us. But start now. Think about Duane Newhouse not only as he was, but as he is. Pray for him. Lift up your hearts and your minds and be with him now. And prepare yourself to join him. None of us will be here very long. Hang on, Duane, we're all coming.

Till then, Duane and Mary Beth have created a heritage that will last for many generations. I have come to know this Newhouse family well. I have watched them in action through a month which can only be described as a living nightmare, and I am impressed. You Newhouse children, young men and young women: what you received from your father will not be lost even in this world. You received from him a great inheritance of love and faith and goodness and kindness. This will be passed down through you to your children and your grandchildren and your great grandchildren, and to all the people you deal with in your lives. What your father has done in his life will affect this world for good long after we all are gone.

Always love him. Always pray for him. Keep your love for him alive, because you will use it again. Our life with Duane Newhouse has not ended; it has just gone into pause mode. We will pick it up again. And when we do, as Uncle David said, we won't need any explanations. We'll be too busy rejoicing.

Chapter Six

Loving

The staretz Silouan emphasized two distinct teachings in his writings. The first was "keep your mind in hell, but do not despair," an exceedingly difficult concept to understand. The second was "love your enemies," an exceedingly difficult one to do. The staretz seemed to make this teaching (from the mouth of our Lord Jesus Christ Himself) an acid test of advanced Christian living.

I recently attended a weekend seminar on conflict resolution for my profession. One of the key principles proposed was "include your enemies in your sphere of influence." The idea here is to realize the value that these individuals can have in one's growth. By gaining some sense of appreciation for what they have to offer, or from their perspective, conflict can have a greater chance for resolution.

For Father Bill it could certainly be stated that one of his "enemies" was the Episcopal Church, or at least those immediate Episcopal representatives who saw to his demise as a priest in that organization. I can testify that I have never heard Father say a bad word or display a bitter, vindictive attitude towards those individuals. As is clear in his homilies and other speaking engagements Father has had a deep appreciation for his Episcopal experience. Certainly he is direct and truthful about the differences he sees between Orthodoxy and the Episcopal Church (Anglican). But this in no way has led him to violate the staretz' teaching.

Imagine if the Episcopal Church had actually allowed Father to stay. It can easily be stated that Father's "enemies" were used by God to bring him to the joys and delights of the Orthodox Church.

For members of the Antiochian Church of Orthodoxy of Arab descent, there likely can be no greater possibility for an enemy than the Middle East conflict with Israeli Jews. Fr. Bill is well aware of this. Several of his most important homilies are not only keenly aware of this but dramatically display his acute sensitivity and loving demeanor. Father communicates an extraordinary balance between historical sensitivity, objectivity, judgment and love for all people.

The homily "Lazarus and the Rich Man" is one of Father's few attempts at an expository style of preaching. More importantly is this theme of love developed. Who could better fit the description of an enemy than the calloused and selfish rich man? Yet there is the Love of God. St. Isaac the Syrian, an Arab Orthodox Father, was one of those few Orthodox Fathers who dared to develop the logical (for him), reasonable end of the Love of God that Bishop Kallistos called "the only interpretation of judgement and hell that makes any sense."* This leads to the difficult topic of the rejection of the Jewish nation as the people of God.

There could not be a more appropriate explanation and follow up to this discussion than Fr. Bill's homily on "Other Faiths: Judaism." For Father this is a common display of his love for Jewish people, sensitivity to the Palestinian persecution at the hands of Israelis with a separation of spiritual and political concerns.

But God's love not only extends to people but to all creation including animals. By Father's request we've included the brief but touching memorial of the death of his family's cat.

Finally, it could be stated that in one sense St. Peter and St. Paul were "enemies." Clearly they came to blows verbally, emotionally and theologically. Father again shines in "Sts. Peter and Paul" regarding not just acceptance but appreciation when there are dramatic differences.

LAZARUS AND THE RICH MAN
Sunday November 5 2006 Text: Luke 16:19-31

There is so much in this reading that I'm going to try to do it in the style of Saint John Chrysostom, verse by verse. I wish I could do it with

---

* Quoted in Bishop Hilarion Alfeyev, *The Spiritual World of Isaac the Syrian*, Cistercian Publications: 2000, p. 10.

the quality of Saint John Chrysostom, who preached wonderful sermons on this passage. They are still in print, a paperback from Saint Vladimir's Seminary Press.

There was a rich man clothed in purple and fine linen who feasted sumptuously every day. At his gate lay the beggar Lazarus covered with sores, desiring only to be fed with crumbs from the rich man's table, and dogs came and licked his sores.

And the rich man stepped right over him. In some ways it was easier to care for the poor in the old days. Once rich and poor lived close to each other. In the village in Ohio where I grew up, there were poor people. Everybody knew them, and I think their needs usually were quietly met. Now community has broken down. For the most part the wealthy and comfortable live here, and the poor and needy live there—only a few miles away—but we drive by them on the expressway and never see them. Although maybe in another way the poor are more visible to us today, for they appear in our living rooms and family rooms on television: starving people in Africa, refugees in the Middle East, still waiting to be cared for. We have to walk by their images in order to get to our dinner tables, where we eat sumptuously every day.

Jesus named the poor man Lazarus. Tradition calls the rich man Dives, but Jesus didn't give him a name. Why not? To make a point. In the end the rich man wound up a nobody, a no-name, forgotten, not remembered. The poor beggar is the one who became somebody, his name was remembered. So this is the parable of Lazarus and the nameless rich man.

Lazarus died and was carried by the angels to the bosom of Abraham.

This was a popular Jewish term for Paradise. Poor Lazarus, so hurt in this world, was now being held, comforted like a little child—"it's alright, everything is going to better now, you can't be hurt any more"—by Abraham, the father of the Jews.

The rich man also died and was buried, and in torment in Hades . . .

The question arose at class last Thursday evening: what happens when we die? Are we awake and aware, or do we sleep until the last judgment? The answer is here. Though after death our bodies "sleep" till the last day—the day of resurrection—yet our souls are awake, aware, alive. The rich man would rather have not been aware.

He lifted up his eyes and saw Abraham far off and Lazarus in his bosom and cried: Father Abraham, have mercy on me and send Lazarus to bring me just a drop of water, for I am in agony in this fire.

Uh huh . . . "Please have Lazarus do for me what I never did for him."

The rich man is in Hades (that's the Greek word, in Hebrew it's "Sheol"), the underworld, the place of departed spirits. In both the Old Testament and the Greek myths, people did not go to heaven when they died. Souls went to the underworld, the place of shadow and darkness. There people were less alive than they were on earth, essentially ghosts; they just lingered and finally faded away. Jesus here adds another element to Hades: fire, flame, torment.

What is the fire? We're not told. Is it the fires of punishment? Protestant revivalist preachers used to emphasize that. Jonathan Edwards drove people into hysteria as he warned them of an angry God dangling souls by a thread over the fires of hell. That's awfully hard to reconcile with the Father of our Lord Jesus Christ who is good and loves mankind. Although . . . Jesus warned us elsewhere to get rid of our sins now, lest we go to the place "where the worm never dies and the fire is not quenched." (Mark 9:43-48)

Or perhaps these are the fires of destruction. One of the Lord's words for hell was "gehenna" or Gehinnon—which was a valley outside Jerusalem, the city garbage dump where the fire was always burning up the refuse, the smoke forever going up. Was the rich man on the cosmic garbage heap? Since while he lived on earth he had had no love, no mercy, no compassion, had God decided he was useless, not worth saving? Perhaps.

Or maybe this is the fire of purification. Fire refines, fire purifies, fire burns away the dross and impurities and leaves pure metal. For all of us, this life is intended to be a refining process. The things that come upon us, both good and evil, the challenges we face are for a purpose. They enable us to purify ourselves—or not. We use them either to become better people, purer and holier—or worse. Either they make us more loving and compassionate and worth saving—or less. They turn us towards God—or away from him. This is our choice, depending on what we do with the events of our lives. But it's clear that we cannot carry our sins with us into heaven. We must get rid of them sooner or later—and sooner is easier, before they become entrenched habits. Lazarus apparently had used his troubles for that purpose; he had been purified. The rich man could have used his opportunities too. There was Lazarus on his doorstep in need of love, mercy, food! What an opportunity for the rich man to do something to save his own soul—but he didn't take it He just walked by.

Was there still hope for the rich man? All Abraham says is that Lazarus cannot come and visit him. There is *a great gulf fixed* between heaven and Hades. Is it a permanent gulf? Or is the rich man being purified so he may someday amount to something worthwhile and join Lazarus? We're not told. If we throw away our chances in this life, is there a chance for repentance after we die? We're not told. Saint Gregory of Nyssa and a few others [St. Isaac the Syrian] dared to hope that in the end all will be saved. In II Corinthians 12, Saint Paul describes a vision in which he was caught up into Paradise and heard inexpressible words "which it is not lawful for a man to utter." Some guess that the thing which must not be told on earth is that in the end all will be saved. Indeed, it is hard to imagine how anyone could finally see God and heaven and reject them. But it would not be good for us to hear that, because I'd say, "Well, no worry!" and I'd never repent. But I don't know if that is the secret Paul could not tell. What Christ actually said was: "Enter by the narrow gate for the way that leads to destruction is wide and many take it, but the way that leads to salvation is narrow and few take that way. (Matthew 7:13-14)

Furthermore God respects our free will. He doesn't force us, doesn't compel us to forsake our sins and become good. The fact is that we sometimes reject God and goodness now don't we? We sometimes say no to God now. If we do it now, why would we not do it in the end? C.S. Lewis wrote that finally there will be only two kinds of people: those who have said to God with all their hearts, "thy will be done," and those to whom God will reluctantly say, "Alright. Thy will be done. If you don't want me, you don't have to have me." It's our choice. I do not know that I will have another chance after death, nor do I know when I will die. Therefore: repent now. Today may be the only chance I'll get.

But I still have hope for the rich man. Saint Matthew (chapter 12) applied one of Isaiah's prophecies to Christ (I love this passage): "Behold my Servant whom I have chosen . . . a bruised reed he will not break, a smoldering wick he will not quench." Christ came to heal, to restore, to save, not to destroy, not to extinguish. In my business I deal with a lot of smoldering wicks, all these candles up here and also some smoldering human wicks—and sometimes they can spring back into flame when you least expect it. If there is even a spark of goodness left in any human being, if the fire hasn't gone completely out, he comes and by the breath of the Holy Spirit he will try to fan that smoking wick back into flame. (Apply this to the issue of capital punishment. How can we give up hope on anyone?) And clearly there is a spark of goodness left in the rich man. He's not completely bad. He still cares about his family. If there's no hope for me, if Lazarus can't help me, *then I beg you, father, send him to my father's house, for I have five brothers, that he may tell them lest they also come to this place of torment.* I think that request means that there is still hope for the rich man. Perhaps his love for his family can be fanned into the flame of love for God and love for all. Perhaps he may still win himself a name in heaven—or not.

Now the story takes another tack. The rich man has asked Abraham to send Lazarus to his brothers to warn them. Abraham answers, *They have Moses and the prophets. Let them listen to them.* Fair enough. If there is anything that is clear in the Old Testament, it is the command to care for the poor and needy. *No, father Abraham, but if one goes to them from the dead they will repent.* Abraham says: *If they don't listen to Moses and the prophets, neither will they be persuaded though one rise from the dead.* Do you get it? Someone soon *would* rise from the dead, and the ones who didn't believe were the Jews.

Now suddenly we have to look back and see this parable in a new context. It means more than we thought. It is not only about caring for the physically needy. It is also about the spiritually rich and the spiritually poor—the Jews and the Gentiles. The rich man is the Jewish nation which has been given spiritual riches—the Law, the prophets, the commandments of God, the support of God. And Lazarus is the Gentiles, the pagan peoples, living right at the door of the Jewish nation, on their borders, even in their midst, not knowing God or his commandments, not knowing to turn to the one true God. And as the rich man, were the Jews sharing their wealth? No, they were keeping it to themselves. But the time was coming when the roles would be reversed. It would be the pagans who would turn to God and be taken to the bosom of Abraham, while the Jews would be rejected. We sing about this in the services before Lazarus Saturday. Jesus said that in the end the unworthy and unwashed would be eating in the kingdom of heaven with Abraham, Isaac and Jacob while the Pharisees and scribes, the leaders of the Jews, would be cast out. Sure enough, when Christ rose from the dead, they were not persuaded. And now the Church is the new Israel of God. We are the true heirs of Abraham.

Do I have to give the moral to this story? Here we are feasting sumptuously every day, most of us, with Lazarus on our doorstep—so many hundreds of millions of people in this world living in poverty and misery. As we approach election day, what I hear from so many of our leaders on both sides is: here is how we can keep what we've got, so "they" won't get it. And here we Orthodox are with the spiritual treasures God has given us—we who are so wealthy, so rich in the faith, with so much to share—living in a culture that day by day seems to be getting shallower and blinder and meaner and poorer in spirit. Watch television, listen to radio, and again listen to the politicians. There is spiritual poverty on our doorstep. You may draw the moral for yourself.

EULOGY FOR AN OLD CAT
October 2008

Our daughter Jennifer found her on the streets of Minneapolis one very cold winter day nearly 20 years ago while she was in college. Her long white hair was dingy and matted; one eye was punctured, one ear torn, she was limping and "squeaking" after her. Jennie took her in and named her Squeaky. Khouria Dianna and I inherited her "temporarily". Her Christian name was Anastasia. A man must have been cruel to her. She ran from me for two years, then only tolerated me, but she was neurotically over-attached to Khouria Dianna. She was scared of almost everyone else; when her savior Jennifer came to visit, she even ran from her. Nevertheless we tried to love her; we fed her and cleaned up after her till the end, which was last Tuesday. We never got much in return. She was often afraid, only occasionally happy.

Squeaky was for us a sign of all the abused, neglected, mistreated people in the world—and spiritually, at least, all of us are damaged merchandise, aren't we? We shouldn't expect too much out of them—or of us, for that matter. Our job is just to love them and each other, as Christ loves us.

Do animals go to heaven? The Bible and the Fathers don't speak to that; pets were not common in those days. But "God so loved the *world*," not only the people in it, and I believe that nothing good will be lost in the end. Perhaps His love and ours can finally pull those who are unloving and unresponsive, often through no fault of their own, into the heavenly Kingdom of love. Even cats. Rest in peace, Squeaky cat. Maybe we'll meet again when he has healed you—and you'll let us love you.

ORTHODOXY AND OTHER FAITHS
Part 3: Judaism
Sunday February 1, 2009

First, let's distinguish three things: 1) Old Testament Judaism, which is our roots. The Old Testament is part of our Christian Bible. Without it we cannot understand ourselves. 2) Modern-day Jews as people. 3)

Today's nation of Israel which is a very different matter, about which some here feel strongly for good reason. So do I. So when I say good things about Judaism and about Jews as people, as I will, please don't misunderstand.

Years ago I heard Father Thomas Hopko say that at inter-religious meetings, at first you find Jews together and Christians together, but that when they get down to the nitty gritty of what religion and life are all about, you find Roman Catholics and Protestants "over there," and Jews and Orthodox Christians together "over here." Granted, he said, we and the Jews have a "slight disagreement" about the identity of the Messiah! His point: many Roman Catholics and Protestants see religion as something external, a law or doctrine to be conformed to, whether it comes from the Bible or the Pope, while most Jews and Orthodox Christians see religion as interior, planted within us, more a way of life than a doctrine or a law. Also, many modern Roman Catholics and Protestants approach religion first as individuals; Jews and Orthodox Christians still approach it first as a community.

Jews are descendants of Abraham. About 4000 years ago this wealthy Semite from what was even then the ancient city of Ur (in southern Iraq) had visions from God—whoever that was, Abraham didn't yet know—calling him to take his wife Sarah, his family, servants, flocks and all he had and go to what is now the Holy Land. There in a series of visions God made with him a covenant (solemn agreement) that if he and his descendants would be faithful to him, *I will make you a great nation . . . in you all the tribes of the earth shall be blessed* (Genesis 12); . . . *I give you and your descendants all the land of Canaan as an everlasting possession* (Genesis 17). (These are two of a number of similar passages.) Thus the Jewish claim to the Holy Land. *You shall be father of many nations: kings shall come from you* (Genesis 17). This prophecy was written while the Jews were a tiny, insignificant tribe. Today nearly three billion people consider themselves heirs of Abraham, whether physically or spiritually. Amazingly, it happened. It came to pass.

Judaism is named after Judah, Abraham's great-grandson, 1 of 12 sons of Jacob, the patriarchs of this people who called themselves God's "chosen people." It has been said: How odd of God to choose the Jews. Why them? Some Jews have said God called everyone; only Abraham answered. Perhaps. I will not take you through Old Testament history. I'll say only that out of this little tribe of Jews came unique world-changing ideas without which our modern world would not exist. (Read Thomas Cahill: *The Gifts of the Jews.*)

From the Jews came: (1) Monotheism—belief in one God, Creator of all. They came to this slowly. Even as late as Moses, the First

Commandment says "Thou shalt have no other god but Me," as if there may be others. Nevertheless long before any other people, long before the great Greek philosophers began to speak of God as well as the gods, all Jews, man, woman and child, knew there is only one real God, the Creator and Ruler. So for the first time, life could be unified, focused in worship and service of one God, not torn apart by serving and placating many lesser spirits as ancient peoples did.

2) God is the source of all that is good and true. It is revealing how the Old Testament treats its heroes. Most nations idealize their great ones ("George Washington never told a lie") and demonize their enemies. But the Old Testament tells of its heroes' virtues and also their sins, and it says some of their enemies were not so bad, even that God sometimes worked through their enemies. Just let an American politician suggest that God might be working through Osama bin Laden! But the Old Testament is not about us good guys versus those bad guys. It's about God working with human beings who each have within us both good and evil. There is nothing like this anywhere in the ancient world and very little in the modern.

3) Out of this monotheism emerged the idea of human brotherhood. If you believe all people have one source, all are made in the image of the same Creator, you must eventually begin to look at all people in a new way.

4) Creation, including matter, is good, not indifferent or even evil. This is the philosophical basis out of which came the development of technology and modern science.

5) The concept of progress. Ancient peoples believed history was cyclical. "What goes around comes around" again and again—and of course there's some truth in that. Lately we seem to be reliving the economics of the 1920s and 1930s. But we all believe things can change, that the future can be not just a recycling of the past. The idea that things can be better is now built into us. But this came from the Jews—the belief that the world, history and we are moving towards some destiny that God works in history, we are going somewhere.

6) The Old Testament Jews integrated religion and morality. The earlier Babylonian Code of Hammurabi hinted at this, but the Jews were the first to take it and run. Most ancient religions had gods or spirits, which had no connection to how you lived, just as long as you offered the proper sacrifices. No one suggested that the gods were good. Then there was ethics, a separate matter for the good of tribe or society. In Judaism these two—worship and morality—were inextricably, continually united. God is good, and he demands goodness of his people. The Ten

Commandments sum it up: "You shall worship me alone," and "Here is how I command you to behave."

7) Finally, out of Judaism came belief in the coming of the Messiah, the Christ, who would be sent from God to set things straight.

How did this little tribe of Jews know all these things? The Jews said God had revealed it all to them. Do you have a better explanation?

The Jews are our fathers and mothers in the faith, the foundation of Christianity. The one God of the Jews we now know in three Persons. The moral life is our way to becoming like Christ our God. We see God moving in history, leading us and the world into his eternal Kingdom. Our Messiah came out of Judaism. As Jesus said to the woman of Samaria, *Salvation comes from the Jews*—and so he did. Old Testament Judaism was fulfilled in him, and after his resurrection Christ taught the apostles how the Law, the Psalms and the Prophets all spoke about him.

However, the New Testament is clear that the situation of the Jews has now changed. Let me quote at length to make the point. Jesus told a parable about vinedressers (the Jews) who rejected God's servants (the prophets) and then killed his Son and so were cast out of God's vineyard. (Matthew 21, Mark 12, Luke 20) Saint Paul saw the Jewish nation as a branch that is cut off, while the Gentiles have been grafted in—not because God was unfaithful but because the Jews as a nation rejected their Messiah. (Romans 11) He wrote that only *those who are of the faith are true sons of Abraham.* (Galatians 3) In the New Testament the Church is the new Israel. As Jesus had predicted the nation of Israel was destroyed by the Romans in AD 70, and the Jews were scattered: *They will not leave one stone upon another*—and why?—*because you did not know the time of your visitation.* (Luke 19) The epistle to the Hebrews, written after the destruction of Jerusalem, says, *The new covenant has made the old obsolete . . . ready to vanish away.* (Hebrews 8) Saint Peter wrote, *They stumbled in their disbelief, but* [applying Old Testament images of the nation of Israel to the Church], now *you are a chosen people, a royal priesthood, a holy nation, his own special people . . . you are the people of God.* (I Peter 2)

Is there still a holy land for God's people? Yes, but it's not in the Middle East or anywhere on earth. Jesus said to Pilate, *My Kingdom is not of this world.* (John 18) You will hear other views on this from some evangelical Christians who must be stuck in the Old Testament, because the New Testament is unequivocal and consistent. Christ said, *The Kingdom of God will be taken away from you and given to another people.* (Matthew 21)

If the Jews are no longer God's chosen people, what should our attitude be towards them? The same as towards all people. The Jews are fellow human beings, made in the image of God. We are to love them. Christ commanded us to love everyone. At first Jews persecuted Christians. Then Christians came to power and often persecuted Jews, claiming they were Christ-killers or whatever. That's absurd. A few Jewish rulers 2000 years ago killed Christ. Most Jews have followed them, as most people follow their leaders, but Jews in general did not kill Jesus. In our treatment of Jews, we Christians have a lot to be ashamed of. Through history Jews have shown an admirable resiliency to survive and prosper under very difficult circumstances, often with a wonderful sense of humor about it. They have been a bright, resourceful, remarkable people.

Now to modern times—World War II and genocide under the Nazis. A few people say the holocaust never happened. It did. Or that Hitler didn't kill 6 million Jews, only 2 million. "*Only 2 million*"?! The holocaust was a catastrophe for the Jews. There had long been some Jews in Palestine as well as a more recent Zionist movement which now came to fulfillment. After the war the western powers, out of sympathy—and guilt since Germany was one of us, part of traditional Christendom—decided to give the Jews a homeland. Many American evangelicals have long said that the Jews still have a right to the Holy Land. So now bad theology made bad politics.

In 1947 the United States took the lead in giving part of Palestine to the Jews as the new nation of Israel, and millions of Jews mostly from Europe poured in. However, there were already people living in Palestine—Palestinians, a large minority of whom were Christians. You will hear some Jews and non-Jews say that Palestine was an empty land, with only a few Arab Bedouins in it. That is a lie. Over the next decades, over 750,000 Palestinians were driven from their homes and lands. The nation of Israel was built on the backs of the Palestinian people. 531 Palestinian villages with their churches and mosques were destroyed. (These are Israeli statistics.) Most fled to nearby countries which couldn't or wouldn't cope with so many; some came to the United States which, thank God, has mostly welcomed them. Today, 61 years later, a third of Palestinians in the old country still live in refugee camps. The nation of Israel now holds 73% of Palestine. The remainder is sometimes occupied by Israel; the rest of the time it is surrounded and controlled like a prison camp by the Israeli army which is financed by the United States. In the Middle East today, only Israel has nuclear weapons, which causes other nations to want them too. Israeli settlements continue to expand illegally into Palestinian territory; they take the best lands and most of the water and make normal life almost impossible for Palestinians. One would think that the Israelis who had their own catastrophe would not impose this catastrophe on others; that those who knew oppression would not become oppressors. Sadly such is not the case.

I don't know the political solution, but let me plead for some understanding on both sides. I am not justifying either Muslim terrorism or Israeli oppression. To understand is not to approve or condone. To those who sympathize with Palestinians, try to understand Israel—a small country surrounded by mostly hostile neighbors who vastly outnumber them. They were traumatized by the holocaust and are terrified of another one. How might you react if you and your family, living in land that you believe (rightly or wrongly) belongs to you, were under almost continual threat of suicide bombers? Some Jews do not support present unjust Israeli government policies, but don't speak up for fear of being socially ostracized.

For any who sympathize with Israel: Consider how you would react if you were driven out of your home and lands or lived under foreign oppression for 60 years and lost hope because the richest, strongest nation in the world finances and unquestioningly supports your enemy? During the recent Gaza war 13 Israelis were killed, 3 of them civilians; *1300* Palestinians were killed, about half of them civilians. Homes, schools and refugee shelters were attacked; the Israelis allowed only the most minimal food and medicine into Gaza. Many American evangelicals actively support all this; they think Joshua is fighting the battle of Jericho all over again, that Israelis have a God-given right to do whatever they like in Palestine. American media pay little attention. The United States Senate recently voted unanimously to endorse Israeli action in Gaza. Now . . . can you think of any reasons why Muslim radicalism and anti-Americanism and anti-Christian attitudes are growing in the Middle East?

To repeat, do not confuse Israeli government policy with Old Testament Judaism which is a wonderful thing, or with individual Jews who are often admirable people. Last week I quoted my professor: most people are better than their religion. Let's expand on that: most people are far better than their politics. No matter, Christ commands us to love all people, even our enemies. Today most Christians have fled the Holy Land. Today Israel and Palestine are dominated by two religions which teach "an eye for an eye and a tooth for a tooth." As someone said, this will leave both sides without eyes and without teeth. As for us, Jesus told us to conquer our enemies with love.

A Sermon on the Feast of the Holy Apostles Peter and Paul
Sunday June 29, 2008

Our old St. Nicholas School director Joan Philosophos *(may her memory be eternal)* used to do a teaching about Peter and Paul. How were they alike? How were they different? I thought at the time it would make a good sermon, so . . .

How were Peter and Paul the same? Both were Jews, as were all the apostles. But immediately we must talk about differences, because they came from very different Jewish backgrounds. Paul (Saul as he was called among the Jews) came from the Diaspora—Jews who had lived out in the Greek world for centuries ever since the Jewish kingdoms had been conquered by the Assyrians and the Babylonians, and many of the Jews had fled. Paul grew up in a Gentile world. He was a city boy; he came from Tarsus in what is now southern Turkey. There's not much left of it now, but then it was a large highly cultured city. Paul's family was so notable that honorary Roman citizenship had been conferred on them, which gave Paul the legal rights of a Roman. He could appeal to Caesar for justice—as he did—and in the end it meant instead of being crucified he could be beheaded—as he was. Paul received the finest education, studied in Jerusalem under the famous rabbi Gamaliel. And he was a strict Pharisee who believed in following the Old Testament Law to the letter and then some. Paul was so zealous that when this "heretical" Christian movement started, he was out to destroy the Church. When Christians fled from Jerusalem, Paul got permission to go to Damascus and bring them back for trial. Paul—the zealot, the intellectual, the theologian who later wrote nearly half the books of the New Testament.

Simon Peter was a fisherman from Galilee, the northern Jewish province, a mostly rural area. If Paul came from Milwaukee, Peter came from "da U.P."* All we know about his family is that his father's name was Jonah. He likely had no special education—which does not mean he was ignorant or narrow-minded. Synagogue school was usual for Jewish boys, and while Galilee was mostly Jewish, many Gentiles lived there, both Greeks and Romans. Also Galilee was a commercial crossroads between east and west, north and south, all channeled along the narrow land between the desert to the east and the Mediterranean to the west. So just to get along, most Galilean Jews had to know three languages—Aramaic,

---

*   [Ed. Note: This is a reference to the Upper Peninsula of Michigan, a very rural area of Scandinavian descent.]

the popular tongue, Hebrew for worship, and Greek, the language of the eastern Empire. Furthermore, great wisdom is often found among those who do not have formal education, especially farmers, shepherds, fishermen who work with nature. So don't make Peter out to be a simpleton. But still if you want to know what sort of person Peter was: his last name so to speak was bar Jonah, son of John. Jesus nicknamed him Cephas/Peter which means Rock. The chief of the apostles was "Rocky Johnson."

What was the same about them? Peter and Paul obviously were both apostles, part of the first generation of men "sent out" to proclaim the Gospel and establish the Church. But they became apostles in quite different ways, so much so that it took a while for Paul's apostleship to be accepted. John's Gospel says that Peter had first met Jesus down by the Jordan, not long after the Lord's Baptism, having been introduced to him by John himself. These fishermen later returned to their work in Galilee. The synoptic Gospels say Simon Peter and his brother Andrew were mending their nets by the Sea of Galilee when Christ called them to be fishers of men. Peter dropped everything and followed. Peter walked with Christ from the beginning as one of his three closest companions. He saw his miracles, heard his teachings, knew him personally, was first to confess Jesus as the Christ, suffered through Holy Week and the Crucifixion, was first into the tomb on Pascha morning and the first apostle to see him risen. In the New Testament Peter is always listed first among the apostles.

Let's look at today's Gospel reading (Matthew 16:13-18), the story of Peter's confession. Jesus said to him: "You are Peter (Rock) and on this rock I build my Church. I give you the keys of the kingdom: what you bind on earth is bound in heaven, what you loose on earth is loosed in heaven." Some say this passage makes it necessary for all Christians to be under the authority of the Pope of Rome, the infallible successor to Peter, the Vicar of Christ on earth who holds the keys of the kingdom. However, the early fathers never read this passage that way. The early Church understood the rock to be Peter's faith, the faith that Christ is the Son of God. Elsewhere Christ gave the keys of the kingdom to all the apostles, that is, to the Church as a whole. Only two chapters later (Matthew 18:18) Christ gives exactly the same authority to all the apostles: "Whatever you *[plural]* bind on earth shall be bound in heaven . . ." In John's Gospel (20: 23) on Pascha night Christ told all the apostles, "If you forgive the sins of any, they are forgiven them; if you retain the sins of any, they are retained." Christ gave this authority not to one man but to the Church. The keys of the kingdom are not the legal authority of the Pope; the key which unlocks the door to the kingdom is the faith of Peter that Christ is Son of the living God. Christ needs no vicar, no representative on earth, because he is still present on earth in the Church which is his Body. "Lo, I am with you always to the end of the age". (Matthew 28:20)

The New Testament does not see Peter as ruler of the Church in the modern Roman Catholic sense. For example, at the first Council in Jerusalem, which Peter attended, it was James the Bishop of Jerusalem who presided and announced the decisions. [Acts 15:6-29] Indeed if being an "apostolic see" founded by Peter makes the Pope of Rome the head of the Church, then the Patriarch of Antioch has just as good a claim to it as does the Pope. If the Pope would again become first bishop among equals, presiding in love, Orthodox would have no trouble being in communion with him again. That is the Orthodox understanding of this passage.

Paul on the other hand was a latecomer, the "new kid on the block." He had not walked with Christ, had persecuted Christians until just outside Damascus he had a vision of the risen Christ who said, "Saul, Saul why are you persecuting me?" That is why Paul so emphasized the Church as the Body of Christ. Paul had been persecuting the *Church*; Christ asked: why are you persecuting *me*? From that moment he insisted that he had been personally called by Christ to be an apostle, to carry the Gospel to the Gentiles, and he called himself by his Greek name Pavlos, Paul. The apparent reaction of the original apostles was understandable. What?! Who does this guy think he is? And I wonder if, at the beginning, Paul had some of the airs of the well educated: what do these fishermen and tax collectors know about theology? It took a while for Paul to prove himself. Paul had to go up to Jerusalem and convince the pillars of the Church (Peter and James) that his teaching agreed with theirs. In time he became the most effective missionary of the early Church, and the other apostles accepted him as an equal.

But Peter and Paul differed profoundly on how to apply the Gospel. Peter was the conservative. He believed that everyone needed to be like him and the earliest Christians; that first people must accept the Old Testament Law and culturally and ethnically become Jewish. And then in addition to that they could believe in Jesus as the Jewish Messiah.

Paul was the liberal; no, from Peter's point of view he was a radical. He said the Old Testament Law could now be left behind, for Christ had fulfilled the Law. All the Gentiles needed was faith in Christ, and to be baptized and join the Church. They did not need to be circumcised and keep kosher meals. Paul prevailed. One day Peter had a vision in which he was directed to go to the home of a Gentile, Cornelius. A good Jew would never enter a Gentile home, lest he be defiled. But Peter obeyed and baptized Cornelius and his family, and he came over to Paul's point of view, as did the rest of the apostles. Paul was right. If Peter's original view had prevailed the Church would have become an ethnic Jewish sect, an eccentric kind of Judaism, small, narrow, inaccessible to the world. Because Paul won, the Church was able to reach out to the world and become multi-ethnic—what we are now, a universal and Catholic Church.

This is still an issue. Some Orthodox think that to be really Orthodox everybody should be ethnically just like them. One of the strengths of our Antiochian approach is that we welcome people of all ethnic backgrounds. The Church is universal; it is for all who believe in Jesus Christ. But that didn't settle the issue. In his epistle to the Galatians (2: 11ff), Paul tells of the time when he thought Peter was backtracking on this principle, and these great apostles had a big argument in public. Paul wrote that before all he accused Peter of being two-faced. We aren't told how Peter responded, but knowing his impulsive personality, very likely he had something to say too.

What was the same about Peter and Paul? Both are the patron saints of our Patriarchate of Antioch. Peter founded the church in Antioch. Paul was brought there by Barnabas, and it was from Antioch that Paul was sent out on his great missionary journeys. We pray today for our Patriarch Ignatius IV who stands in direct apostolic succession from Peter, chief of the apostles.

How else were they different? Peter was married, Paul was not. One of Christ's early miracles was to heal Peter's mother-in-law of a fever. He whom some say was first Pope had a mother-in-law! Paul mentions in I Corinthians 9:5 that Peter and other apostles took their wives with them on their missionary travels. We don't know Peter's wife's name or whether they had children. Paul never married; he said he wished all could be like him, but it was better to marry than to burn with passion. On the other hand, Paul came to think so highly of marriage that in Ephesians 5 he used marriage as an analogy for the Kingdom. He says the love of husband and wife are symbols, signs of the love between Christ and the Church.

How were they the same? They both gave their lives to the Lord and the Church. Both gave up social standing, were both thrown out of the synagogue. Both spent the rest of their lives traveling from place to place like the Son of Man who said he had no place to rest his head, no earthly home.

In today's epistle (2 Corinthians 11:21-33; 12:6-9) Paul speaks about false apostles who bragged about how superior they were. Paul felt strongly about this. He had once been suspected of being a false apostle. So here he uses doubletalk. He tells the Corinthians all the things he could brag about but won't! "I speak as a fool . . . I am more [than they]" in labors, in beatings, in prison, in deaths. He lists all the troubles he has had as an apostle. [One of his trials by sea was the one I told you about last week, the harbor I visited in southern Crete where his ship took refuge from a storm.] And besides these was his "daily concern for all the churches." I have so little power, so little prestige that in Damascus I had to be let down in a basket through a wall to escape arrest. This was the life of an apostle. Paul goes on "not to boast" about his revelations and visions and concludes by telling about his "thorn in the flesh." We don't know what this was—a physical infirmity, a particular temptation or weakness?—which despite begging God, he couldn't get rid of. Paul even thought it hindered him in his apostolic work. But then he learned. God said to him, "My grace is sufficient for you, for my strength is made perfect in weakness." So he concluded: "I boast about my infirmities, so that the power of Christ may rest upon me."

This was something Peter also had to learn, the hard way. You know Peter's weaknesses—his impetuosity, his big mouth, his instability of purpose. He had promised Holy Thursday night that even if the other apostles fell away, he would go with Christ to death. Then before dawn he denied three times that he even knew him. In that beautiful, terrible resurrection appearance the risen Lord asked Peter three times, "Peter, do you love me more than these? . . . Do you love me? . . . Do you love me?" Both Peter and Paul were by nature strong men, tough guys. They had to have been to have survived the kind of life they led. But they both learned that they were also weak men and that God often works more through our weaknesses and failings than through our strengths, so that we will know the real power lies in God.

Peter and Paul were both martyrs for Christ. Nero was emperor. Peter had been in Rome for some time. Paul was being held in prison there because of his Christian activities. Nobody knows how the city of Rome caught fire, but rumor was spreading that Nero had ordered some of his men to do it for his enjoyment—Nero was often out of his mind—and that he had sat and played on his lyre while he watched the city go up in flames. (Nero fancied himself a musician and a poet, and woe to you if you didn't applaud heartily at his excruciating performances.) So Nero accused the Christians of doing it. A smart move. People were already suspicious of these "atheists" who refused to worship the gods. It certainly pleased the Jews, and it got the heat off Nero. So he had Christians burnt at the stake around his garden parties, and he crucified many including Simon Peter, the head of the church in Rome. Jesus had told Peter that one day he would be "bound and led where he did not want to go"—and so he was. Tradition says Peter asked to be crucified upside down, that he was not worthy to die as his Master had. He was martyred on Vatican Hill in Rome on June 29, probably in the year 65.

In the same persecution, perhaps on the same day, Paul also was executed at a place on the highway to Ostia the port of Rome. His body was long said to lie in a church nearby, and was rediscovered in 2006. I'd like to go there someday. When we were in Rome in 1985, we went to Saint Peter's Basilica. We had seen many churches in Europe, most of which, as I said last week, seemed more tourist traps than places of prayer. I was afraid Saint Peter's would be the same. But Saint Peter's is a holy place. When I came to the place where Peter's body lies and looked down at his tomb, I began to cry. Dear Peter, dear fallible, impetuous, all too human Peter. Look at the eternal Church Christ our God has built on you. Christ was right: you turned out to be the Rock.

In the icon for today, Saints Peter and Paul are shown embracing. They were very different men, once suspicious of each other, sometimes arguing with each other, but they were united in Christ, united in apostleship, united in martyrdom, and united in this feast day which they have shared for almost 2000 years now. God uses people of many different backgrounds, types, temperaments and talents to build his Church. We don't always all get along. All of us, like Peter and Paul, have our strengths and our virtues. But all of us like Peter and Paul are also weak, all of us fail him, all of us are sinners, all of us still have a lot to learn. That didn't stop the Lord Jesus then. It certainly won't stop him now.

Epilogue

I have mentioned what seems to me to be two absolute "rules" in Orthodoxy. 1) One must never state that one does not have pride. To speak or think thus is a sure sign that one is filled with it. 2) One can never state that one is humble. To speak or think thus is a sure sign that one is not.

I've also discovered what seems to be a third "rule." One must absolutely never entertain real or imagined praise from anyone. To do so is to fall into the trap of the first rule which then leads to sure violation of the second rule. St. Pinouphrios of Egypt is a ubiquitous example of one of many saints who went to extreme lengths to avoid praise fearing its dire impact and consequences.

Where does this leave us who have now praised Fr. Bill for his exemplary traits as a priest, evidenced through his homilies and life? Are we now guilty of temptation of another to a great fall? Does the presence of praise consequently require the intended recipient of this praise to flee in extreme measures?

About the time that coeditor James Scarpaci and I initiated this project, James coincidentally gave me a copy of a collection of newly translated material of the Syriac Fathers by the eminent Syriac scholar Sebastian Brock. My heart leapt with joy as I came across the following statement by the Syriac Father Babai in his *Letter to Cyriacus*:

*Hold in honour those who have grown old in the fear of God; honour them as though they were our Lord, and not men. **For no one is greater than he who honours the person who holds the Lord in awe.*** (emphasis mine)

I can't think of a better description of the intent and purpose of this work. Without a doubt Fr. Bill meets the criteria of "the person who holds the Lord in awe." We shall then trust the advanced spiritual life of Fr. Bill to the degree that he can receive our honor without having to flee to the remote areas of the Egyptian desert (or Greece).

Perhaps a final word should be mentioned about the relationship between a priest and his congregation—a priest nearing his retirement. Fr. Bill is the only priest St. Nicholas Church has known. There can be no doubt that there is a great attachment by the congregation to him.

As preparation for the people of St. Nicholas Church, Father has addressed this publicly and in no uncertain terms. The priest who will follow Fr. Bill is to be received and honored in the same manner as he has been.

Here there is often a stark contrast between Orthodoxy and many Protestant churches. In many Protestant churches the pastor plays the "star" role consistent with American culture. Not so with Orthodoxy. In Orthodoxy the "star" role is the experience of worship of our Lord Jesus Christ in and through the Liturgy and Sacraments regardless of the charismatic or noncharismatic disposition of the priest. The priest is not called to intentionally or unintentionally draw attention and praise to himself by his "star" performance.

Fr. Bill, the earthly tool of the indispensable work of the Holy Spirit with the help of St. Nicholas himself, has laid the initial foundation for a model of the American Orthodox Church. Dare we have the boldness of St. Paul to say "Be imitators of us?"

Heavenly Father, grant that in our honoring of your obedient, knowledgeable and loving servant, Fr. William Olnhausen, your work through him may be magnified and multiplied as fruitful life in the congregation of your American people. May the reader who meditates on the words of these homilies be deeply and profoundly blessed in their advancement of becoming like your Son, our Lord and Savior Jesus Christ.

Appendix

A Sermon on the Feast of the **Archangels Michael and Gabriel and All the Bodiless Powers of Heaven Sunday November 8, 2009** Father Bill Olnhausen Saint Nicholas Antiochian Orthodox Church Cedarburg, Wisconsin

From the Children's Sermon: *What do angels look like? They don't look like anything, they don't have bodies. Our pictures of angels aren't what they really look like; they just tell us what angels are. We show them like human beings because often they appear that way.*

Michael and Gabriel are archangels, chiefs, leaders of angels. Michael is a warrior angel: in the book of Revelation he and his angels fight against the devil, and sometimes he carries a sword. Gabriel brought messages to Zachariah that he and Elizabeth would be parents of John the Baptist, to the Virgin Mary that she was to be Mother of Jesus. That icon is on the royal doors.

Look at our beautiful new icons. Angels have halos to show they are holy, wings because they move through all times and spaces. They hold a staff of power because they are very powerful, and orbs, almost invisible, which look like the round earth, a symbol of the new world they bring to us which we can just barely see. Look closely at our icons. They are extraordinary—their great spiritual depth (look into their eyes); these orbs are gorgeous. These things like ribbons behind their necks are like radio waves to show that the angels receive messages directly from God.

Both Michael and Gabriel lean towards Jesus because they worship him, serve him. The Church says each of us has a guardian angel, an invisible friend who looks after us and protects us. When you say your prayers to night, always add: Holy angel, protect me. If you're worried about seeing an angel, don't worry. Very few people ever see them; I never have. And those who do say it's wonderful—scary at first but then it's wonderful. Because the angels are on our side, they're here to help us. Look at these icons: the angels are holy and beautiful and good.

DIVINE LITURGY:
The Proanaphora, Part 1
Sundays of January and February, 2000

Today we will go on to the public Liturgy.

The first thing to be said is: try to be on time! For the most part, I'm not complaining here. Most Saint Nicholas people are in church more or less on time, and some come early. And I know sometimes there are extenuating circumstances—dealing with little children or traffic or whatever. However, the truth is that some Orthodox make little effort to get to church on time. When the deacon sings, "The doors! the doors!" midway through the Liturgy, anciently this was the time when the doors were guarded to make sure no pagans got in to disturb the most solemn part of the service. Sometimes I'm tempted to have our ushers guard the doors at that time to make sure that no more careless Orthodox get in! Do be careful about this. You try not to show up late for work. I presume most of you make it to the movies on time, or ball games or dinner engagements. Is Divine Liturgy less important? This is God's salvation made present for you, God's Banquet offered to you. How will the Host react if you show up only for dessert at the end? Try hard to be here by 9:30. If Liturgy starts a bit late—as it often does—consider that a grace period. Probably it won't harm you to hear a few minutes of Matins . . .

"Divine Liturgy" is the Orthodox term for what Roman Catholics title the Mass, or Protestants variously call the Lord's Supper, Holy Communion or the Holy Eucharist. "Divine" means "holy," belonging to God. "Liturgy" is the Greek λειτουργεία ("leitourgia"); it was the ancient pre-Christian word for "public ceremony," deriving from λάος ("laos", people) and έργον ("ergon", work). This tells us something. The Divine Liturgy belongs to all Christian people; it is not the special sphere of only a few—the clergy or monastics or choir. And the Liturgy is intended to be work—not chiefly entertainment or education or a spiritual uplift, but something we all *do* together. That is why our Antiochian Archdiocese urges all to participate, to sing, to make the responses, as was the case in the early Church. Don't let the clergy and choir do it alone. Liturgy is the work of all God's people.

Now let's approach the Divine Liturgy itself. The Great Doxology which appears to begin the Liturgy is actually the end of Matins, according to Antiochian and Greek usage. It begins with the hymn of the angels over Bethlehem ("Glory to God in the highest, and on earth peace, good will toward men"), announcing the coming of Christ. During it, the deacon does the great censing of the entire church, and we ring bells and light candles to prepare the Lord's way. Towards the end of the Great Doxology, priest and deacon quietly conclude their preparatory prayers. The deacon says to the priest, "It is time for the Lord to act." It is the Greek word καίρος ("kairos", time) again. As I mentioned last time, this means not clock time (χρόνος, "chronos" as in the English word chronology) but rather a period of time. "Kairos" here means: it is time for us to be lifted up from our linear time into the eternity of the Kingdom of God.

And that is what the Divine Liturgy is all about. The priest's opening audible words are "Blessed is the Kingdom of the Father and of the Son and of the Holy Spirit." These words proclaim the purpose of the Liturgy. The Liturgy is the manifestation on earth of the Kingdom of Heaven. To come at it the other way, the Liturgy is our entrance, our journey into the eternal Kingdom. There is much more also going on in the Liturgy. There is education, fellowship, intercession, spiritual nourishment. It can even be seen as a reenactment of the life of Christ. Most things in life have multiple functions. Family meals, for example, feed us physically, strengthen family bonds, celebrate special occasions, and even educate us (on those occasions when we can get our children to tells us anything that's going on in their lives!). But all of it is an experience of what it means to be family. Just so, many things are taking place in the Liturgy, but the chief is that here we experience the reality of our heavenly family, the eternal Kingdom of God. The Liturgy is heaven on earth. The Liturgy is earth lifted up to heaven. Here, while we are still dwellers on earth, living in time and space, we are (as John Chrysostom said) "endowed with the Kingdom which is to come."

This first section of the public Divine Liturgy is usually titled the Pro-Anaphora or the Liturgy of the Catechumens. Pro-Anaphora means it precedes the Anaphora, the Offering of the Holy Gifts, which we will describe later. It is called the Liturgy of the Catechumens (literally "learners"), because anciently those who were taking instructions preparing for Baptism could attend only this part of the Liturgy. Some also title the Proanaphora the Liturgy of the Word, since it centers on the reading of the Holy Scriptures and the sermon—the proclamation of Christ, the Word of God.

Now the deacon begins the Litany of Peace, also called the Great Ektenia. The deacon's chief role throughout the Liturgy is to stand between priest and people, often speaking for the people. This is why he spends so much time outside the altar, on the peoples' side of the icon screen. During the Liturgy, again and again we pray for people and their needs. This is the chief function of the priestly people of God: to lift up the world to God. The response "Lord, have mercy" is an inadequate translation of the Greek Κύριε Ελείσον ("Kyrie eleison"). In English, "mercy" means chiefly pity and compassion. But the New Testament Greek "eleos" has a more positive connotation. It means saving love, all the good things that God wills for us. Anciently "Kyrie eleison" was the popular cry addressed to kings and rulers as they passed by. There is no good English translation for it. I'm tempted to put this response back into Greek.

Next come three antiphons with accompanying litanies. An antiphon is a psalm or hymn with alternate parts; that is, we sing it back and forth. The first Christian antiphonal singing is attributed to Saint Ignatius of Antioch. In our case, a cantor sings the verses, and the congregation sings the refrain. Our antiphons were originally used in Constantinople. It was the custom there that on each saint's day, Divine Liturgy would be celebrated at the church dedicated to that saint, and everybody would process there, picking up people from various congregations along the way. (It sounds like fun.) As they walked they would sing hymns with refrains, interspersed by prayers with a response. People loved them so much that, even outside Constantinople, they came to be sung as a kind of permanent introduction to the Liturgy—thus our present Antiphons and Little Litanies.

The Antiphons vary on certain festivals, and in Russian and other Slavic practice two psalms and the Beatitudes are sung here. In Antiochian and Greek practice, the Sunday Antiphons commemorate the Mother of God ("Through the intercessions of the Theotokos, O Saviour, save us") and the Resurrection ("O Son of God, who art risen from the dead, save us who sing unto thee: Alleluia.") The hymn "Only begotten Son and Word of God" was added by the Emperor Justinian in the sixth century to safeguard the doctrine of Christ's Incarnation. All this provides a good spiritual warm up exercise for the more important things to come.

Why are we still singing 1500-year-old antiphons and hymns? Why do we Orthodox scarcely ever change the Divine Liturgy? Why are we not revising and modernizing our worship as other Christians are doing today? Actually we're not completely unchanging. We change from one language to another. When people took to flying, without controversy we added "and air" to our petitions for those who travel. In recent years, Orthodox are returning to the ancient customs of congregational singing and frequent Holy Communion. But there is absolutely no movement in Orthodoxy to revise the Liturgy. Why not? Because Orthodox people love it as it is. It truly is the *peoples'* service. Families where things are not going well, or which have lost their sense of identity and history, often change their customs. But families that are united and know who they are, and where people are happy, keep the old family customs. You parents know this. Propose to your children opening Christmas presents at another time, or having something other than turkey on Thanksgiving, and you'll have rebellion in the ranks. Because your children are happy and therefore like things the way they are. This means you have a functional loving family. Despite our occasional problems, the Orthodox Church is a functional loving family. We know who we are, and the sign of this is that nobody wants to change things. Propose to change the Divine Liturgy, and there would be rebellion in the ranks. But in fact nobody proposes it. When we had some visitors from a Protestant congregation several weeks ago, a woman asked me, "How do you handle it when your people visit other churches and see new things and come back and want to try them here?" I answered truthfully, "The subject has never come up."

Next week: the Pro-Anaphora, beginning at the Little Entrance.

DIVINE LITURGY INSTRUCTIONS
Part 3: Proanaphora 2
Sundays of January and February, 2000

Now we come to the Little Entrance, which has a triple significance.

(1) The Little Entrance is the clergy's formal entrance into the Holy Place—also called the altar (area) and the sanctuary. Anciently the clergy remained in front of the icon screen during the Antiphons, entering the sanctuary for the first time at the Little Entrance. (This is still the bishop's practice at Hierarchical Liturgy, and it makes more sense.) But at the ordinary Sunday Liturgy, you need to pretend that Deacon John and I haven't already been in the altar for 90 minutes! Now we formally enter the Holy Place through the royal doors, just as the priests of Israel entered into the Holy Place, the place where God dwelt, in the temple in Jerusalem. Both in Old Testament Judaism and in the Orthodox Church, the altar area has been especially sacred. In the early Church, only clergy entered the sanctuary. Today acolytes are

allowed to join them, but no one enters the altar except on business. Even the priest enters only to worship or to prepare for worship, and when I do so I always wear at least the gibby, the clergy's black robe (cassock). This is the Holy Place.

(2) The Little Entrance is the symbolic entrance of all the people into the Kingdom of Heaven. I said last time that the first words of the Divine Liturgy define our goal. We are here to enter "the Kingdom of the Father and of the Son and of the Holy Spirit." The clergy and acolytes act out this entrance for the people. We pray before the icon screen, so that in spirit we can take this first step in our journey, moving together into God's Kingdom. "Wisdom! Let us attend [pay attention]!" cries the deacon, and the priest prays: "Cause that with our entrance there may be an entrance of holy angels serving with us and glorifying thy goodness."

(3) The Little Entrance is the beginning of that section of the Liturgy which contains Scripture readings, culminating in the Holy Gospel reading and the sermon. The carrying of the Gospel Book announces this. The Troparia and Kontakion of the Day are hymns originally designed to help cover the Little Entrance, which, in the great church Agia Sophia in Constantinople with its many clergy, took some time. These have become the "theme songs" of the day. A troparion is a hymn on the topic of the day or season. A kontakion is a concluding hymn. These vary according to the day and season. For example, each Sunday's primary troparion is on the theme of the resurrection. On most days we also commemorate the saint(s) of the day, as well as our patron saint. The Kontakion is usually related to the season. Does the priest or the choir director ever get to choose hymns and anthems they like, as is done in other churches? No. Never. We do have some flexibility about music, but otherwise all things are appointed in the Orthodox Church. This is the Church's Liturgy, and we worship with the Church.

Next comes the Trisagion Hymn, the "thrice-holy" hymn. When Isaiah had his great vision of heaven (Isaiah 6) the seraphim were singing "Holy, Holy, Holy." Likewise, when the holy apostle John was lifted up to heaven, the angels were singing, "Holy, Holy, Holy." Twice in the Liturgy we sing versions of this thrice-holy hymn, specifically after each Entrance. The point is that we have now entered heaven and we join in the song of the angels. The priest prays quietly to the "holy God, who restest in the holy place, who art hymned by the Seraphim with thrice-holy cry and glorified by the Cherubim and worshipped by every heavenly power . . . Receive even from us sinners the thrice-holy hymn . . ." Why do we sing this particular version of the thrice-holy hymn?

Here is the story that is told. During a series of severe earthquakes in Constantinople, the people gathered in Agia Sophia to pray for deliverance. There a young boy had a vision and heard the angels singing, "Holy God, Holy Mighty, Holy Immortal, have mercy on us," and he awoke still singing the hymn. The congregation joined with him, and with that the earthquakes stopped, and the emperor decreed that this should be sung forever in the Divine Liturgy—and we still do.

Now that we have arrived in the Kingdom of Heaven, and have sung to the three-personed, thrice-holy God, it is time to listen to what God has to say to us. We hear readings from the Holy Scriptures. Anciently there were sometimes more readings at Liturgy. In places at least two Old Testament readings, an Epistle and a Gospel, each usually followed by a sermon, all separated by Psalms. Sometimes at Vespers, Vesperal Liturgies and special services, we still use the Old Testament readings. We still always use the Psalms at Liturgy, even if very briefly. The Psalms were the Old Testament Jewish hymn book—150 hymns of the utmost spiritual depth. I love them. We sing them much at Matins and Vespers. The traditional monastic services require all 150 psalms to be sung weekly, and twice weekly during Lent. At Divine Liturgy the Church uses them in the same way we use everything in the Old Testament: to point to Christ and his work. In Psalm 18 [sung this morning], for example, "God gives me the victory," the "me" is Christ. Though the psalm was written about King David, the "king," the "anointed one," the Christ, we sing about is David's descendant Jesus.

Next come readings from the New Testament. This book is the Church's first written witness to the revelation of God in Jesus Christ. Our faith must be in accord with the Holy Scriptures, or it isn't Orthodox, it isn't authentically Christian. We say in the Creed that the Church is "apostolic." Our daily lectionary (daily order of readings) likely goes back to the 4th century. The epistles originally were personal letters written by the apostles to the early Christians. Today they are still the word of the apostles to us. Listen to those who knew Christ personally, the message of the first Christians.

The word "Gospel" means "good news." Jesus came proclaiming the good news of salvation to the world, the news that God "is good and loveth mankind." As Orthodox we do not try to confine the presence of Christ to Holy Communion. As one of our prayers says, Christ our God is "in all places and fills all things," and here in the Gospel reading Christ is present. All stand and sing "Alleluia" (Hebrew for "praise the Lord") and "Glory to thee, O Lord." For just as Christ once came from heaven to earth, so now he comes to us from the Holy Place, and in the

Holy Gospel we hear the story of Jesus Christ, we hear the words of Jesus Christ, we hear Jesus Christ.

In these Scripture readings, we are also acting out the fact that the Bible is the Church's book. The New Testament was written by the Church and authorized by the Church, and is interpreted by the Church out of her experience with God. The Bible can only be rightly understood in the midst of the Church. You can't take the Bible off in a corner by itself and get it right, as some try to do. To show how we Orthodox treasure the Gospel, how central it is to Orthodoxy, we adorn it in a beautiful cover, and we keep the Gospel book at the holiest of all possible places—at the center of the altar in the heart of the sanctuary. The Gospel of Jesus Christ is the heart of Orthodoxy.

Next comes the homily (sermon). An ordained clergyman (bishop, priest or deacon) proclaims the meaning of the Gospel. This is why the sermon was anciently placed (and still belongs) immediately after the Gospel reading. His job is to proclaim the Church's teachings, not his own opinions or theories. Some preachers are better than others. Some sermons are better than others. (Some, like this one, are too long.) But listen, no matter. In my time I have heard some truly inspiring sermons and also some really dreadful ones, but there has never been one that I couldn't get something out of, not one in which I did not hear some word of God spoken to me.

And with that the Pro-Anaphora, the Liturgy of the Catechumens, the Liturgy of the Word ends.

The ANAPHORA of the DIVINE LITURGY
OF SAINT BASIL
Lent 2007

PART I. God: Father Son and Holy Spirit.

Saint Basil's Anaphora (the prayer of offering and consecration of the Holy Gifts) is used on Lenten Sundays. Anciently the Anaphora was always said aloud, but we clergy got lazy and secretive. In the 5th century the Emperor Justinian directed that these prayers must be said aloud, but the clergy ignored him. Thus in most places for many centuries they have been said quietly by the priest. But these are the peoples' prayers. Although Christ is the one true Priest, the whole Church is priestly (Revelation 1:6). In Baptism and Chrismation we are anointed into the priestly Body of Christ, and we all make this offering to God. In recent years the trend is to restore the Anaphora to the people. I think that, just in order to be who we are as Orthodox Christians, we who live in this non-Orthodox, increasingly sub-Christian society need to hear and participate in this great offering, this central and focal prayer of the Divine Liturgy, the Anaphora.

Did you know, by the way, that for many centuries Saint Basil's Liturgy was used every Sunday? Saint John Chrysostom's was for weekdays. Now Saint Basil is reduced to only ten times a year. And, I know, Saint Basil's Anaphora is five minutes longer than Saint John Chrysostom's. But what a five minutes! In it is, I think, the best summary of Orthodox teaching and salvation history ever written, and a model for our personal prayers. And the language is simply gorgeous, too beautiful to hide away. Many people tell me how much they love to hear it. So don't tune it out: pray it with me.

Today we will cover the introduction to the Anaphora, the section preceding the Thrice-holy Hymn. As with the entire Liturgy, the Anaphora is addressed to God the Father. We begin by telling God that he is the *existing One, Master, Lord, God, almighty and adorable Father.* On the surface of it, this is an odd thing to do, to tell God things about himself. Surely the Father already knows who he is! So why do we say it? Because we are establishing relationship with him. Someone pointed out that most conversation consists not of conveying information but just of establishing contact, telling the other person what he already knows. Last week, as I shoveled the walk, I said to my neighbor, "This snow is really heavy isn't it [pant pant]?" "Yeah, it sure is [pant pant]," he responded. We both already knew that. We were just staying in touch. Just so, in the Anaphora. God has no need to be informed that he is worthy of praise or that he sent his Son to save us. But for our soul's salvation, for us to truly live, we need to be in contact with the living God. Indeed, *it is truly meet and right and befitting the majesty of thy holiness that we should praise thee, hymn thee, bless thee, worship thee, give thanks unto thee and glorify thee.*

This praise and worship of God is what establishes us and who we are as Church. This unites the Body of Christ with the head and through him with the Father. Let me add a word on that first title *Existing One.* This comes from Moses' vision of God in the burning bush. When he asked, *What is your name? What shall I tell my people?* God answered, *I am who I am* or *I am the One who is, the existing One.* (Exodus 3:14) Only God truly *is*, only God truly exists. We exist only in a contingent way, because moment by moment he causes us to be.

What we offer to the Father is *rational worship*, worship with our minds, not just our feelings. Orthodox worship is not "feel good" worship, designed primarily to move the emotions; it is rational; it has doctrinal content. What we believe and what we are as Orthodox Christians is expressed chiefly in our worship, both in the words and in the ceremonies and actions. Someone said: if you want to know what Orthodox believe, come and see us worship. But the term *rational* here has a deeper meaning. The original Greek derives from *logos*, usually translated as "word" (self-expression) in English, as in the prologue to John's Gospel: *the Word was made flesh and dwelt among us.* The *logos* of God is Jesus Christ. But in Greek *logos* also means the rational power of God that under girds and fills the universe. So *rational worship* means worship which is caught up in the reality of Christ himself, true to God's self-expression, and cosmic in its sweep, universal in its concerns—as we shall see.

We offer this worship *in contrite heart and spirit of humility*—because of who God is and who we are, or rather what we are not. He is so much greater than we—infinite, holy, so utterly beyond our words—that the Old Testament Jews did not dare even to speak his name aloud. (How different from the modern irreverent attitude towards God! Never say "O my God," unless you're praying!) Saint Basil reflects this:

Who is able to speak of thy mighty acts, to make thy praises to be heard, or to tell of all thy wonders at every season? For the Father is *Master of all, Lord of heaven and earth and of all creation both visible and invisible.*

Then Saint Basil gives us some challenging words. God is (1) *unoriginate:* He has always existed, beyond time, dwelling in the eternal "now"; (2) *invisible—dwelling in unapproachable light, whom no man has ever seen or can see* (I Timothy 6:16); (3) *incomprehensible:* If you think you've got him proved, defined and explained, that's not God; (4) *uncircumsript:* without limits, infinite. Someone said God is a circle whose circumference is nowhere and whose center is everywhere. I can't even bear to think of that for very long; (5) *immutable:* he never changes. Notice: all these words are negative (what theologians call "apophatic"), because we believe God is too great to be described by any positive human words. Nothing we can say does him justice, so it is safer to say what he is not and leave the mystery of God undefined. All this, by the way, is why cheap "hokey" worship just doesn't cut it. God is too great for that. I must approach him with humility and awe, for he is the holy God, and I am not. Our Orthodox worship expresses God's holiness.

But also, he is *the Father of our Lord, the great God and Savior Jesus Christ.* Why do we call God our Father? It did not naturally occur to human beings—limited, fallible, sinful, mortal and material as we are—to look at the unoriginate, invisible, incomprehensible, infinite, unchanging God and say, "Hi, Daddy!" In the Old Testament there are only two or three passing references to God as being like a father. It was Jesus only who taught us that God is the Father. In the New Testament God is called Father more than 300 times, because Jesus Christ is the only-begotten Son of God who has made us his brothers and sisters, children of his Father. Only because of Jesus Christ do we *dare* to speak the name of God, *to call upon the heavenly God as Father and to say: Our Father.* Christ taught us to call the infinite God *Abba*, Aramaic for "daddy"! Our Orthodox worship likewise reflects the warm, family relationship we have with God and the saints.

It is Jesus Christ who has revealed the invisible God to us. Any positive words and names we ascribe to God we take from him; anything Christ did not teach or show us about God we do not accept. For he is *the image of thy goodness.* When the apostle Philip begged, "Lord, show us the Father," he responded, "Philip . . . whoever has seen me has seen the Father." (John 14:8-9) That is, in Christ we see the character of the invisible God. Jesus *shows forth . . . the Father,* for he is the Father's *living Word;* Christ is himself *the true God, the Wisdom* of God who existed *before the ages.* Jesus Christ is *Life, Sanctification* (holiness), *Power, the true Light.* He is God incarnate. There is nothing else the Church knows to call him. It is what he said of himself in a multitude of ways, *making himself equal with God.* (John 5:18) *I and my Father are one.* (John 10:30)

The introduction to the Anaphora has a third part: *Through whom the Holy Spirit was manifested.* Christ taught that the Holy Spirit *proceeds from the Father.* (John 15:26) God the Father is the origin, the source of all things including the Son and the Spirit. Christ also taught that he himself would *send* the Spirit to us (John 16:7), that as the universal Word of God, he directs the work of the Holy Spirit. For example, after the resurrection he breathed upon the apostles and said *Receive the Holy Spirit* (John 20:22). Saint Basil himself did a major Scriptural study (now in paperback titled *On the Work of the Holy Spirit*) showing that the Holy Spirit is divine, the third Person of God.

He here describes him as (1) *the Spirit of truth* who, as Christ promised, leads his people into the truth. The Truth is Christ himself (John 14:6); (2) *the Gift of adoption* given in Baptism when we are adopted as God's children; (3) *the pledge of the inheritance to come* who plants eternal life in our hearts; (4) *the First fruits of eternal good things* through whom we already begin to experience and participate in the Kingdom of heaven; (5) *the life giving Power,* "the Lord and Giver of life," whose invisible power is the cause of all that exists and lives in this world and every world; (6) *the fountain of Sanctification:* Christ promised the woman of Samaria *a fountain of water welling up to eternal life . . . whoever drinks this water shall never thirst again* (John 4:14), *living water . . . , the Spirit whom those who believed in him would receive* (John 7:38-39); (7) by whose power *every rational and intelligent creature serves thee:* the Holy Spirit is at work not only in the visible Church but wherever and in whomever there is truth, goodness, beauty, joy, love. Why do we call the Holy Spirit "he", addressing him in personal terms? Again, because Jesus did. He spoke of the Holy Spirit *whom I will send from the Father.* God is never a blind force; he deals with each of us personally, one by one. Once again, in describing the Holy Spirit, Saint Basil exclusively uses Scriptural terms. He never attempts to explain or define the Spirit. God's Holy Spirit remains a mystery. Here, too, our Orthodox worship expresses the mystery of the Holy Spirit. It is supremely Spirit-filled, alive with the presence and power of the living God, in a way that can be experienced but never understood or fully put into words.

So the mystery of God consists of three Persons, three centers of personality in the one God. The one God is a Family, a Community. Why do we believe this unbelievable thing? Again, because of Jesus Christ. The clearest example is found on Holy Thursday night when we find Christ our God, one Person, praying to God his Father, a second Person, promising to send the Holy Spirit, a third Person. But there is only one God. How to explain this? Don't even try. We believe it because we believe Jesus. But as we live in the Church we do begin to experience this inexplicable mystery of the Holy Trinity . . .

. . . who is praised by *every rational and intelligent being* and by all the ranks of heavenly bodiless powers mentioned in the Scriptures, *angels, archangels, thrones, dominions, principalities, authorities, powers, . . . the many-eyed cherubim,* and finally, around the throne of God, *the six-winged seraphim.* This comes from Isaiah's vision, often portrayed around the Pantocrator icon in the dome of Orthodox churches, his call to be a prophet:

In the year that King Uzziah died I saw the Lord sitting upon a throne, high and lifted up and his train filled the temple. Above him stood the seraphim; each had six wings: with two he covered his face, with two he covered his feet, with two he flew. And one called to another and said: Holy, holy, holy is the Lord of hosts; the whole earth is full of his glory. And the foundations of the threshold shook at the voice of him who called, and the house was filled with smoke. (Isaiah 6)

And so at every Divine Liturgy as we approach the highest heaven, the throne of God, the heavenly banquet, we join with the seraphim and sing to the Holy Trinity, one God in three Persons: *Holy, holy, holy, Lord God of hosts heaven and earth are full of thy glory.*

The ANAPHORA of the DIVINE LITURGY
OF SAINT BASIL
Lent 2007

**PART III.   What are we doing at Divine Liturgy?
The purpose of the Anaphora**

The Divine Liturgy is a journey into the Kingdom of God. We are here to experience heaven on earth, earth lifted up into heaven. We are here to offer ourselves to God at the heavenly altar, and to share in the eternal Banquet in heaven. This requires an introduction.

As Father Alexander Schmemann pointed out, the first words of the Divine Liturgy (which sadly many Orthodox never hear, as they straggle in late) tell us where we're headed. *Blessed is the Kingdom of the Father and of the Son and of the Holy Spirit.* That's where the Liturgy takes us if we have eyes to see and hearts that are open to it. This is why the Liturgy has a series of entrances. First we all enter the church, then the Little and Great Entrances into the altar, physical entrances which symbolize the spiritual journey we are making, carrying us further and further into God's Kingdom. And as we begin the Anaphora we have words which Father Schmemann said are the key to the whole Liturgy: *Let us lift up our hearts. We lift them up unto the Lord.* Through the Great Entrance, we arrived in the highest heaven; we have come to the holy of holies. Here, first, we praised God (Part I of this series of talks); then we thanked God for all he has done for us, for how we got here. (Part II) Now we prepare for the Heavenly Banquet.

We take bread and wine as Christ commanded at the Last Supper. We Orthodox call these the Holy Gifts, our gifts to him which were originally his gifts to us. They symbolize the fundamentals of life, food and drink, wheat and grapes. These are gifts of God, the products of his seeds, his soil, his sun, his rain, which have been made into bread and wine by human work and ingenuity which are also gifts of God. Our bread is also called the prosphoron or "offering" (plural: prosphora). At each Liturgy the bread is provided, offered by a member or family from the church. Usually they bake it themselves.

Early on Sunday morning (before or during Matins), the Holy Gifts are prepared by the priest (and deacon, if there be one present) in the Proskimidi service. Placing bread on the paten (plate) the priest constructs a picture of the Church—a large piece for Christ in the center, the Theotokos and saints around, and at the bottom a particle of bread for each person he prays for. Each Sunday I place a particle there and pray by name for each member and friend of Saint Nicholas Church, living and departed, and for each person for whom you have asked prayers—all united with Christ. This is what the priest carries to the altar at the Great Entrance—you and those you love, to be part of Christ's great sacrifice. The Cherubic Hymn then calls us to *lay aside all earthly cares*—all our concerns for ourselves and loved ones, offering them up to God, trusting them to his love—in those little particles of bread. So "there are you on the paten; there are you in the chalice; there are you on the altar."

Now we *lift up our hearts unto the Lord, Let us give thanks* (Greek ευχαριστίσωμεν: eucharistisomen) *unto the Lord.* From this comes one of the popular titles for Holy Communion, the Eucharist, the thanksgiving. And having entered the heavenly Holy of holies, we sing with all the ranks of angels the thrice-holy hymn of the seraphim *Holy, holy, holy, Lord God of hosts, heaven and earth are full of thy glory,* first heard by the Prophet Isaiah in his vision of God "high and lifted up" in the temple. To it we add the Messianic acclamation made to Christ on Palm Sunday: *Hosanna* (save us) *in the highest. Blessed is he that cometh in the name of the Lord.* Who has come? The Messiah has come to us. We have come to him. We are now with Christ in heaven. *Hosanna in the highest.*

At the Anaphora of the Liturgy, we are doing what Christ commanded at supper on Holy Thursday night:

1) *For when he was about to go forth to his voluntary and ever-memorable death, in the night in which he gave himself up for the life of the world, he took bread in his holy and immaculate hands, and when he had shown it unto thee, the God and Father . . .* We have already done this at the end of the Great Entrance.

2) *and given thanks . . .* We did this beginning with "Let us give thanks."

3) *and blessed it and hallowed . . .* This is what we now do.

4) *and broken it . . .* This will take place after the Lords' Prayer.

5) *he gave it to his holy disciples and apostles, saying: Take, eat.* We will do this in Holy Communion.

The Lord continued: *This is my Body which is broken for you, for the forgiveness of sins.* And likewise with the wine: *This is my Blood of the new covenant which is shed for you and for many for the forgiveness of sins.* We identify this bread and wine with Christ's sacrificial life, especially his crucifixion and all that proceeded out of it.

This is my Body. This is my Blood. What did he mean by those words? Christians have argued much about it. Should we take them literally? Yes, of course. He didn't say these are *like* my Body and Blood. He said this *is* my Body, this *is* my Blood. Does this mean the bread and wine are changed chemically? No. (Nor have any Christians ever officially believed this.) Materially they remain the same. Orthodox have never tried to explain precisely what does happen to the bread and wine. We don't attempt philosophical explanations of divine things. I think Orthodox would agree with Queen Elizabeth I of England who reputedly said: "Christ was the word that spake it, He took the bread and brake it, And what his word doth make it, That I believe and take it." Do we need more explanation?

But we can try to make the meaning of Body and Blood clear. Consider: Christ is God who "is in all places and fills all things," who by nature had no body. He took on a human body born of Mary—a body, a locatable place of his presence, through which he had worked—teaching, healing, saving us. Now it was his Last Supper before his death. Next day his body would die, and after his Ascension his human body would no more be on earth. So now he took bread and said: *This is my Body*; you will find me here; I will now work through this. *This is my Blood,* my power, my life for you; I will save you through this. He identified the holy bread and wine specifically with his death: *My Body . . . given for you, my Blood . . . shed for you.* All that I will now accomplish for you will be accessible in this bread and wine, in this Liturgy. *Do this in remembrance of me.* The New Testament Greek word is "anamnesis"; there is no English equivalent. "Remembrance" is a very inadequate translation. "Anamnesis" means to make present again, to re-call in the literal sense. So put it together: this is where I will be, this is where I will save you. This is my power and strength for you. Do this to call me back. Holy Communion is not simply a mental "remembering" of Christ and his life. Holy Communion is a meeting place with Christ, our access to him and his power.

Is Holy Communion the only place we can find Christ? Certainly not. He is God; there is nowhere he is not. But we are limited; it is hard for us to find him everywhere. We need times and places. Someone said, "God is everywhere, but if you don't find him somewhere you won't find him anywhere." So start here in Holy Communion—and also with that other holy thing called the Body of Christ: the Church, the people of God. Christ is just as "present" in his people as he is in bread and wine. But that is a topic for another talk.

Saint Basil continues: *Wherefore O Master . . . having in remembrance* (calling to be present) *his saving passion and life-giving cross, his three day entombment and resurrection from the dead, his ascension into heaven and sitting at the right hand of . . . the Father, and his glorious and fearful second coming . . .*

All these are present with us, including his future second coming—for we are now in heaven, beyond our time and space, in the eternal "now" with Christ our God, where the past and the future are present. So now, united with Christ's sacrifice, we offer up all things to God the Father—our whole lives, the whole world, past, present and future, all of it. This is cosmic, it is all-encompassing.

The priest lifts up the holy bread and wine: *Thine own of thine own, we offer unto thee in behalf of all and for all.* And offering it all up to God, losing it all in his glory: *We praise thee, we bless thee, we give thanks unto thee, O Lord. And we pray unto thee, O our God*—clinging to nothing for ourselves, claiming nothing for ourselves, *no good deed upon earth,* trusting only in God's *mercies and compassions which* he has *poured out on us,* offering it all to God in these *antitypes* of the Body and Blood of Christ. An antitype is something that was prefigured beforehand. It means that the Last Supper was the prefiguring, the symbol—but *this*, this Holy Eucharist now before us, is the Real Thing.

Now the direction of the Liturgy changes. So far it has been a movement in, an offering up. But now *we pray and implore thee . . . that thy Holy Spirit may descend upon us and upon these gifts . . . and hallow them.* It is a new creation, the Holy Spirit again descending, "moving over the face of the deep." (Genesis 1) Christ again comes down and becomes incarnate, embodied as when the Holy Spirit first *overshadowed* the Virgin. (Luke 2) Notice what is hallowed here: not only *these gifts* but also *us.* We also become his dwelling place, and he works through us, for we are the Church, the Body of Christ, *and show this bread to be itself the precious Body . . . of Christ . . . and this cup to be itself the precious Blood . . . of Christ.*

Is this the "moment of consecration" of the bread and wine? Is this finally the "real presence" of Christ? We Orthodox don't look at it that way. As Father Schmemann once said: if the Liturgy is about five minutes of Real Presence, then what's the rest of the Liturgy? What's the rest of life? Real absence? No, Christ is present in all of the Liturgy. This prayer is the focus of the consecration, but the whole of the Divine Liturgy is consecratory. The holy bread is treated with reverence from the moment it is prepared before Liturgy. Nor is Christ absent from the rest of life. Christ our God is present in all things at all times. He is never absent. So what happens here in the Anaphora? Saint John Chrysostom's Liturgy speaks of *making* the bread and wine to be Christ's Body and Blood, *changing* them, as all things must be changed if they are to be taken up into heaven. Nothing, none of us can remain the same. Saint Basil speaks here of *showing* them to be the Body and Blood of Christ—as if they have been so all along, and now our eyes are opened, and we are allowed to see it. All things lifted up into the Kingdom, offered up to the Father, radiate the presence of Christ who has always been present in them, but we couldn't see it before.

The process of opening our spiritual eyes begins with seeing and knowing Christ in this holy bread and wine. But the Divine Liturgy is, in the end, outward directed, so that we can now return into the world and be able to begin to see Christ our God and know him and receive him, radiant, really present in all things and especially in all people. And that, finally, is the purpose of the Holy Anaphora.

THE SEVEN DEADLY SINS: Part 3—Lust
October 26, 2003

Lust, the third of the deadly sins may not be what you may think. It is defined in the Pocket Prayer Book as "impure and unworthy desire for something evil." Sexual lust is only one kind of lust. We often use the word that way, saying that people have a lust for power or revenge. I think desire for addictive substances also comes under this category. The word lust implies strong desire—compelling, potentially out of control—so that we find ourselves doing things we know we ought not to do, doing what we do not even want to do, so we fall into it again and again. The fathers called these "passions": unworthy desires which feel nearly irresistible, or perhaps we have become so attached to them that we choose not to resist. Saint John of the Ladder says these demons [especially that of fornication] darken our minds, urging us to do things which when we return to our senses seem completely mad, and we're ashamed. (*The Ladder of Divine Ascent,* Step 15)

Some call these "besetting sins," strong temptations which attack us, then withdraw for a time so that we think we've got them conquered, and then they hit us again. It is said that each of us has at least one besetting, persistent, tormenting sin. Different people have different besetting sins. One person may be greatly tempted by alcohol but not at all by anger. Another person may be the opposite. One besetting sin may lead to another. Lust for alcohol can lead to lust for nicotine and sexual lust. What causes these passions? Is it heredity or environment? Is it chemical or psychological or habit resulting from many bad choices? It may be any or all of the above. Could we have resisted the sin? If we yield we are never sure. God only knows, he who knows us better than we know ourselves. This means that it is not our job to judge peoples' guilt, for we are not even capable of judging our own. Remember, sin means simply "missing the mark." Our goal is not chiefly to evaluate our personal guilt, but rather to repent and get our lives back on target.

In popular usage our lusts and besetting sins are sometimes called our "demons". Orthodoxy says the ultimate cause really is demons. The devil hits us at our weak points. He is the great enslaver, who tries to destroy our freedom and get control of us. In today's Gospel story (Luke 8:27-39) Christ came upon a man possessed by demons, which caused him to do irrational, antisocial things and made him a danger to others. He had to be kept under guard, bound in chains. But he would break out again and was driven into the wilderness, where he dwelt in the tombs, a living death. This also describes our demons and what they can do to us, and what they have done to people we know and love.

Let's look at some of the more common lusts. (1) Lust for addictive substances such as drugs, drink and nicotine. We understand now that some peoples' chemistry makes them particularly subject to this, so that it is very difficult for them to resist. This is a medical condition which can afflict anyone, rich or poor, high or low. However, the person with the addiction, this particular lust, has a responsibility to get help. If there is moral culpability here, usually it is not in the addiction, but rather in being too proud to get help. See, we're back to pride again—pride which is the root cause of all sin. "I don't have a problem. I can stop anytime. I can handle it by myself." That's pride. Dealing with addiction may require "tough love" on the part of family and friends. Out of mercy and compassion, they may need to stage a painful intervention to save the addicted person from destruction. From this we can learn why God, who is merciful and loves us, is not always "nice" to us. Sometimes he must show all of us tough love. He intervenes and causes us pain, lest we destroy our souls with one of the deadly sins.

2) Lust for power, the desire to control: "I must have my own way." Like all sins, this is something good twisted out of shape. God has given us power and authority to be used not to please ourselves but rather humbly and responsibly for the good of others, submitting ourselves always to God's will and power and authority. How common is lust for power? The answer: "It is very common in others, but not in me!" Married people, you know how often you feel that your spouse thinks he or she is always right, always gets his or her way. And your spouse claims that you always think you're right, that you always get your way. This is because our lust for control is often hidden from us, but not from the people around us. Lust for power is particularly dangerous, for we do not know to repent

of sins that we are unaware of. The people we deal with and who love us are forever saying to themselves, "Oh, I'll just shut up and let him have his way, it's not worth the fight." And we never know it. Those with addictions or sexual lust often repent, because their sin is so obvious, and they're ashamed. But lust for control can have us in its grip before we even know it. And when that happens it is a terrible demon. I'm sure you have dealt with people (I hope you have not been one of those people) who must always dominate, whether by force or intimidation or manipulation, playing on other peoples' guilt or taking advantage of their love. Lust for control can do horrible things to marriage, family and friendship, creating resentment, anger and alienation. When lust for power gains control of a person in high position or of a nation (for example, Hitler and Nazi Germany), horrible things can happen in the world.

3) Finally, what you all are waiting to hear about: sexual lust. Here again, sin is something good twisted into evil. Sex is a good thing, given by God who created us male and female in his image and told us "be fruitful and multiply." (Genesis 1:27-28) However, contrary to popular myth, sexual activity is not a need but only a desire. Our witness to that once again is the monastic life, where for higher purposes men and women live entirely fulfilling lives without sexual self-expression. It's often a struggle for them; not many are called to that life. But they don't die, as they would if they gave up food and drink. The God-given purpose of sexual desire is to draw man and woman together, so that they can express their love and complete commitment within marriage, and to produce and raise children in a stable family. Sexual intercourse creates a permanent spiritual union and therefore should be confined to marriage, lest peoples' interior lives be torn apart spiritually. (I Corinthians 6:16-18) Therefore the teaching of the Church, and of Judaism before it, has always been absolutely uniform and for many people very difficult to keep. Sexual union belongs only within marriage, which by the Church's definition is heterosexual. There are no exceptions. The desire for sex for other purposes is sexual lust.

C.S. Lewis married late in life. When he wrote *Mere Christianity* he was still a middle-aged bachelor (though not a prude, by any means). Nevertheless he had some profound insights. He wrote that either Christianity is wrong or our sexual instinct has gone wrong. He thought it self-evident that our sexual instinct has gone especially astray. He says the biological purpose of sex is to procreate the race, but a healthy young man, if he indulged his desires as much as he wanted, might populate an entire village. Our sexual instinct has become excessive. Lewis said that if one attended a certain kind of theatre and there was raucous music while something was progressively unveiled, exposed bit by bit, and in the end it turned out to be a pork chop or some such thing, one would conclude that something had gone very wrong with our appetite for food. Lewis wrote (this was in the early 1940s): "They tell you sex has become a mess because it was hushed up. But for the last twenty years it has . . . been chattered about all day long. Yet it is still a mess . . . . I think it is the other way round. I think the human race originally hushed it up because it had become such a mess." (*Mere Christianity*, Book III, chapter 4)

Now sixty more years have passed, and our culture is saturated with sex. With what results? More children born out of wedlock (in Milwaukee it's now the majority), an ever-increasing number of children living in poverty, more sexual disorders, rampant sexual diseases, more adultery, more broken families, a flourishing pornography industry, millions of abortions and the accompanying devaluing of human life, and a great coarsening of our culture. Little children today are exposed to things that I never heard of in the high school locker room. And still the propaganda in the media advocates more sex, less restricted sex, more bizarre sex, continually further inflaming sexual lust. Only in regard to sex do people argue that if it feels good, you should do it. What if we applied that principle to excessive drinking or wife beating or thievery?

Lewis was right. Our sexual instinct has gone wrong, and on this subject the modern world is particularly disordered. Anyone who advocates sensible Christian sexual morality today is made to feel like a fool, is called a prude or homophobic or (worst of all) "judgmental". No, we do not judge people. That's forbidden by the Lord. But we do judge sins. And we Christians need to stand firm and say: Sorry, modern world. Sorry, MTV. Sorry, Episcopalian bishop-elect of New Hampshire. Sex outside the bonds of marriage is lust. It is a deadly sin.

But this needs to be kept in perspective. The modern attack on Christian sexual morality has been so extreme that it has led some to suspect that sexual sins are the worst sins. This is not so. As I said before, because sexual sins usually are obvious, they are more often repented of. Sinners and harlots repented and turned to Jesus. The proud Pharisees did not. I quote C.S. Lewis again: "The sins of the flesh are bad, but they are the least bad of all sins. All the worst pleasures in the world are purely spiritual: the pleasure of putting other people in the wrong, of bossing and patronizing and playing spoilsport, and backbiting; the pleasures of power and of hatred. For there are two things inside me, competing with the human self which I must try to become. They are the animal self and the Diabolical self. The Diabolical self is the worse of the two. That is why a cold, self-righteous prig who goes regularly to church may be far

nearer to hell than a prostitute. But, of course, it is better to be neither."
(*Mere Christianity*, Book III, chapter 5)

What is the cure for lust—whether for addictive substances or for power and control or for disordered sex? At the beginning "just say no" is good advice. If you fix it in your mind that you will not even consider adultery or drugs, you're probably safe. But once you enter into dialog with the temptation it's usually all over. Saint John of the Ladder says we can't defeat the demons by arguing with them. They're stronger than we are. (*The Ladder of Divine Ascent*, Step 15) To fight the lust, we must change on the inside. Jesus said "Whoever looks at a woman to lust for her has already committed adultery with her in his heart." (Matthew 5:28) And if you are already drinking or being bossy or fornicating, just trying to control yourself will not work, at least not for long—or if it does, you will become proud of yourself and even more of a target for the devil. It's the heart, the inner self, the mind and will that need to change. Unless we do that, the temptation, the lust will just keep coming back. The way to eliminate the symptoms is to be cured of the disease.

That means we've got to turn to God. Only God is stronger than the demons. In the Gospels, it is Christ our God who has power to cast out demons. No one else can do so except by his power. That is why even secular alcoholics use the 12-step program in which they turn themselves over to a "higher power." What is required if you really want to conquer your demons is to let the power of God into your life—much prayer, regular examination of conscience, repentance, frequent use of the sacrament of Confession, frequent Communion, and the fellowship of healthy-minded Christian people. Find yourself a good spiritual director, or someone else who can guide you. As Saint John of the Ladder says, "when dealing with sin, one man's medicine is another man's poison," and you need a skilled doctor of the soul who can give you the right prescription. If you have a chemical addiction, you also need the services of a medical doctor and a professional counselor or a support group. And then you need patience. The ingrained bad habit of giving in to the demon can take a long time to break. Often the only gift that comes from confession and absolution is the grace not to give up when you fall again. When the time is right, God may give the gift of victory. The lust is driven out, and the demon is gone. God can do that. I have seen it happen. But don't count on it—not in this life.

This is hard. If lust is your great temptation, you must be prepared for lifelong vigilance, never-ending war for the rest of your life. But if we never give up, we have the promise of a Kingdom where "there shall be no more . . . sorrow or crying [or] pain, for the former things have passed away." (Revelation 21: 4)

10514966R00104

Made in the USA
San Bernardino, CA
16 April 2014